I N D E X

Missing page

Missing page

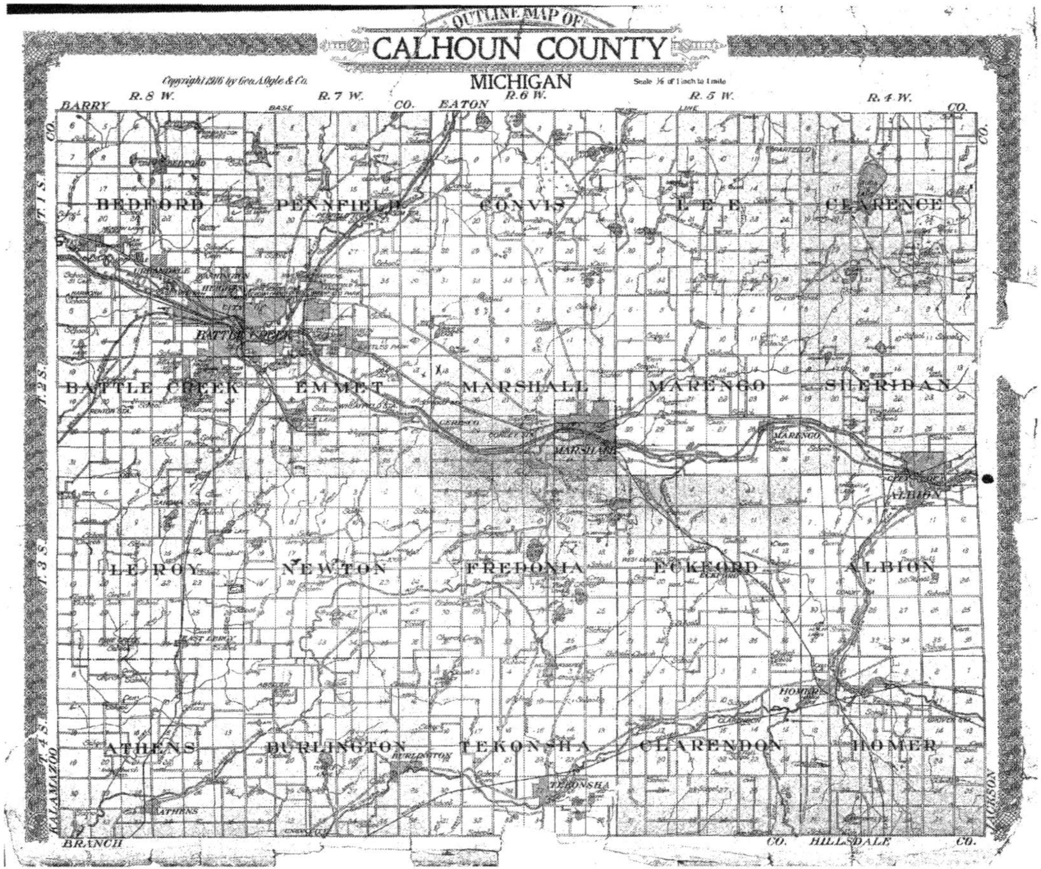
OUTLINE MAP OF
CALHOUN COUNTY
MICHIGAN
Copyright 1916 by Geo. A. Ogle & Co.
Scale ½ of 1 inch to 1 mile
R. 8 W.
R. 7 W.
R. 6 W.
R. 5 W.
R. 4 W.
BARRY
CO.
EATON
CO.
T. 1 S.
T. 2 S.
T. 3 S.
T. 4 S.
KALAMAZOO
BRANCH
CO.
HILLSDALE
CO.
JACKSON
BEDFORD
PENNFIELD
CONVIS
LEE
CLARENCE
BATTLE CREEK
EMMET
MARSHALL
MARENGO
SHERIDAN
LE ROY
NEWTON
FREDONIA
ECKFORD
ALBION
ATHENS
BURLINGTON
TEKONSHA
CLARENDON
HOMER
MARSHALL
MARENGO
ALBION
HOMER
TEKONSHA
BURLINGTON
ATHENS

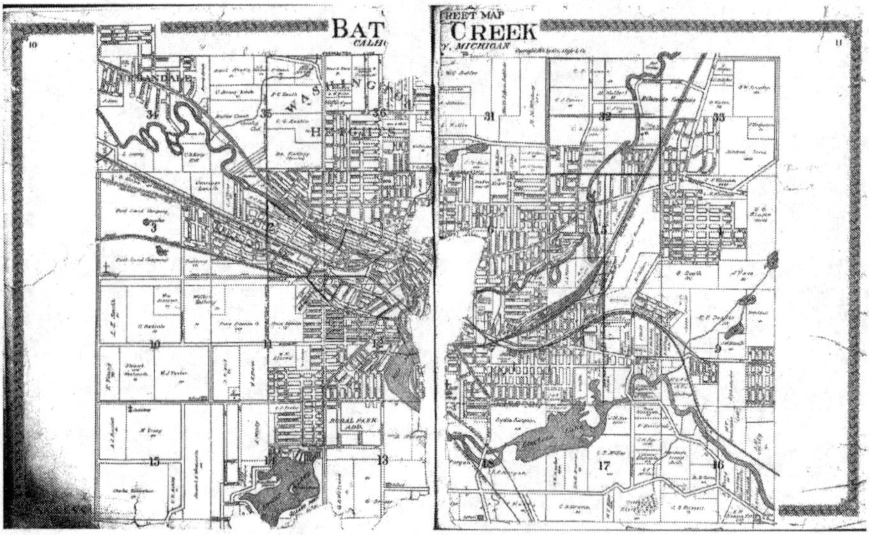
BAT
CALHO
REET MAP
CREEK
Y, MICHIGAN

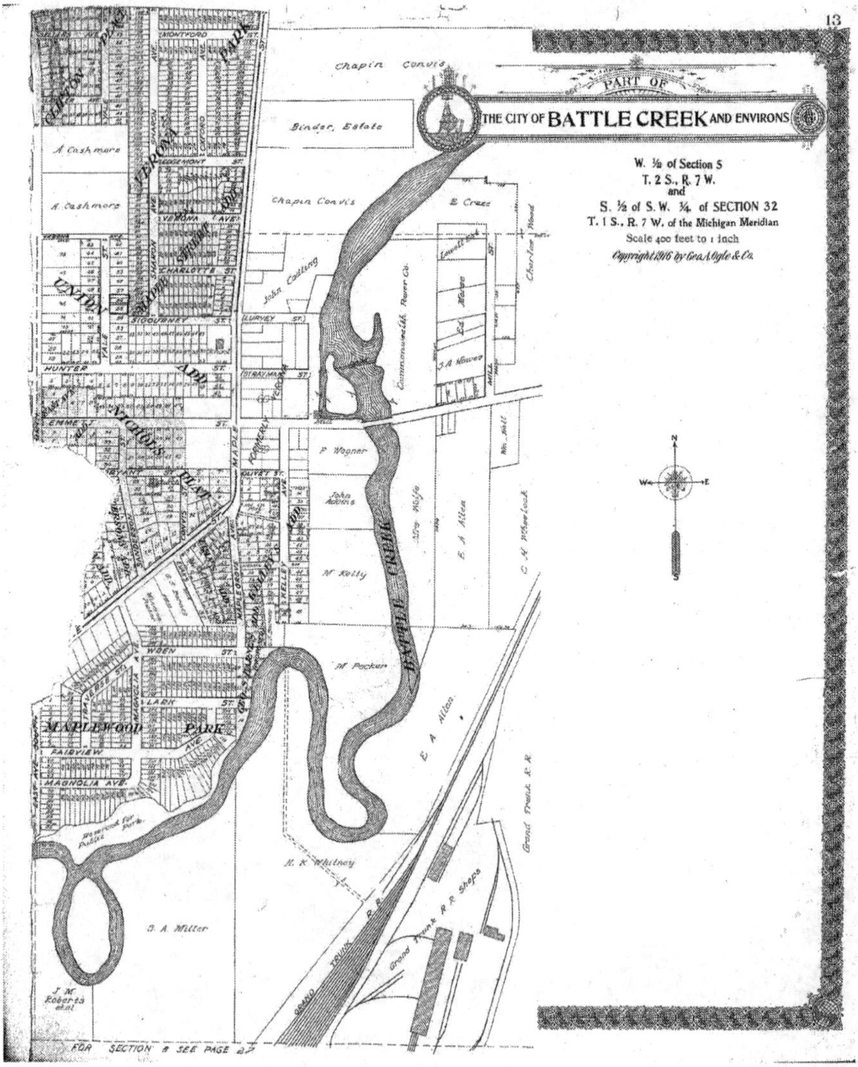
PART OF
THE CITY OF BATTLE CREEK AND ENVIRONS
W. ½ of Section 5
T. 2 S., R. 7 W.
and
S. ½ of S. W. ¼ of SECTION 32
T. 1 S., R. 7 W. of the Michigan Meridian
Scale 400 feet to 1 inch
Copyright 1916 by Geo. A. Ogle & Co.
N
S
E
W
Chapin Convis
Binder, Estate
Chapin Convis
E Crane
John Cosling
Commonwealth Power Co.
Charlie Wood
J. A. Nowes
P Wagner
John Adams
M Kelly
M Packer
Mrs Wolfe
E A Allen
C. H. Wheelock
E. A. Allen
BATTLE CREEK
H. K. Whitney
S. A. Miller
J. M. Roberts et al
Grand Trunk R.R. Shops
Grand Trunk R.R.
GRAND TRUNK R.R.
MONTFORD
PARK
CLINTON
VERONA
A. Cashmore
A. Cashmore
LEDGEMONT ST.
VERONA AVE.
CHARLOTTE ST.
UNION
SIGOURNEY ST.
LURVEY ST.
HUNTER ST.
ADD.
STRAYMAN ST.
EMMET ST.
NICHOLS
BRYANT
PLAT
OLIVET ST.
MAPLE
WREN ST.
LARK ST.
MAPLEWOOD PARK
FAIRVIEW
MAGNOLIA AVE.
Reserved for Public Park
FOR SECTION 8 SEE PAGE 27

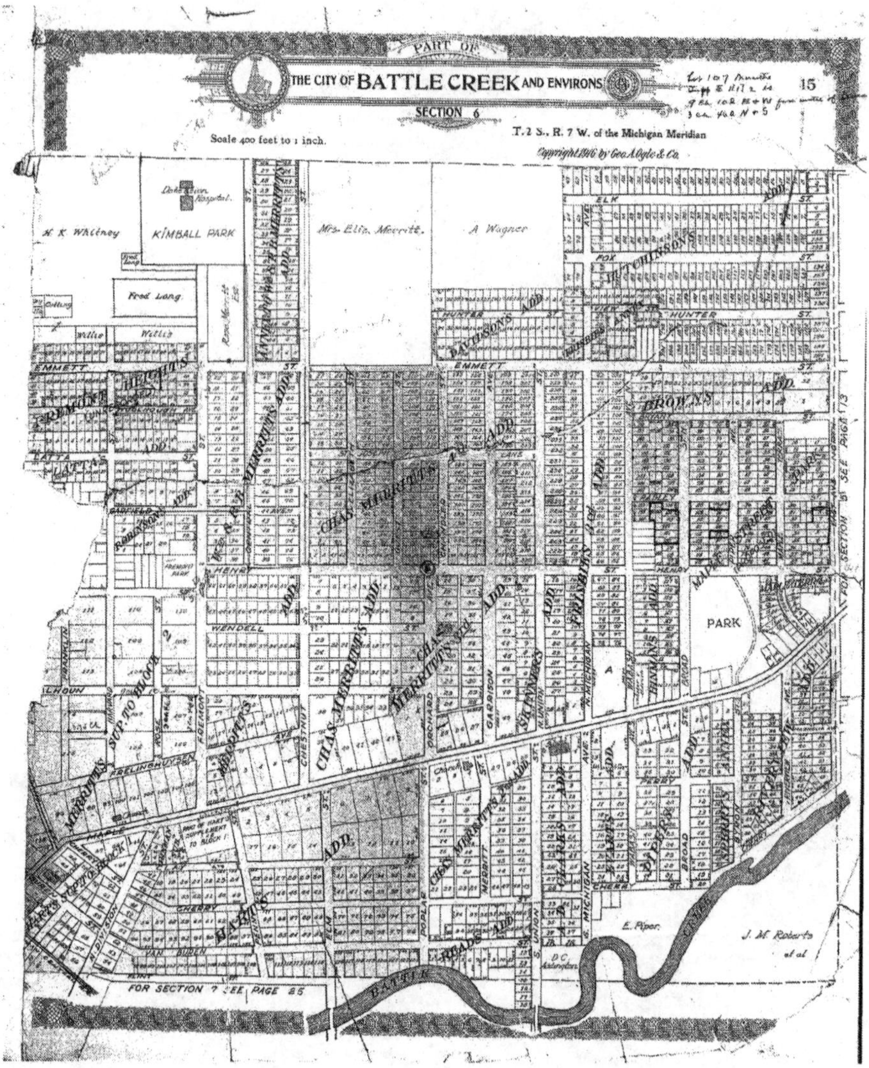
PART OF
THE CITY OF BATTLE CREEK AND ENVIRONS
SECTION 6
15
Scale 400 feet to 1 inch.
T. 2 S., R. 7 W. of the Michigan Meridian
Copyright 1916 by Geo. A. Ogle & Co.
H. K. Whitney
KIMBALL PARK
Mrs. Eliz. Merritt
A. Wagner
Fred Lang
EMMETT
ELK
FOX
HUNTER
HUTCHINSON'S
DAVIDSON'S ADD.
BROWN'S ADD.
FREMONT HEIGHTS
CHAS. MERRITT'S ADD.
HENRY
WENDELL
PARK
GARRISON
ORCHARD
MICHIGAN
UNION
CHERRY
MAPLE
VAN BUREN
BROAD
HARTS ADD.
CLARK'S ADD.
E. Piper
J. M. Roberts et al
FOR SECTION 7 SEE PAGE 85
FOR SECTION 31 SEE PAGE 13

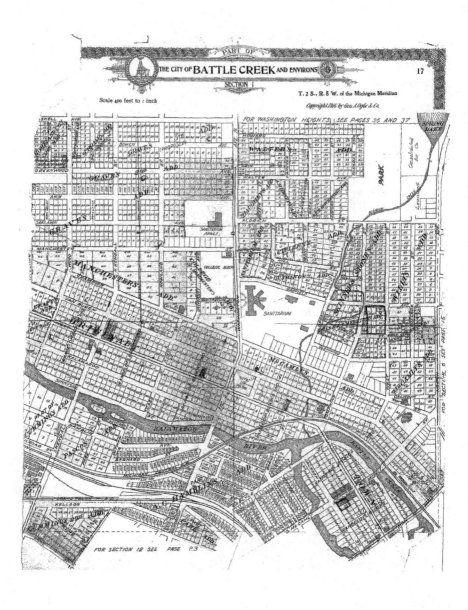

PART OF
THE CITY OF BATTLE CREEK AND ENVIRONS
SECTION 1

T. 2 S., R. 8 W. of the Michigan Meridian

Scale 400 feet to 1 inch

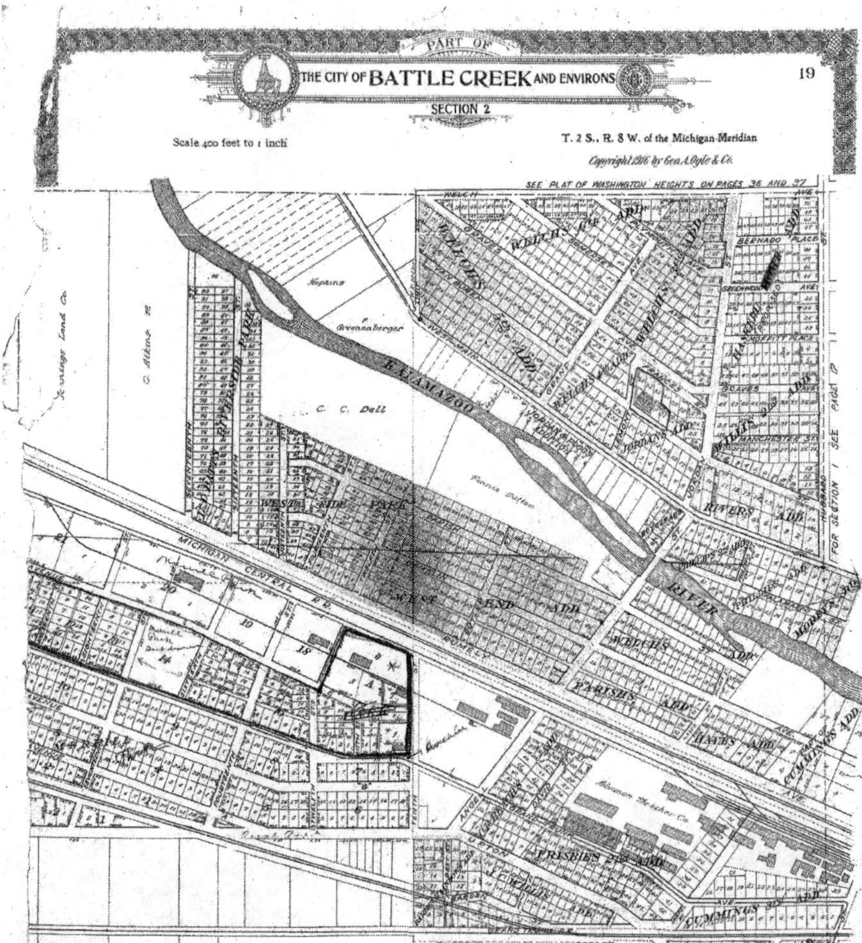
PART OF
THE CITY OF BATTLE CREEK AND ENVIRONS
SECTION 2
19
Scale 400 feet to 1 inch
T. 2 S., R. 8 W. of the Michigan Meridian
Copyright 1916 by Geo. A. Ogle & Co.
SEE PLAT OF WASHINGTON HEIGHTS ON PAGES 36 AND 37
KALAMAZOO
RIVER
MICHIGAN CENTRAL R.R.
WEST SIDE PARK
WEST END ADD
WELCHS ADD
PARISHS ADD
HAYES ADD
RIVERS ADD
JORDANS ADD
WILLIS ADD
FRISBIES ADD
CUMMINGS ADD
C. C. Dell
Hopkins
Grenenberger
Jennings Land Co.
BERNARD PLACE
GRAVES
MANCHESTER ST.
Home Fire Side Co.
J. S. Upton Est.
FOR SECTION 1 SEE PAGE 17
FOR SECTION 11 SEE PAGE 81

PART OF
[C]ITY OF BATTLE CREEK AND ENVIRONS
East Part of SECTION 3
T. 2 S., R. 8 W. of the Michigan Meridian
Scale 400 feet to 1 inch
Copyright 1916 by Geo. A. Ogle & Co.

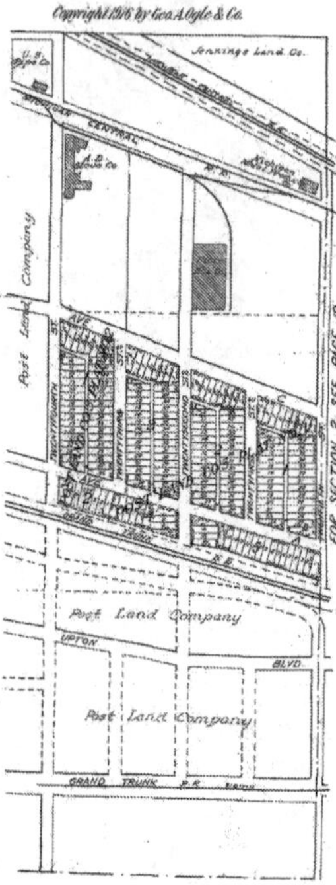

PART OF
THE CITY OF BATTLE CREEK AND ENVIRONS
East ½ of Section 11
T. 2 S., R. 8 W. of the Michigan Meridian
Scale 400 feet to 1 inch
Copyright 1916 by Geo. A. Ogle & Co.

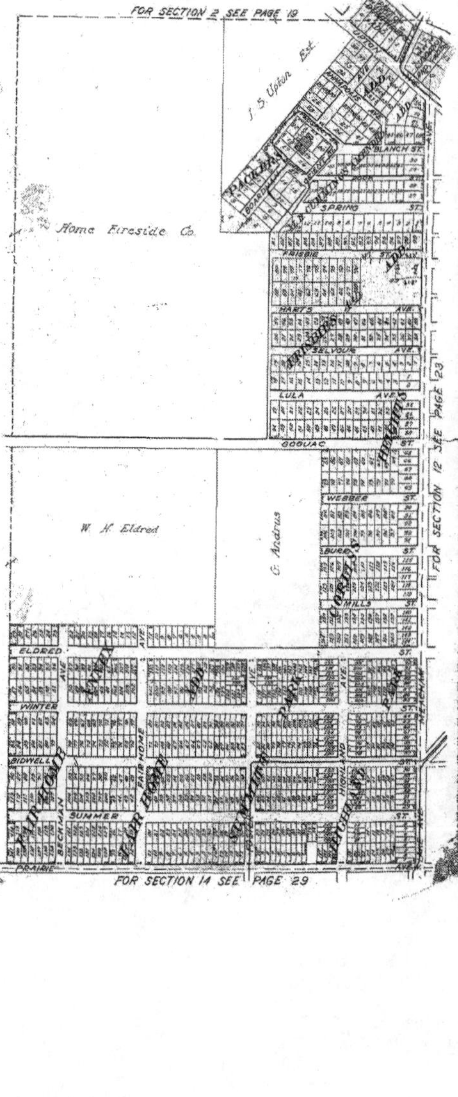

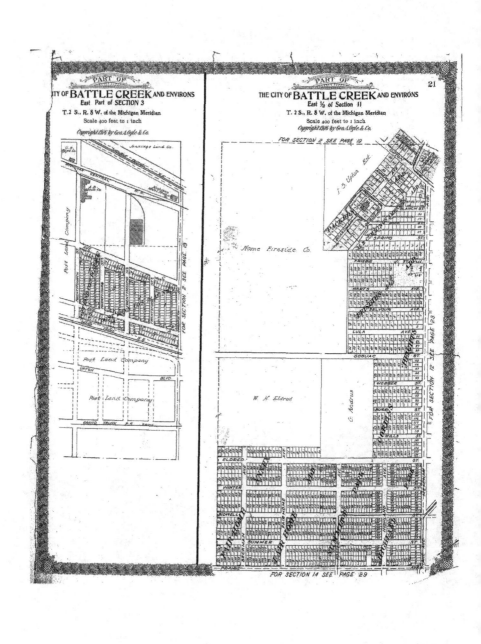

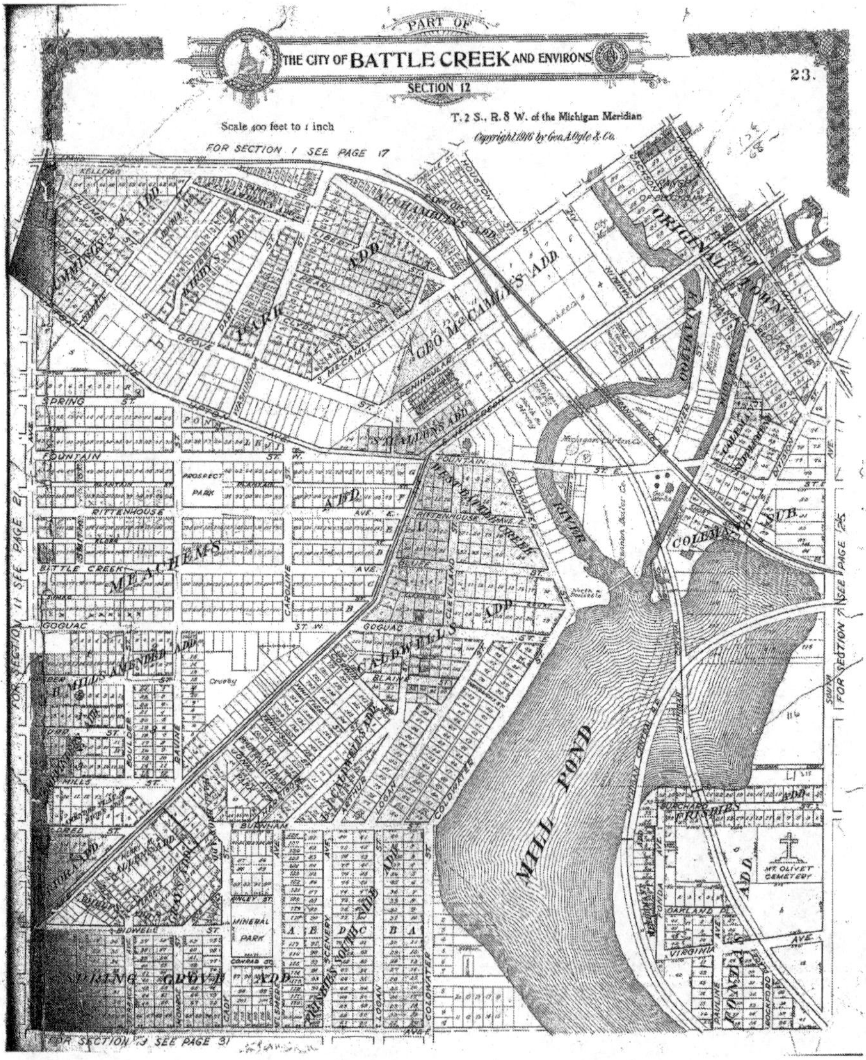

PART OF
THE CITY OF BATTLE CREEK AND ENVIRONS
SECTION 12
23.
Scale 400 feet to 1 inch
T. 2 S., R. 8 W. of the Michigan Meridian
Copyright 1916 by Geo. A. Ogle & Co.
FOR SECTION 1 SEE PAGE 17
FOR SECTION 11 SEE PAGE 21
FOR SECTION 13 SEE PAGE 31
ORIGINAL TOWN
GEO McCAMLY'S ADD
PARK ADD
MEACHEM'S ADD
CALDWELL'S ADD
SPRING GROVE ADD
COLEMAN'S SUB
FRISBIES ADD
MILL POND
RIVER
PROSPECT PARK
MINERAL PARK
MT. OLIVET CEMETERY
SPRING ST.
FOUNTAIN ST.
RITTENHOUSE AVE.
BATTLE CREEK AVE.
GOGUAC ST.
HILLS ST.
BURNHAM
BIDWELL ST.
GROVE
CAROLINE
CLEVELAND
COLDWATER
BLAINE
VIRGINIA
OAKLAND
PAULINE
KELLOGG
LIBERTY
WASHINGTON
PENINSULAR
HOUSTON
Michigan Carbon Works

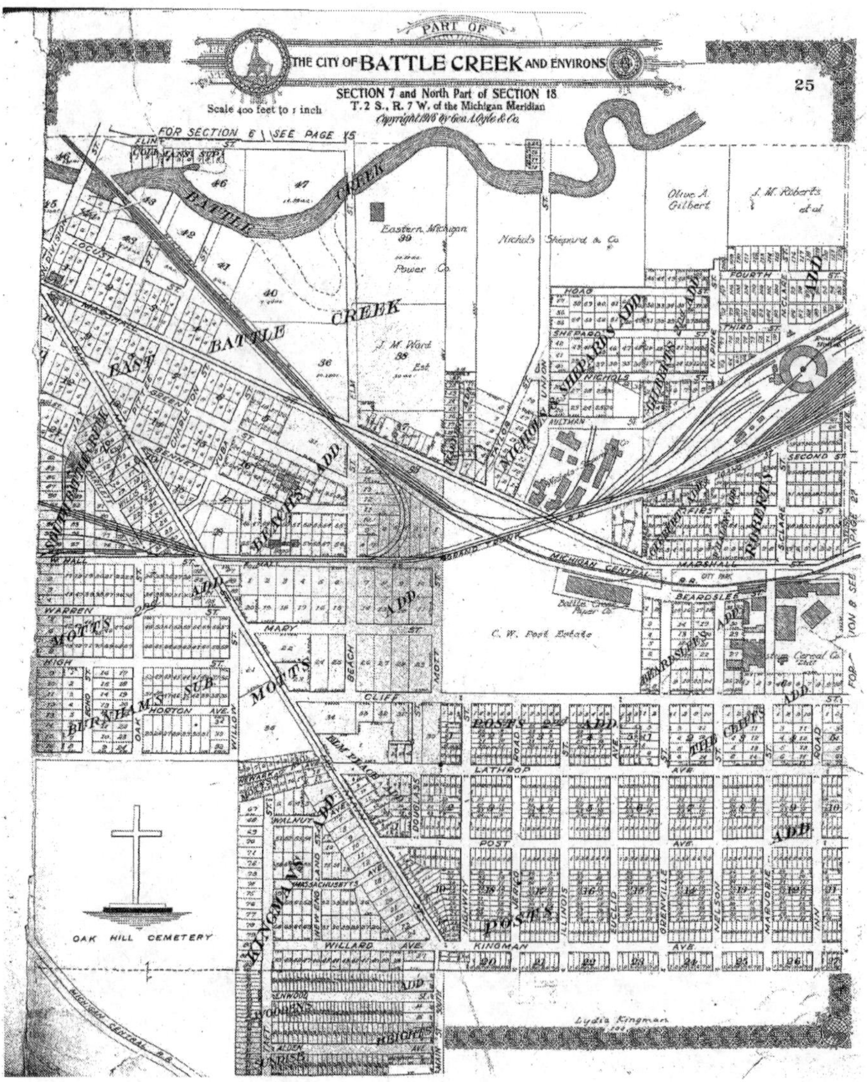
PART OF
THE CITY OF BATTLE CREEK AND ENVIRONS
SECTION 7 and North Part of SECTION 18
T. 2 S., R. 7 W. of the Michigan Meridian
Scale 400 feet to 1 inch
Copyright 1916 by Geo. A. Ogle & Co.
25
FOR SECTION 6 SEE PAGE 15
BATTLE CREEK
EAST BATTLE CREEK
Eastern Michigan Power Co.
Nichols Shepard & Co.
Olive A. Gilbert
J. M. Roberts et al
J. M. Ward Est.
NICHOLS & SHEPARDS ADD
ROBERTS ADD
MOTTS ADD
BURNHAMS SUB
BEACHS ADD
C. W. Post Estate
Battle Creek Paper Co.
Postum Cereal Co.
POSTS 2ND ADD
THE CLIFFS ADD
POSTS ADD
KINGMANS ADD
ELM PLACE ADD
OAK HILL CEMETERY
MICHIGAN CENTRAL R.R.
GRAND TRUNK
Lydia Kingman
LATHROP AVE.
POST AVE.
KINGMAN AVE.
WILLARD AVE.
CLIFF ST.
MARSHALL ST.
BEARDSLEE ST.
WARREN ST.
HIGH ST.
HORTON AVE.
MARY ST.
MASSACHUSETTS AVE.
WALNUT ST.
FOURTH ST.
THIRD ST.
SECOND ST.
FIRST ST.
HOAG ST.
SHEPARD ST.
NICHOLS ST.
AULTMAN ST.
LOCUST ST.
FOR SECTION 8 SEE PAGE 27

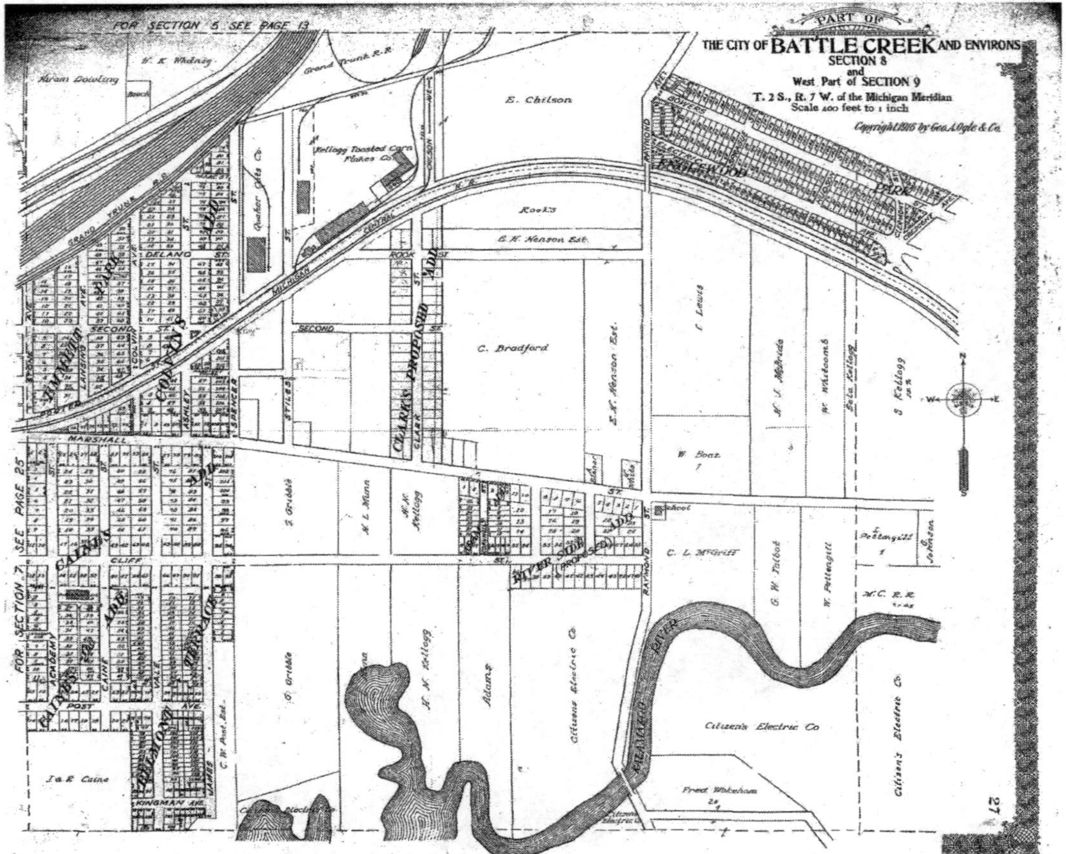
PART OF
THE CITY OF BATTLE CREEK AND ENVIRONS
SECTION 8
and
West Part of SECTION 9
T. 2 S., R. 7 W. of the Michigan Meridian
Scale 400 feet to 1 inch
Copyright 1916 by Geo. A. Ogle & Co.
FOR SECTION 5 SEE PAGE 13
FOR SECTION 7 SEE PAGE 25
E. Chilson
Kellogg Toasted Corn Flakes Co.
Quaker Oats Co.
Grand Trunk R.R.
ENGLEWOOD PARK
Rooks
E. H. Henson Est.
C. Bradford
CLARK'S PROPOSED ADD.
COLVIN'S ADD.
EMMETT PARK
CAINES ADD.
BELMONT TERRACE
RIVER SIDE ADD. (PROPOSED)
KALAMAZOO RIVER
Citizen's Electric Co.
I. Lewis
W. Boaz
C. L. McGriff
G. W. Talbot
W. Pettengill
H. H. Kellogg
H. L. Mann
Adams
G. Gribble
S. Kellogg
W. Whitcomb
Fred Wakeham
J & R Caine
C. W. Post Est.
MARSHALL
MICHIGAN
RAYMOND
School

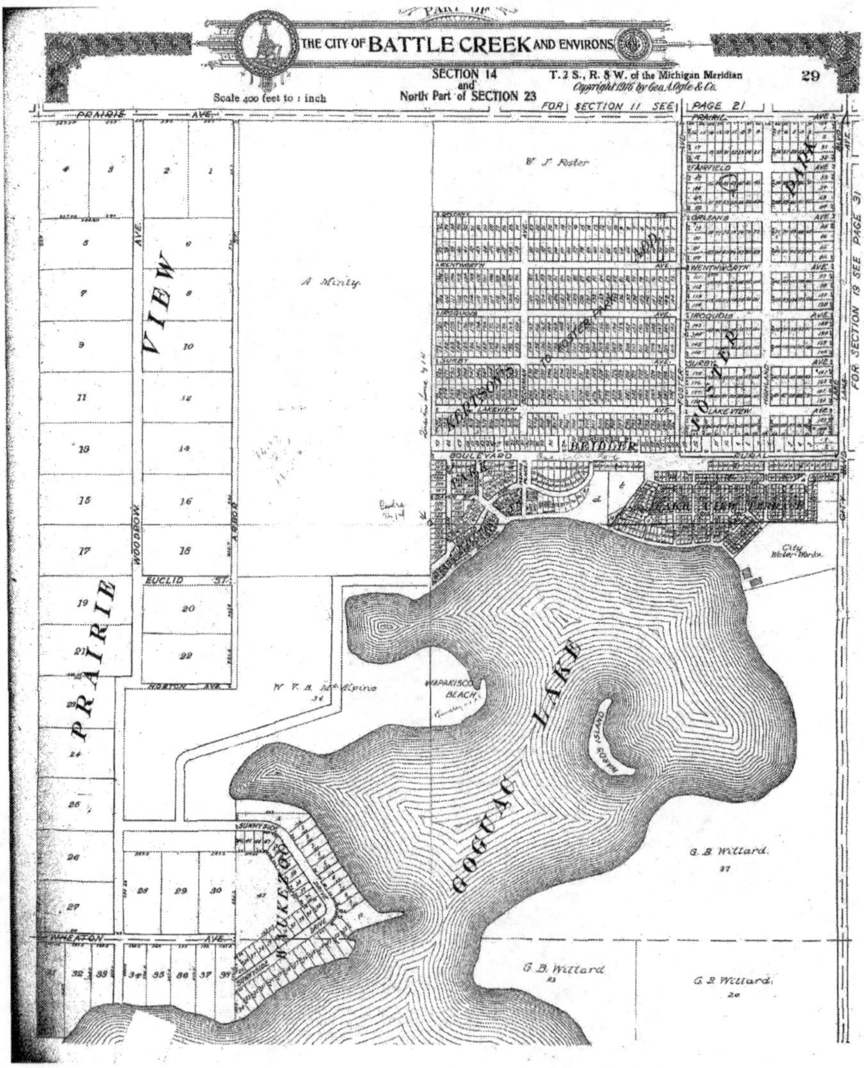
PART OF
THE CITY OF BATTLE CREEK AND ENVIRONS
SECTION 14
and
North Part of SECTION 23
T. 2 S., R. 8 W. of the Michigan Meridian
29
Copyright 1916 by Geo. A. Ogle & Co.
Scale 400 feet to 1 inch
FOR SECTION 11 SEE PAGE 21
FOR SECTION 13 SEE PAGE 31
PRAIRIE AVE.
PRAIRIE VIEW
WOODROW AVE.
ARBOR
EUCLID ST.
NORTON AVE.
WHEATON AVE.
A. Minty
W. J. Foster
W. V. B. McAlpine
WENTWORTH AVE.
IROQUOIS AVE.
SURBY AVE.
LAKEVIEW AVE.
FAIRFIELD AVE.
ORLEANS AVE.
HIGHLAND
FOSTER PARK
KERTSON'S
BOULEVARD
BEYDLER
WAPAKISCO BEACH
GOGUAC LAKE
City Water Works
WAUKETOO
SUNNYSIDE
G. B. Willard

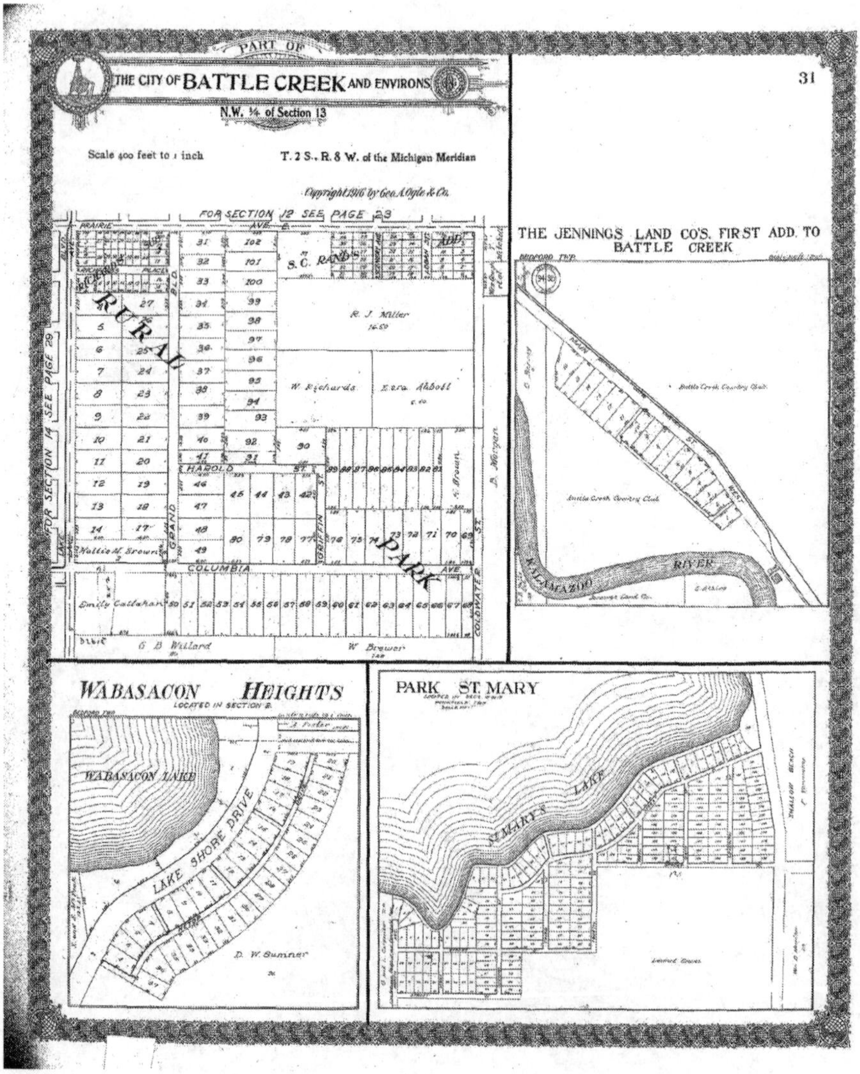
31
PART OF
THE CITY OF BATTLE CREEK AND ENVIRONS
N.W. ¼ of Section 13
Scale 400 feet to 1 inch
T. 2 S., R. 8 W. of the Michigan Meridian
Copyright 1916 by Geo. A. Ogle & Co.
FOR SECTION 12 SEE PAGE 23
FOR SECTION 14 SEE PAGE 29
PRAIRIE AVE.
S. C. RANDS ADD.
RURAL PARK
R. J. Miller
W. Richards
Ezra Abbott
HAROLD ST.
GRAND BLD.
GRIFFIN ST.
COLUMBIA AVE.
COLDWATER ST.
Nattie M. Brown
Emily Callahan
G. B. Willard
W. Brewer
THE JENNINGS LAND CO'S. FIRST ADD. TO BATTLE CREEK
BEDFORD TWP.
MAIN ST. WEST
Battle Creek Country Club
KALAMAZOO RIVER
WABASACON HEIGHTS
LOCATED IN SECTION 8.
WABASACON LAKE
LAKE SHORE DRIVE
D. W. Sumner
PARK ST. MARY
ST. MARY'S LAKE
SHALLOW BEACH

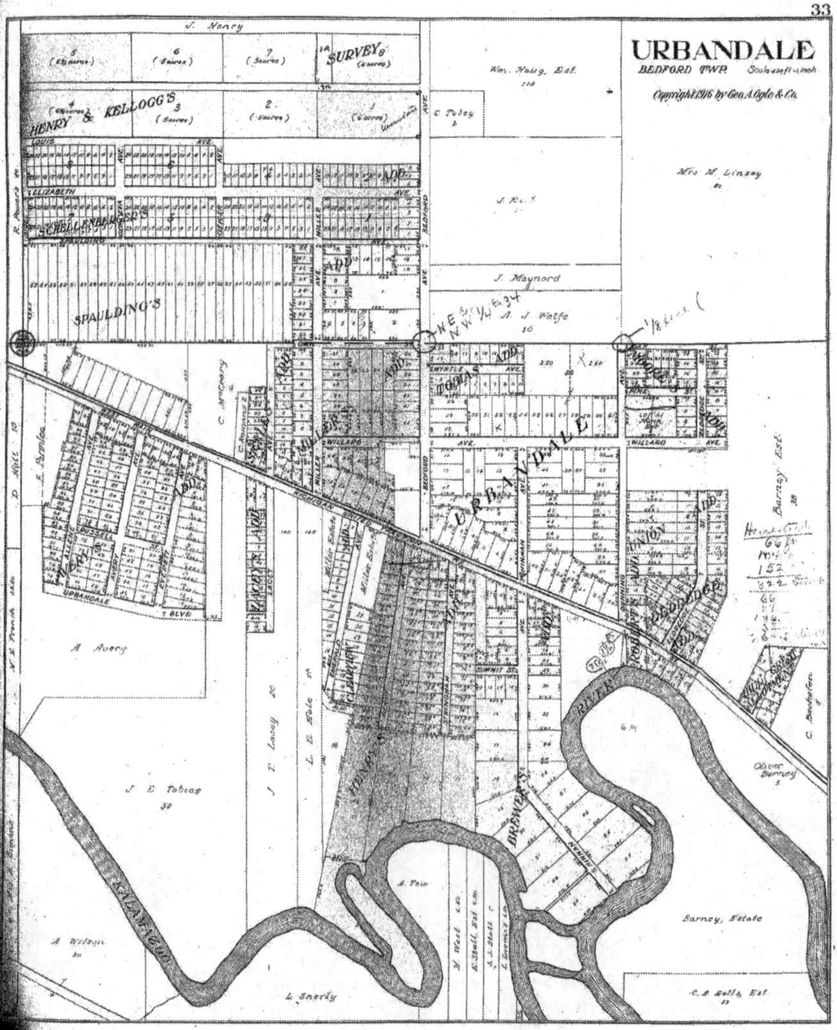
URBANDALE
BEDFORD TWP.
Copyright 1916 by Geo. A. Ogle & Co.
J. Henry
SURVEY
HENRY & KELLOGG'S
SCHELLENBERGER'S
SPAULDING'S
Wm. Haug, Est.
C. Tobey
Mrs M. Linsey
J. Maynard
A. J. Wolfe
TOBIAS ADD.
MILLER'S ADD.
URBANDALE
UNION ADD.
Barney Est.
A. Avery
J. E. Tobias
J. T. Lacey
L. E. Hale
A. Wilson
L. Snerly
Barney Estate
C. E. Kells, Est.
Oliver Barney
BREWER'S
RIVER
KALAMAZOO

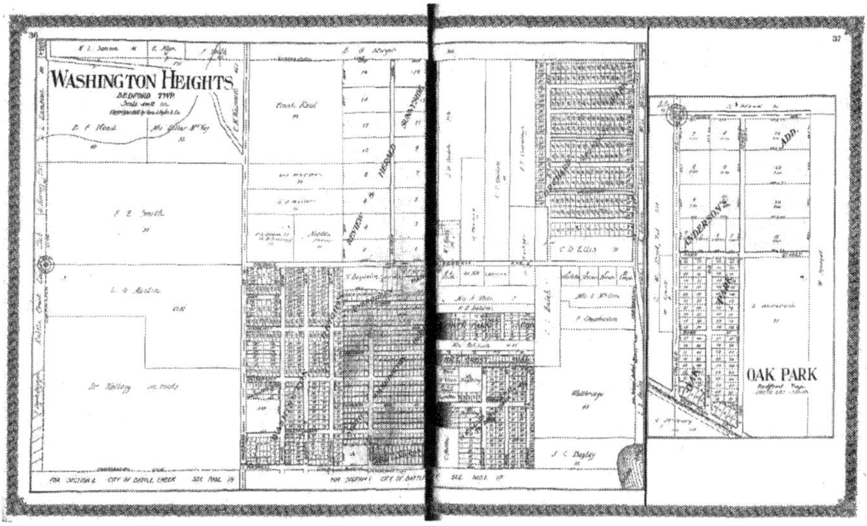
WASHINGTON HEIGHTS
BEDFORD TWP.
OAK PARK
ANDERSON'S ADD.
F. E. Smith
L. G. Austin
C. D. Ellis
J. C. Bagley

RIVERSIDE GARDENS, GREENFIELD PARK, GREENFIELD PARK ANNEX, BROWNLEE PARK and PINE LODGE

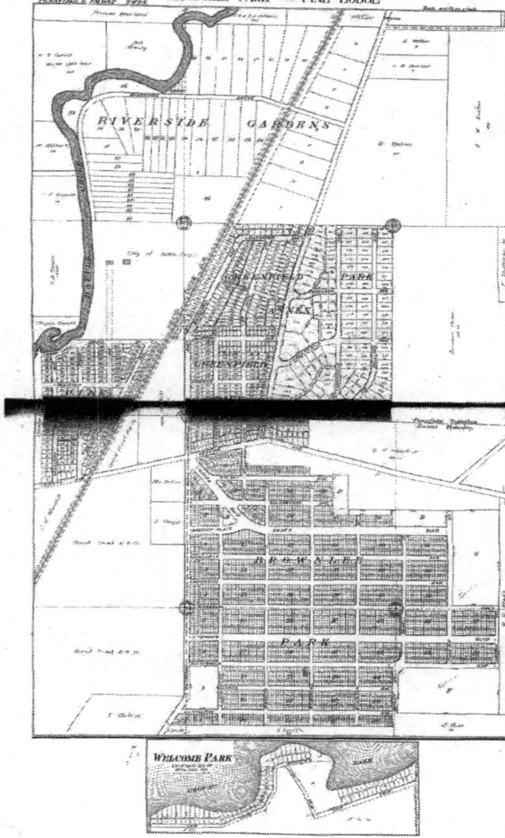

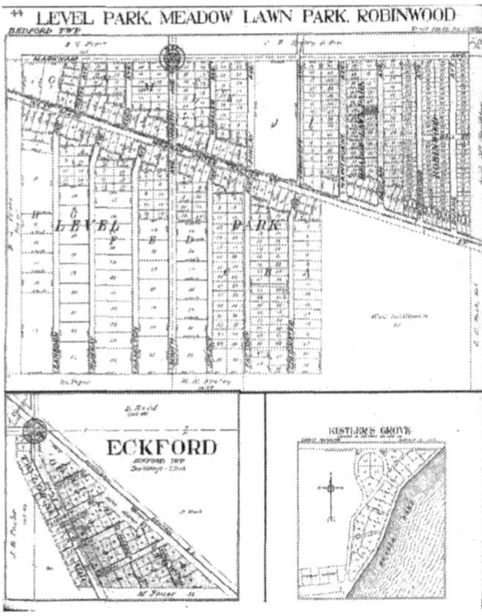
44
LEVEL PARK, MEADOW LAWN PARK, ROBINWOOD
BEDFORD TWP
LEVEL PARK
ECKFORD
ECKFORD TWP
KISTLER'S GROVE

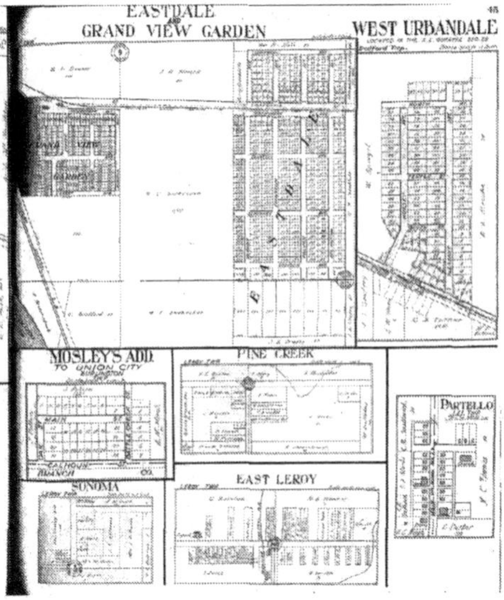
45
EASTDALE AND GRAND VIEW GARDEN
WEST URBANDALE
MOSLEY'S ADD. TO UNION CITY
MAIN
CALHOUN
BRANCH CO.
PINE CREEK
SONOMA
EAST LEROY
PARTELLO

WATTLE'S PARK GREEN ACRE AND GREEN ACRE EXTENSION

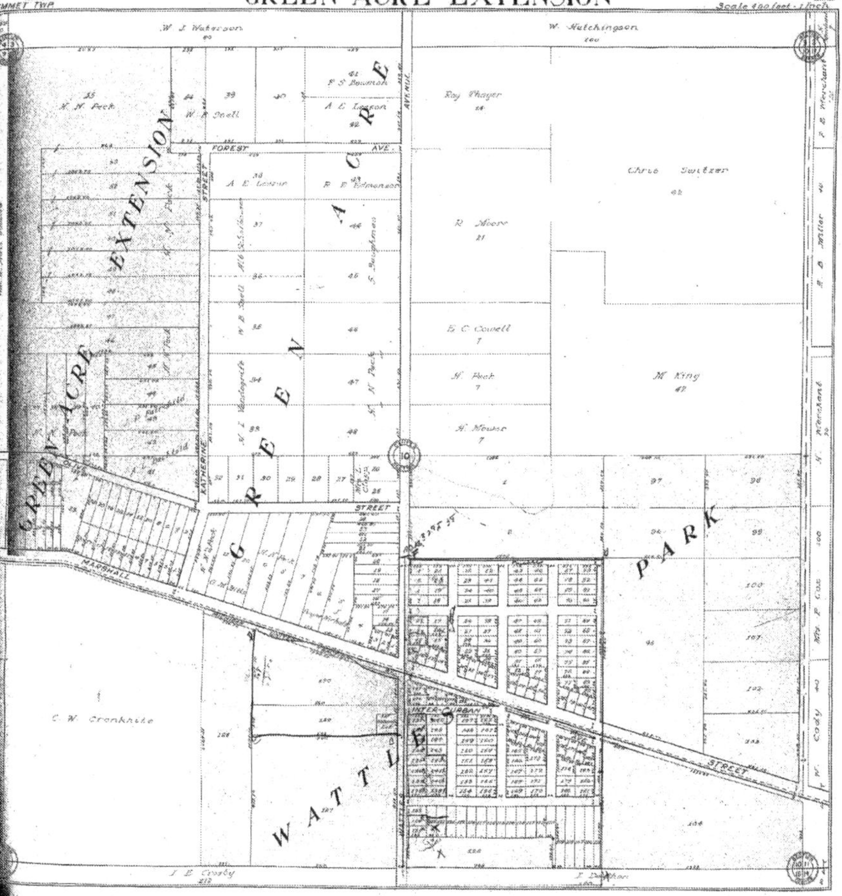

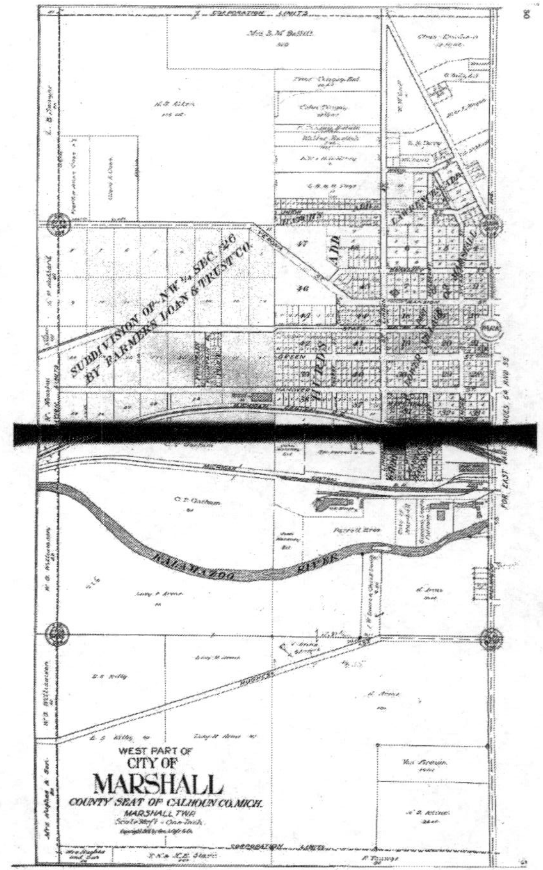
WEST PART OF
CITY OF
MARSHALL
COUNTY SEAT OF CALHOUN CO. MICH.
MARSHALL TWP.
SUBDIVISION OF NW ¼ SEC. 26
BY FARMERS LOAN & TRUST CO.
KALAMAZOO RIVER
CORPORATION LIMITS

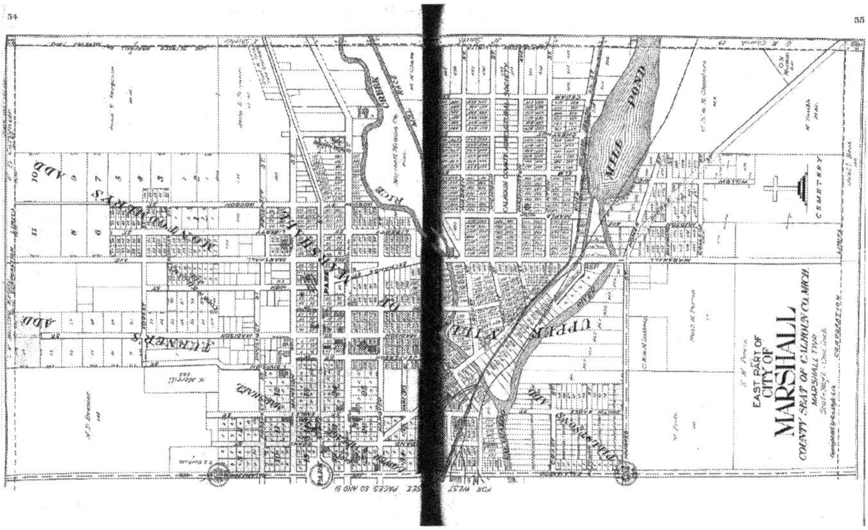
EAST PART OF
CITY OF
MARSHALL
COUNTY SEAT OF CALHOUN CO. MICH.
MILL POND
CEMETERY

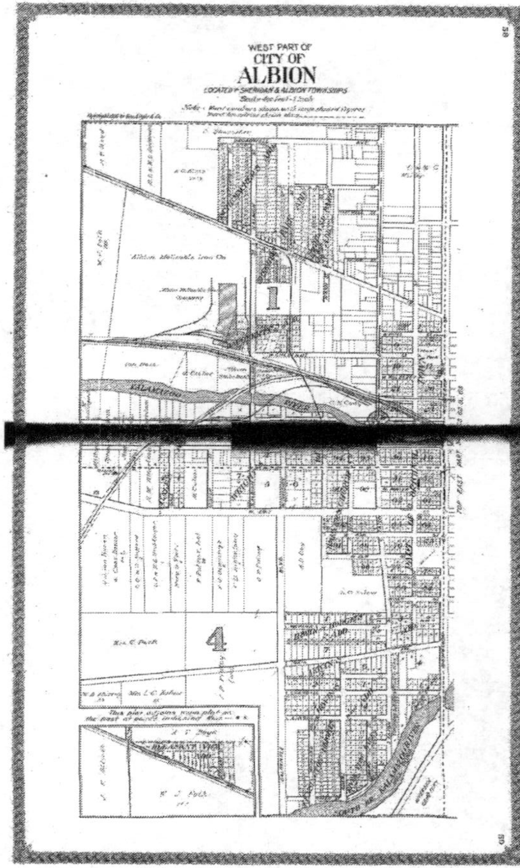
WEST PART OF
CITY OF
ALBION
LOCATED IN SHERIDAN & ALBION TOWNSHIPS
Albion Malleable Iron Co.
1
4

EAST PART OF
CITY OF ALBION
LOCATED IN SHERIDAN & ALBION TOWNSHIPS

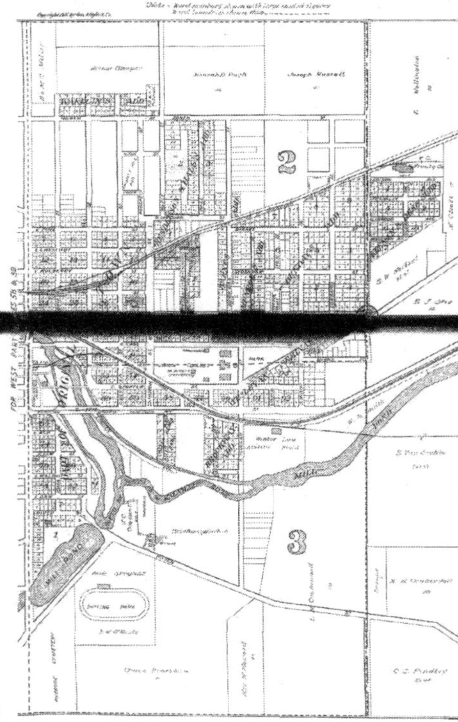

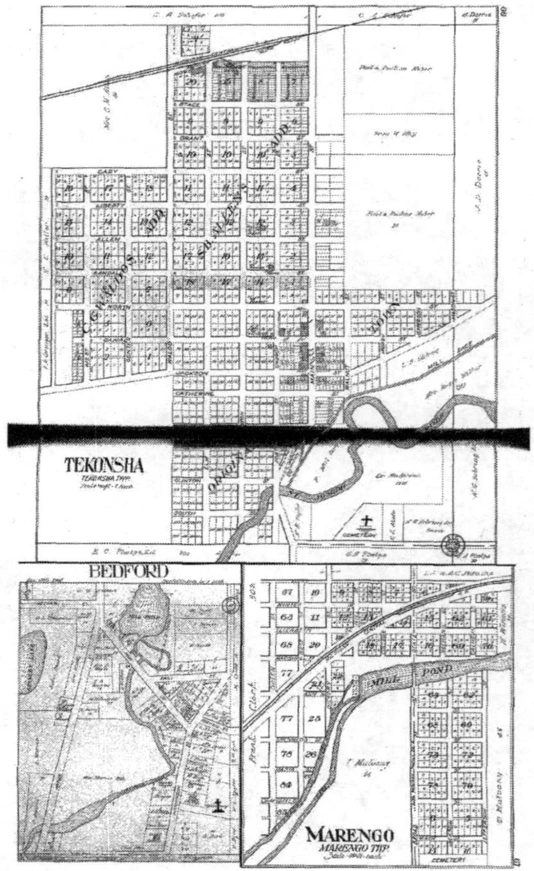

TEKONSHA
TEKONSHA TWP.
ORIGINAL
UNION
BEDFORD
MARENGO
MARENGO TWP.
MILL POND
CEMETERY

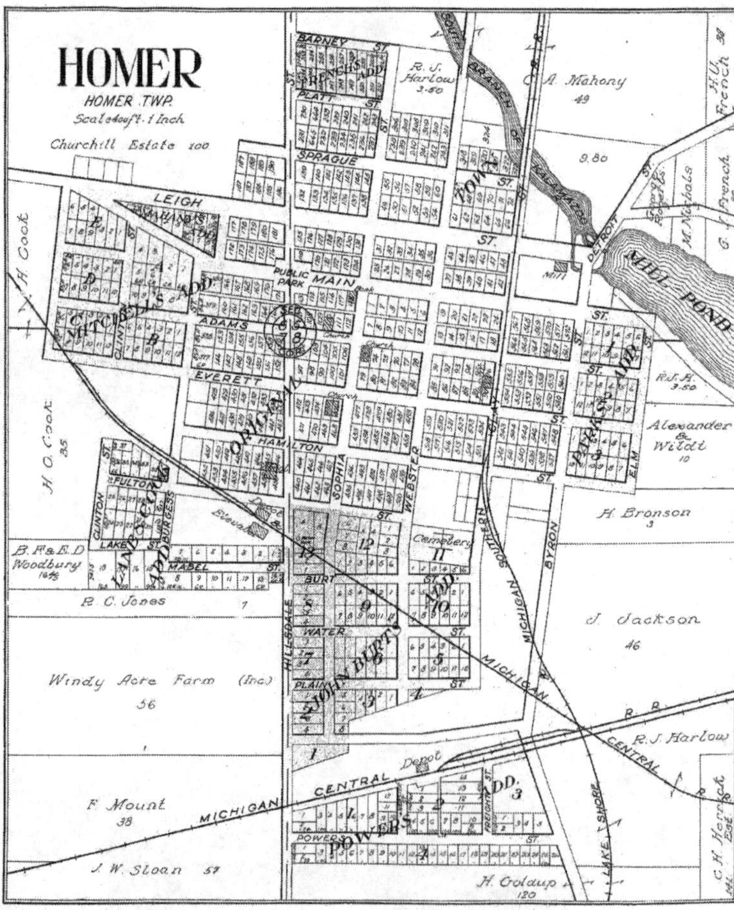
HOMER
HOMER TWP.
Scale 400 ft. 1 Inch
Churchill Estate 100
R. J. Harlow 3.50
C. A. Mahony 49
9.80
H. U. French 38
M. Nichols
G. F. French 30
MILL POND
Mill
R. J. H. 3.50
Alexander & Wildi 10
H. Bronson 3
J. Jackson 46
R. J. Harlow
C. H. Herrick Est. 141
H. Coldup 120
J. W. Sloan 57
F. Mount 38
Windy Acre Farm (Inc.) 56
R. C. Jones 7
B. F. & E. D. Woodbury 16
H. O. Cook 35
H. Cook
MICHIGAN CENTRAL R. R.
LAKE SHORE
MICHIGAN SOUTHERN
SOUTH BRANCH OF KALAMAZOO R.
MITCHELL'S ADD.
ORIGINAL
JOHN BURT'S ADD.
POWERS ADD.
FRENCH'S ADD.
PARKS ADD.
LANDON & COOK ADD.
LEIGH
MAIN
ADAMS
EVERETT
HAMILTON
SPRAGUE
PLATT
BARNEY
DETROIT ST.
BYRON
WEBSTER
SOPHIA
HILLSDALE
BURT
WATER
PLAIN
POWERS
FREIGHT ST.
CLINTON
FULTON
LAKE ST.
MABEL
BURGESS
ELM
PUBLIC PARK
Cemetery
Depot
Elevator
Church

ATHENS

ATHENS TWP.

Scale-35oft-1in.

BURLINGTON

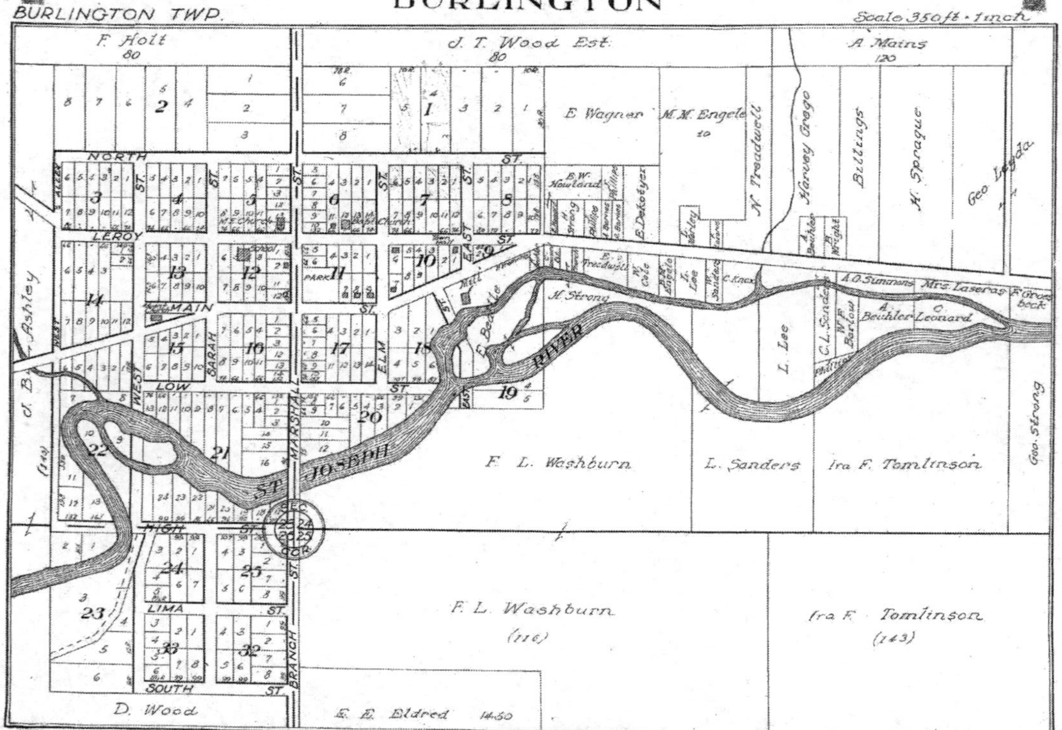
BURLINGTON TWP.
Scale 350 ft. = 1 inch
F. Holt 80
J. T. Wood Est. 80
A. Mains 120
E Wagner
M. M. Engele 10
N. Treadwell
Harvey Grego
Billings
H. Sprague
Geo. Legda
NORTH ST.
LEROY ST.
MAIN ST.
LOW ST.
HIGH ST.
LIMA ST.
SOUTH ST.
WEST ST.
SARAH ST.
MARSHALL ST.
ELM ST.
EAST ST.
BRANCH ST.
PARK
Bapt. Church
School
E.W. Howland
E. Dekotyer
H. Strong
A.O. Summons
Mrs. Laseras
F. Groesbeck
A. Beuhler
C. Leonard
W.F. Barlow
C. L. Sanders
L. Lee
L. Sanders
Ira F. Tomlinson
Ira F. Tomlinson (143)
Geo. Strong
F. L. Washburn
F. L. Washburn (116)
E. E. Eldred 14.50
D. Wood
J. B. Ashley (144)
ST. JOSEPH RIVER
SEC. COR. 24 25
Burlington Village

MAP OF
CLARENCE
TOWNSHIP
Scale 2 inches to 1 mile
Township 1 South, Range 4 West of the Michigan Meridian
EATON
CO.
BASE
LINE
TWP
CO.
DUCK LAKE
LEE
SHERIDAN
TWP
JACKSON
Wm Butterfield
A Baum
Mrs W. Porter
D.G. Allen
John Schmidt
A.B. Cooper
W.C. Luattia
Fred Kopp
Wm. Krenerich

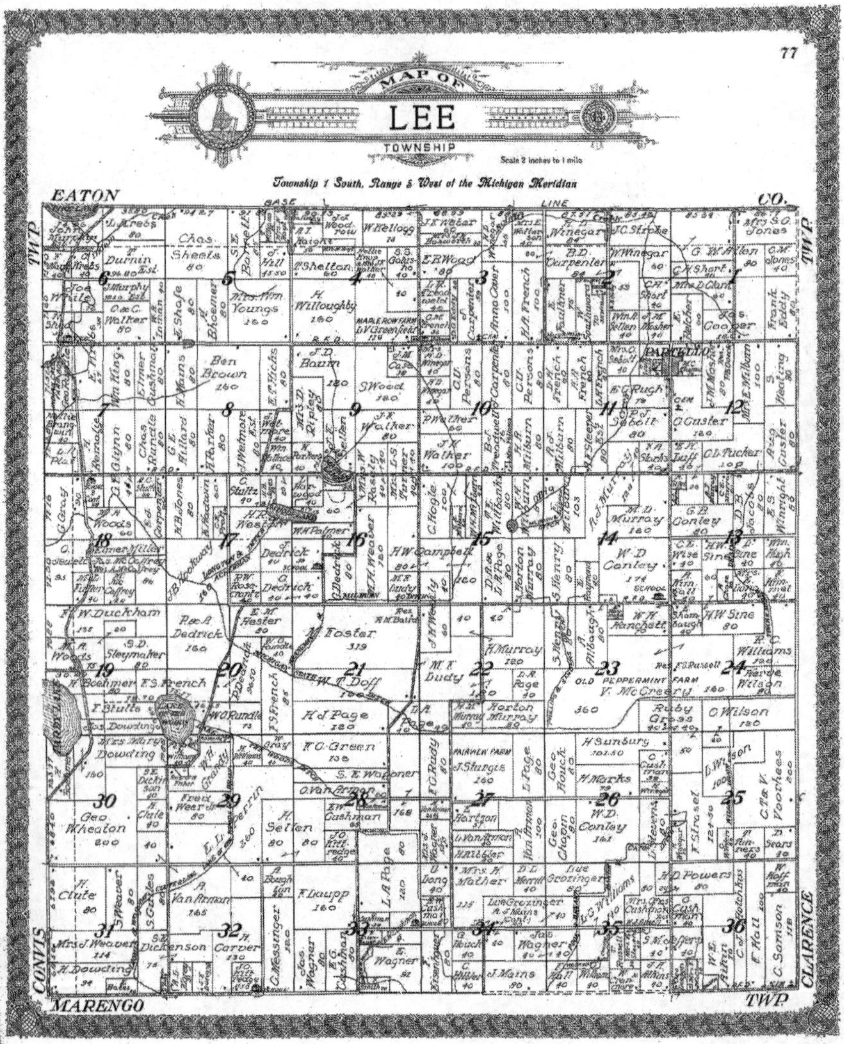
MAP OF
LEE
TOWNSHIP
Scale 2 inches to 1 mile
Township 1 South, Range 5 West of the Michigan Meridian
EATON CO.
BASE LINE
TWP.
CONVIS TWP.
MARENGO TWP.
CLARENCE TWP.
PARTELLO
OLD PEPPERMINT FARM
FAIRVIEW FARM
MAPLE ROW FARM

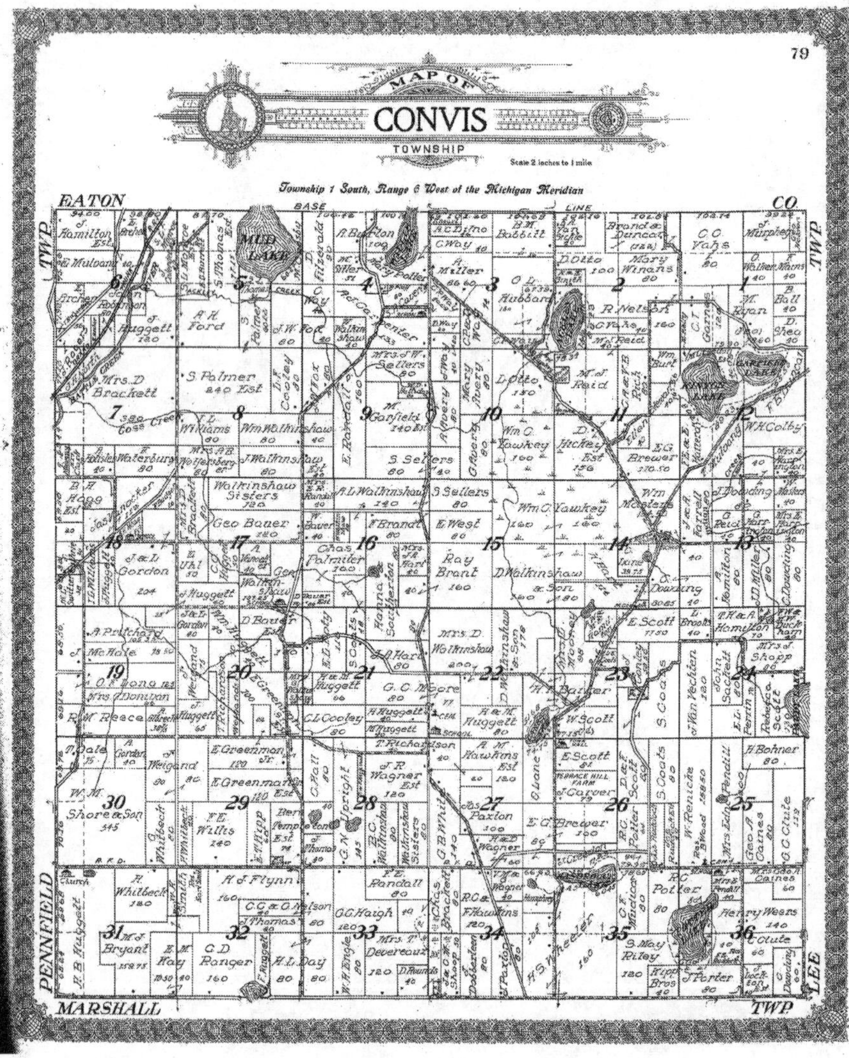
MAP OF
CONVIS
TOWNSHIP
Scale 2 inches to 1 mile
Township 1 South, Range 6 West of the Michigan Meridian
EATON
CO
BASE LINE
TWP
PENNFIELD
MARSHALL
LEE
TWP
MUD LAKE

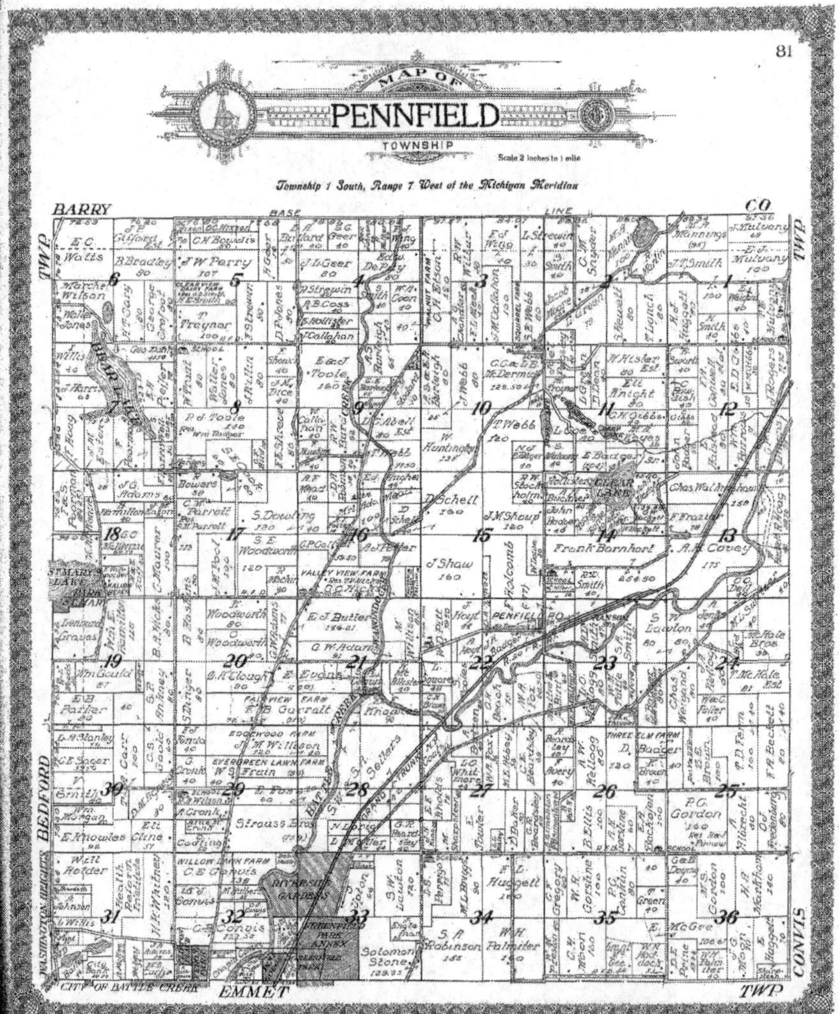
MAP OF
PENNFIELD
TOWNSHIP
Scale 2 inches to 1 mile
Township 1 South, Range 7 West of the Michigan Meridian
BARRY
BASE
LINE
CO
TWP
BEDFORD
TWP
CONVIS
TWP
EMMET
CITY OF BATTLE CREEK
CLEAR LAKE
PENNFIELD
RIVERSIDE GARDENS

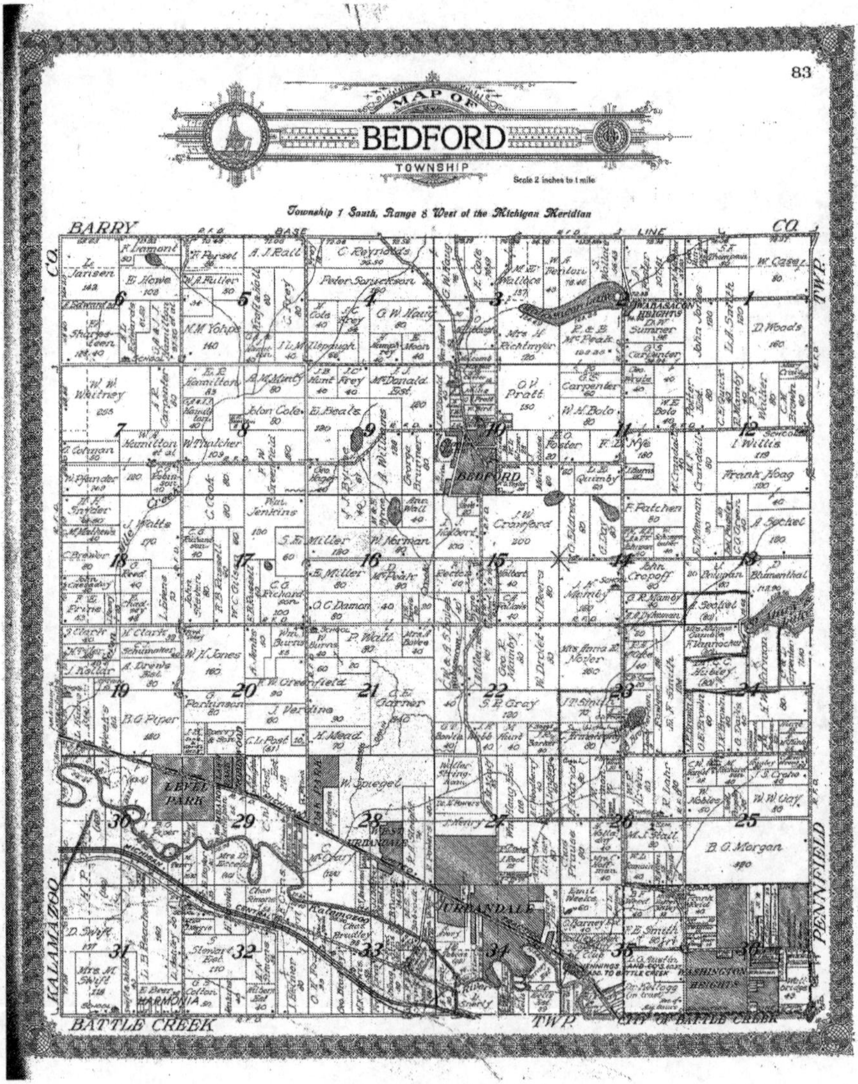
MAP OF
BEDFORD
TOWNSHIP
Scale 2 inches to 1 mile
Township 1 South, Range 8 West of the Michigan Meridian
BARRY
BASE
LINE
CO.
TWP.
KALAMAZOO
PENNFIELD
BATTLE CREEK
TWP.
CITY OF BATTLE CREEK
BEDFORD
URBANDALE
WEST URBANDALE
LEVEL PARK
HARMONIA
WASHINGTON HEIGHTS

MAP OF
BATTLE CREEK
TOWNSHIP
Scale 2 inches to 1 mile
Township 2 South, Range 8 West of the Michigan Meridian
BEDFORD
TWP.
CITY OF BATTLE CREEK
FOSTER PARK
WELCOME PARK
RENTON STA.
KALAMAZOO
CO.
LEROY
EMMET
TWP.

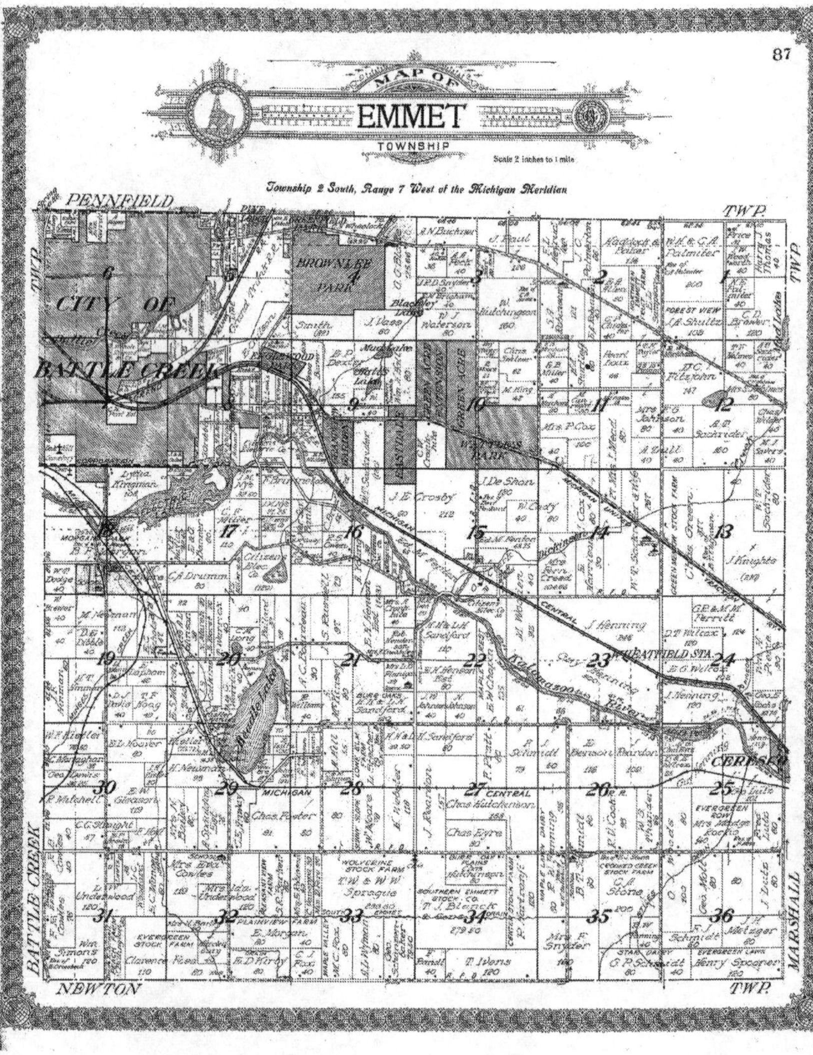
MAP OF
EMMET
TOWNSHIP
Scale 2 inches to 1 mile
Township 2 South, Range 7 West of the Michigan Meridian
PENNFIELD TWP.
TWP.
BATTLE CREEK
TWP.
MARSHALL
NEWTON TWP.
CITY OF
BATTLE CREEK
BROWNLEE PARK
WHEATFIELD STA.
CERESCO
MICHIGAN CENTRAL R.R.
J. E. Crosby
J. Henning
Chas. Foster
Chas. Hutchinson
Chas. Eyre
WOLVERINE STOCK FARM
T.W. & W.W. Sprague
SOUTHERN EMMETT STOCK CO.
PLAINVIEW FARM
EVERGREEN STOCK FARM
EVERGREEN LAWN
Henry Spooner
G.P. Schmidt
T. Ivens

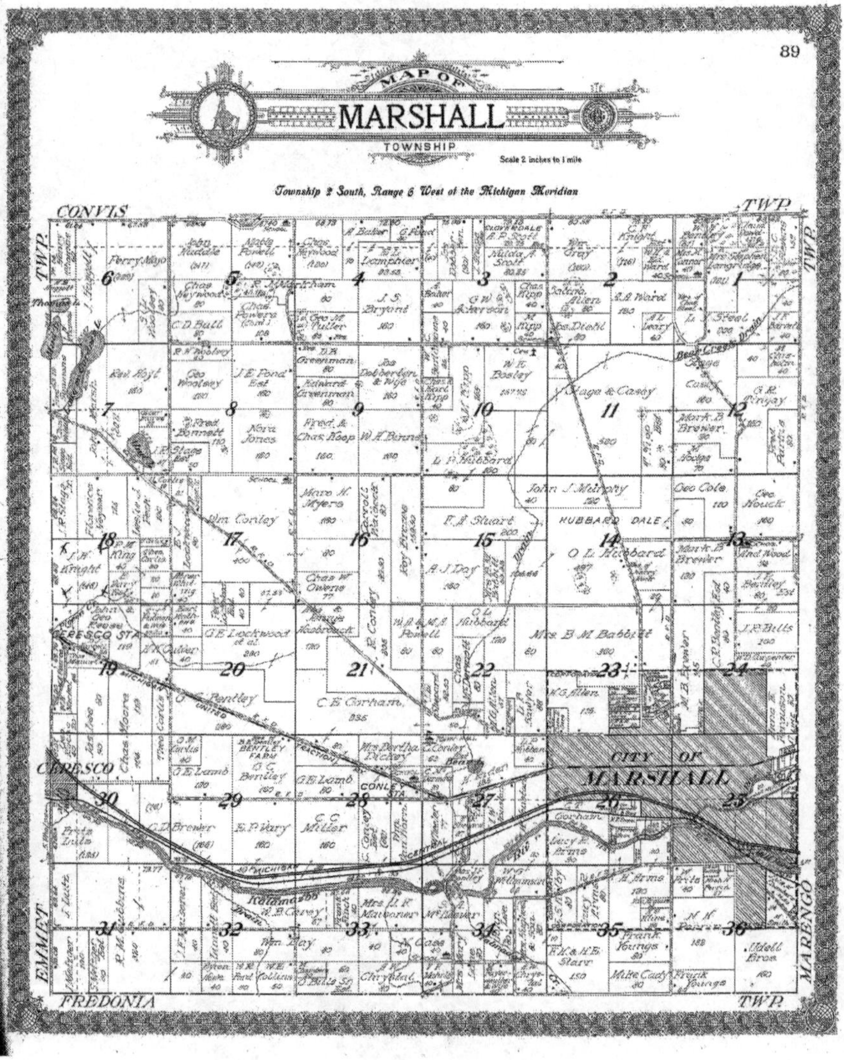
MAP OF
MARSHALL
TOWNSHIP
Scale 2 inches to 1 mile
Township 2 South, Range 6 West of the Michigan Meridian
CONVIS
TWP.
EMMET
FREDONIA
MARENGO
CITY OF MARSHALL
CERESCO
HUBBARD DALE

MAP OF
MARENGO
TOWNSHIP
Scale 2 inches to 1 mile
Township 2 South, Range 5 West of the Michigan Meridian
LEE TWP
TWP
MARSHALL
SHERIDAN
ECKFORD
TWP
J. B. Carver
E. W. Henry
J. J. Flynn
J. J. Flynn
E. D. Washburn
O. D. Townsend
Wm. G. Forman
E. F. Chapin Est.
R. W. Dean
J. H. Storrs Est.
S. Bossard
R. Frink
H. D. Powers
M. Bolles
C. A. Miller Est.
M. B. Pain
W. E. Doolittle
N. F. Wilder
John Adams
Van Suckle
R. Beattie
R. A. Leggett
O. Raesley
T. E. Tanner
F. E. Smith
W. W. Williams
W. Newton
D. Shutz
F. A. Avery
Harry Youngglove
C. Seaman
County Farm
Dr. L. V. Rogers
C. F. Perritt
C. D. Cooper
O. R. Fish
Mulvany
F. Shebel
R. Hughes
R. Graham
A. Barkley
H. O. Tucker
C. Godfrey
C. H. Hess
R. Rose Est.
J. C. Page
F. Graham
A. C. Pollison
J. H. McClure
L. Perrin
MARENGO
RICE CREEK
MICHIGAN
KALAMAZOO
RIVER
1
2
3
4
5
6
7
8
9
10
11
12
13
14
15
16
17
18
19
20
21
22
23
24
25
26
27
28
29
30
31
32
33
34
35
36

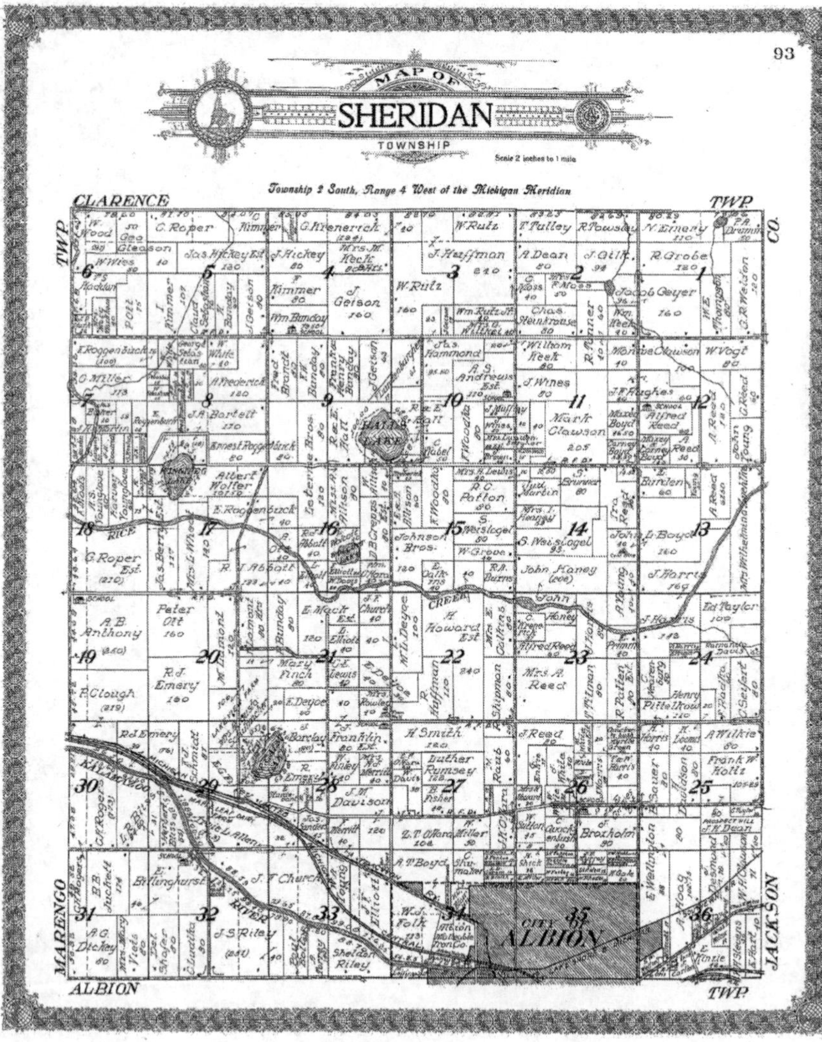
MAP OF
SHERIDAN
TOWNSHIP
Scale 2 inches to 1 mile
Township 2 South, Range 4 West of the Michigan Meridian
CLARENCE
TWP.
TWP.
CO.
MARENGO
JACKSON
ALBION
TWP.
CITY OF
ALBION
HALLS LAKE
RICE
CREEK
RIVER

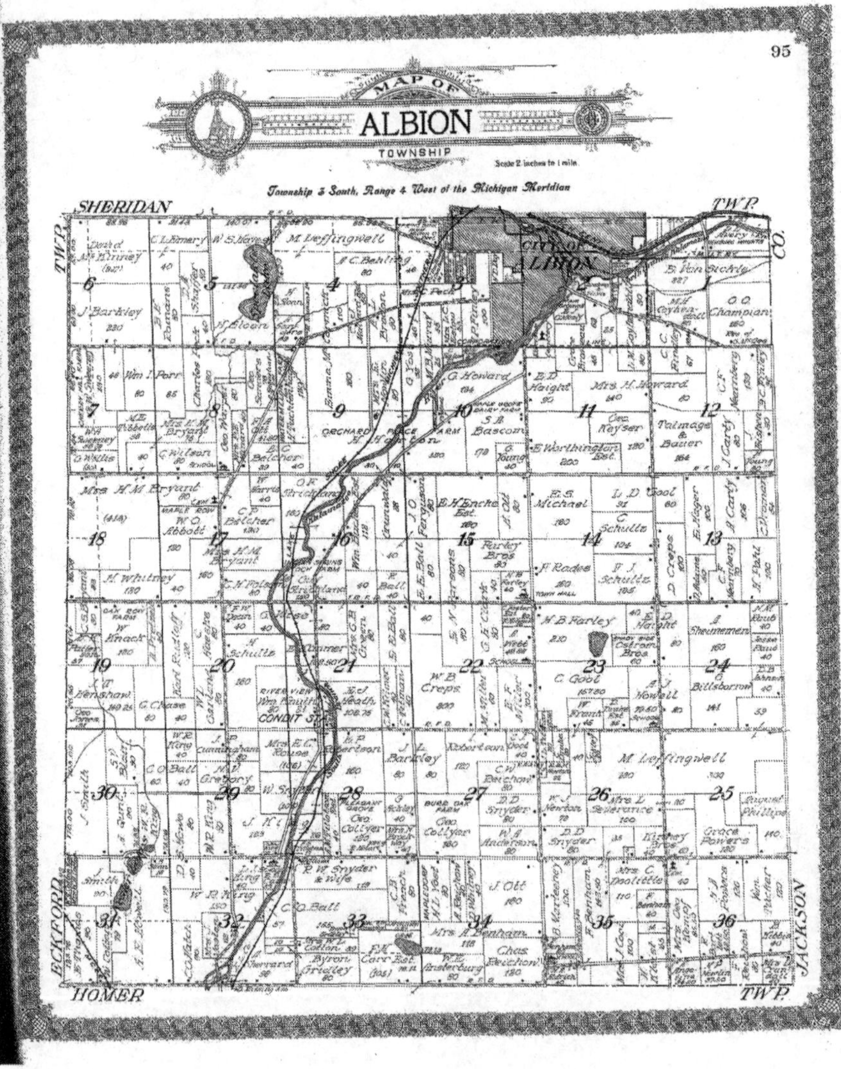

MAP OF
ALBION
TOWNSHIP
Scale 2 inches to 1 mile.
Township 3 South, Range 4 West of the Michigan Meridian
SHERIDAN
TWP.
TWP.
CO.
ECKFORD
HOMER
TWP.
JACKSON
CITY OF ALBION
M. Leffingwell
J. Barkley
C. L. Emery
E. Van Sickle
O. C. Champian
G. Howard
S. B. Bascom
Mrs. H. Howard
E. Worthington Est.
Talmage & Bauer
Mrs. H. M. Bryant
W. O. Abbott
C. P. Belcher
M. Whitney
E. S. Michael
L. D. Gool
F. J. Schultz
M. B. Farley
W. B. Creps
C. Gool
M. Leffingwell
Grace Powers
Geo. Collyer
J. Ott
Chas. Reichow
Byron Gridley
CONDIT

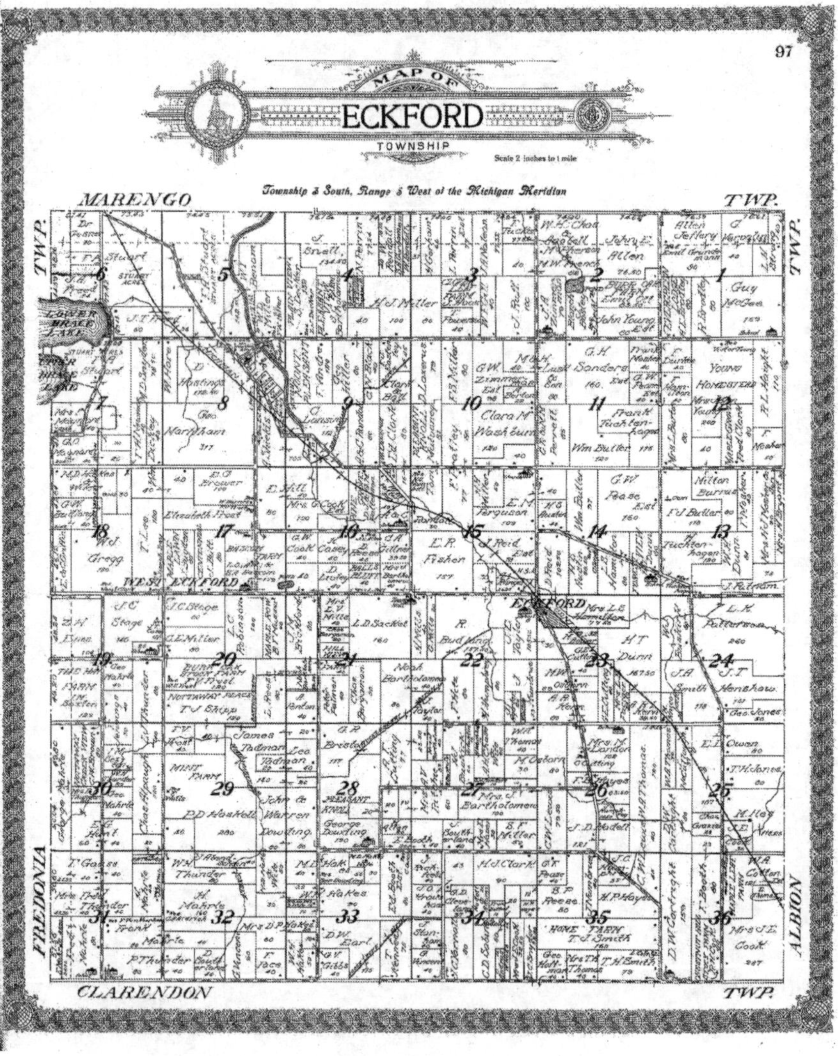
MAP OF
ECKFORD
TOWNSHIP
Scale 2 inches to 1 mile
Township 3 South, Range 5 West of the Michigan Meridian
MARENGO TWP.
CLARENDON TWP.
FREDONIA TWP.
ALBION TWP.
LOWER BROCK LAKE
WEST ECKFORD
ECKFORD
NOTTAWAY PLACE
MINT FARM
PLEASANT KNOLL
HOME FARM

MAP OF
FREDONIA
TOWNSHIP
Scale 2 inches to 1 mile
Township 3 South, Range 6 West of the Michigan Meridian
MARSHALL
TWP.
NEWTON
TEKONSHA
TWP.
ECKFORD

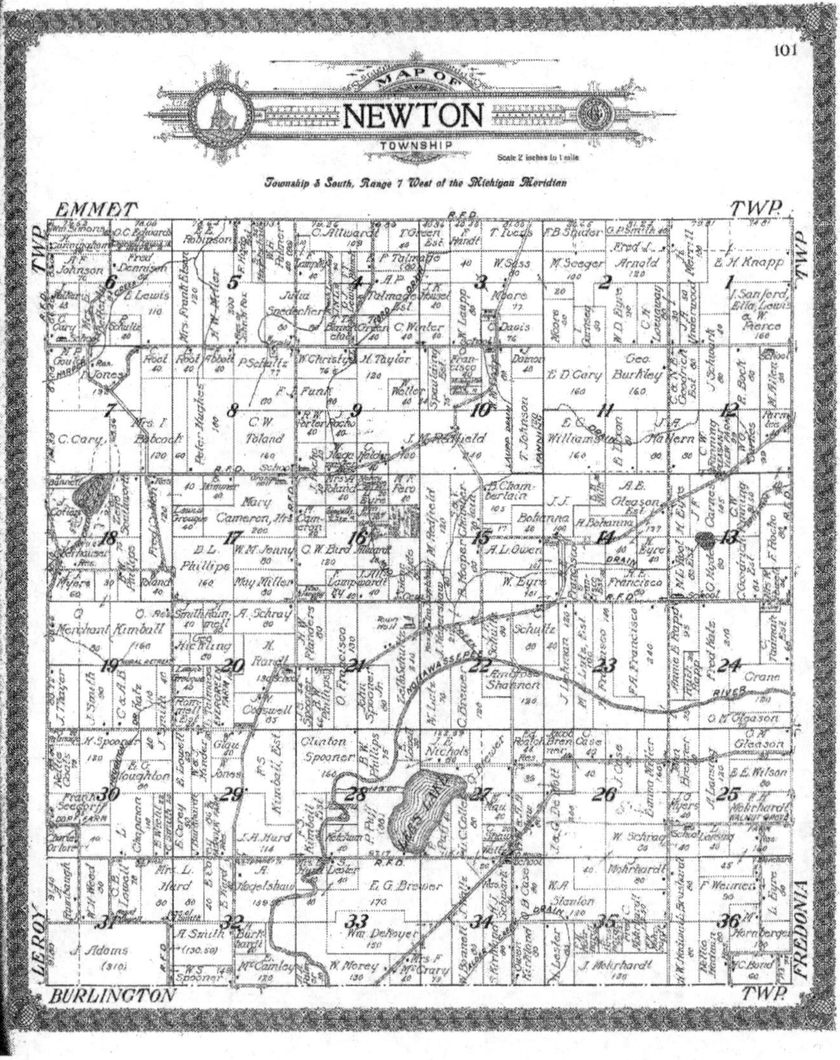
MAP OF
NEWTON
TOWNSHIP
Scale 2 inches to 1 mile
Township 3 South, Range 7 West of the Michigan Meridian
EMMET TWP.
LEROY TWP.
BURLINGTON TWP.
FREDONIA TWP.

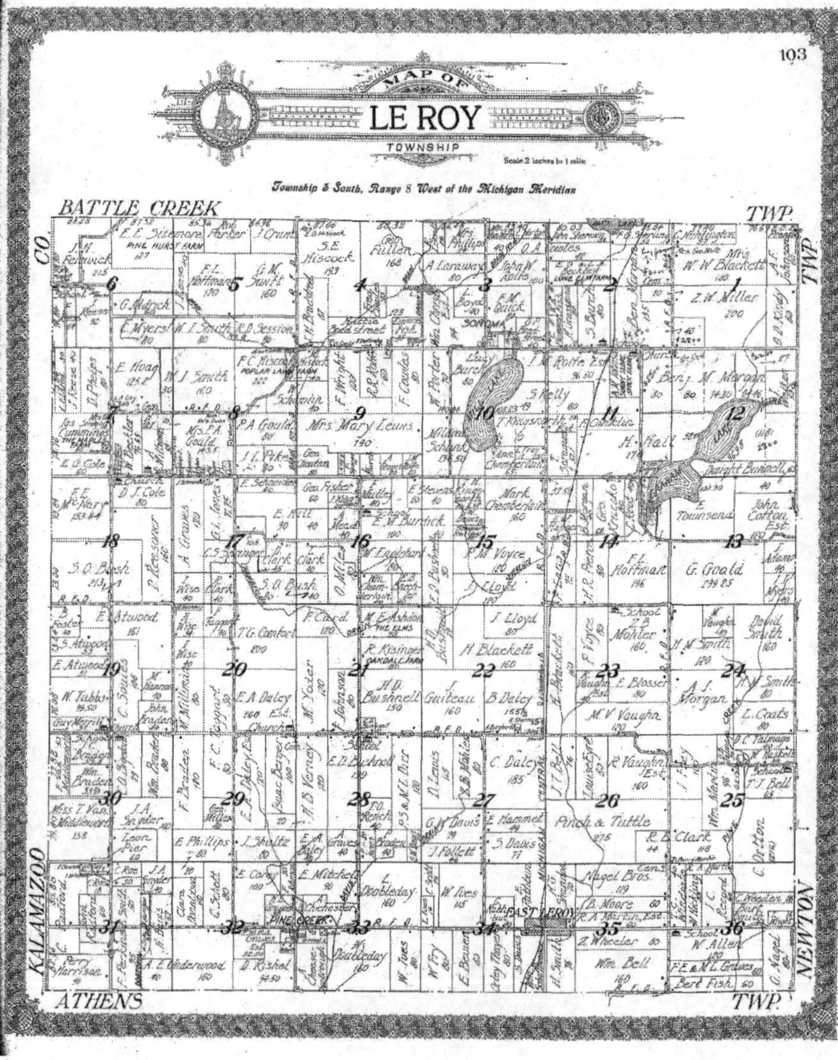
MAP OF
LE ROY
TOWNSHIP
Scale 2 inches to 1 mile
Township 3 South, Range 8 West of the Michigan Meridian
BATTLE CREEK
TWP.
CO.
TWP.
KALAMAZOO
NEWTON
ATHENS
TWP.
SONOMA
PINE CREEK
EAST LEROY
PINE HURST FARM
POPLAR LAWN FARM
THE ELMS
OAKDALE FARM
E. E. Sitemore
S.E. Hiscock
Geo. Fullen
A. Laraway
W. W. Blackett
Z. W. Miller
F. L. Hoffman
G. M. Swift
C. Myers
W. I. Smith
R. D. Session
E. Hoag
F. C. Hiscock
Mrs. Mary Lewis
S. Kelly
Benj. M. Morgan
H. Hall
Dwight Bunnell
E. G. Cole
D. J. Cole
Mark Chamberlain
E. Townsend
John Cotton Est.
S. O. Bush
F. L. Hoffman
G. Goald
E. Atwood
T. G. Comfort
R. Kisinger
H. Blackett
J. Lloyd
H. W. Smith
David Smith
W. Tubbs
F. A. Daley
H. D. Bushnell
J. Guiteau
B. Daley
M. V. Vaughn
A. J. Morgan
L. Coats
E. D. Bushnell
C. Daley
R. Vaughn Est.
Pinch & Tuttle
R. B. Clark
G. W. Davis
E. Hammet
S. Davis
E. Phillips
E. Mitchell
L. Doubleday
Nagel Bros.
B. Moore
A. E. Underwood
D. Rishel
A. Doubleday
Z. Wheeler
Wm. Bell
W. Allen
Bert Fish
Perry Harrison
1
2
3
4
5
6
7
8
9
10
11
12
13
14
15
16
17
18
19
20
21
22
23
24
25
26
27
28
29
30
31
32
33
34
35
36

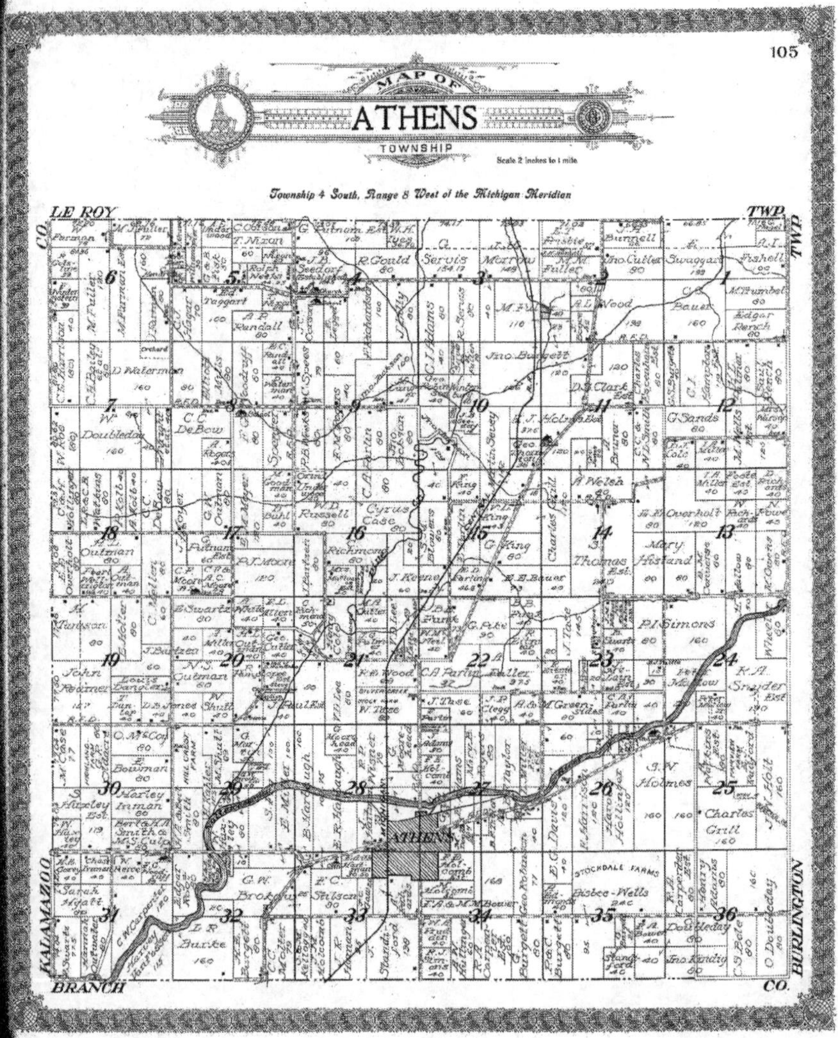
MAP OF
ATHENS
TOWNSHIP
Scale 2 inches to 1 mile
Township 4 South, Range 8 West of the Michigan Meridian
LE ROY
TWP.
CO.
TWP.
KALAMAZOO
BRANCH
CO.
BURLINGTON
ATHENS

MAP OF
BURLINGTON
TOWNSHIP
Scale 2 inches to 1 mile
Township 4 South, Range 7 West of the Michigan Meridian
NEWTON
TWP.
TWP.
ATHENS
TEKONSHA
BRANCH
CO.
BURLINGTON
ABSCOTA
FAIRVIEW FARM
UNION CITY
MICHIGAN CENTRAL

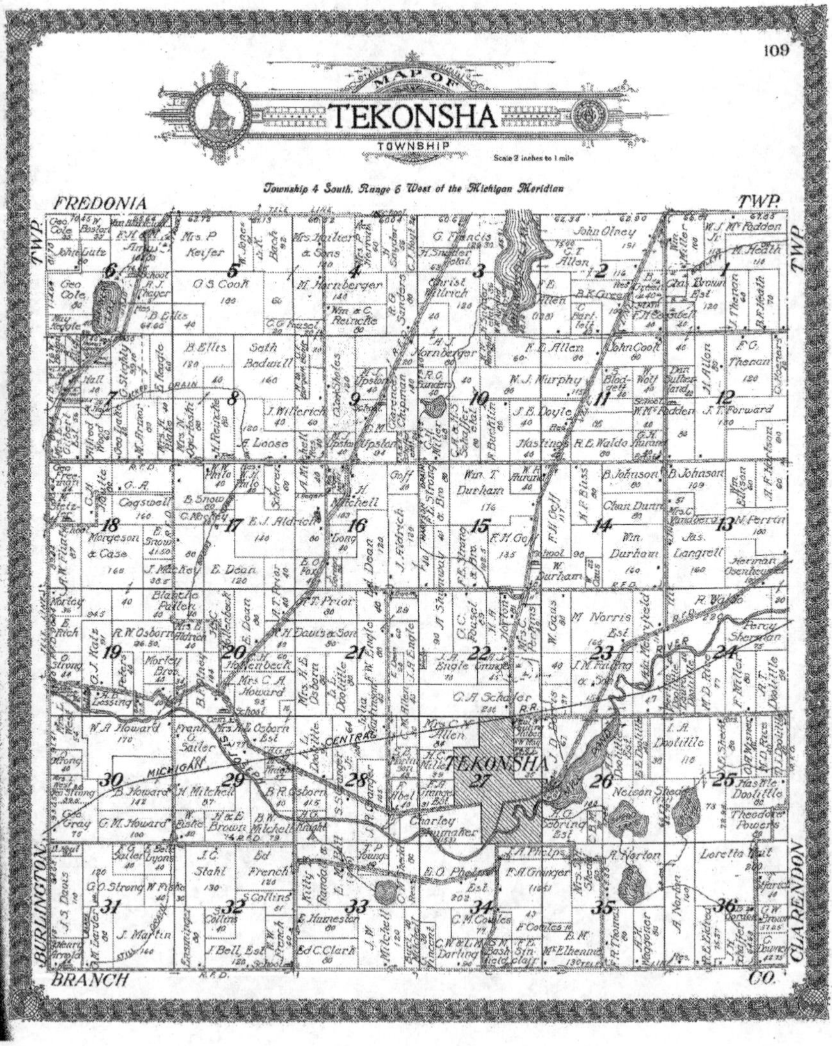
MAP OF
TEKONSHA
TOWNSHIP
Scale 2 inches to 1 mile
Township 4 South, Range 6 West of the Michigan Meridian
FREDONIA
TWP.
TWP.
TWP.
BURLINGTON
BRANCH
CO.
CLARENDON
TEKONSHA
MICHIGAN CENTRAL R.R.
RIVER

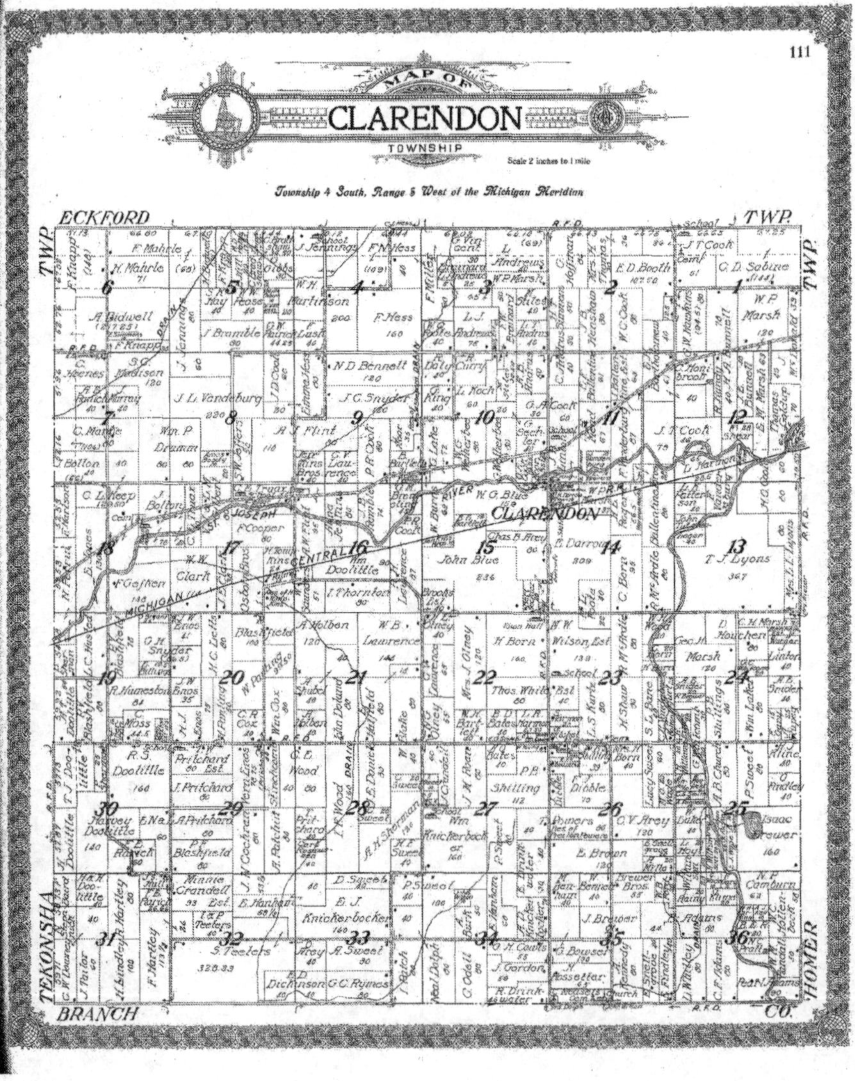
MAP OF
CLARENDON
TOWNSHIP
Scale 2 inches to 1 mile
Township 4 South, Range 5 West of the Michigan Meridian
ECKFORD TWP.
TWP.
TEKONSHA TWP.
HOMER TWP.
BRANCH CO.
CLARENDON
ST. JOSEPH RIVER
MICHIGAN CENTRAL
1
2
3
4
5
6
7
8
9
10
11
12
13
14
15
16
17
18
19
20
21
22
23
24
25
26
27
28
29
30
31
32
33
34
35
36

MAP OF
HOMER
TOWNSHIP
Scale 2 inches to 1 mile
Township 4 South, Range 4 West of the Michigan Meridian
ALBION
TWP.
TWP.
CO.
CLARENDON
JACKSON
HILLSDALE
CO.
HOMER
MILL POND
MICHIGAN
CENTRAL
KALAMAZOO
RIVER
MAPLE GROVE FARM
THE ISLAND FARM
A. C. Conger
Geo Carder
Ed. Linton
Geo. D. Cleveland
L. H. Champion
J. E. Champion
W. McKennan
Geo. Wildt
Geo. H. Kiefer
Mary Fisher
Thomas Dawson
S. A. Riddle
Mrs. O. Peabody
W. C. Wolland
H. Goldup
J. Jackson
E. J. Foller
H. Hardt
G. A. Finley
A. H. Sherrard
F. Mount Est
W. Van Wert
C. M. Shaw
Chapman
1
2
3
4
5
6
7
8
9
10
11
12
13
14
15
16
17
18
19
20
21
22
23
24
25
26
27
28
29
30
31
32
33
34
35
36

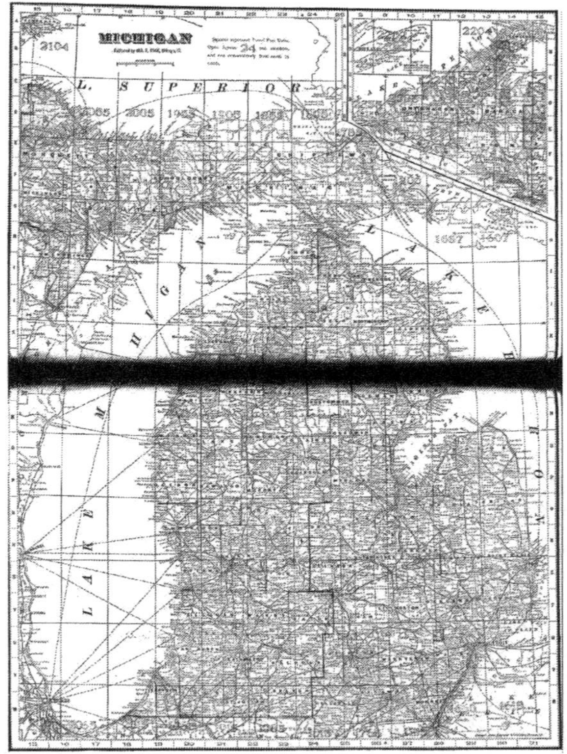
MICHIGAN
L. SUPERIOR
LAKE MICHIGAN
LAKE HURON
LAKE

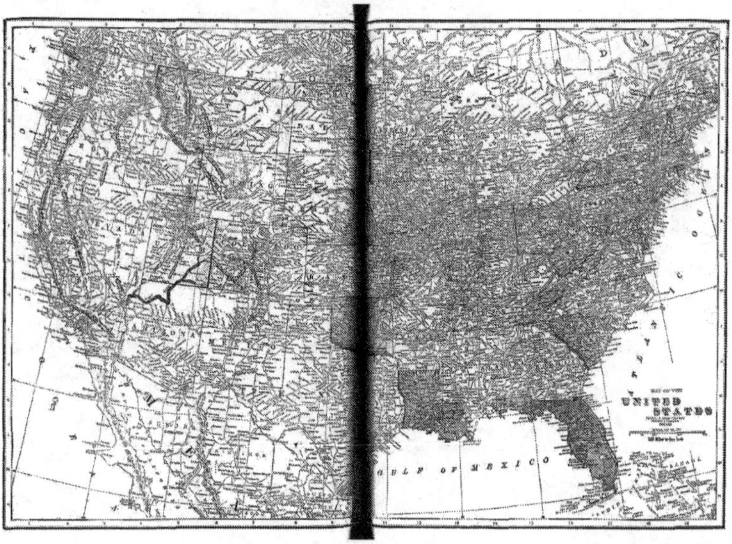
UNITED
STATES
GULF OF MEXICO

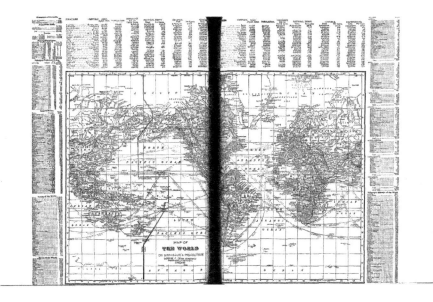

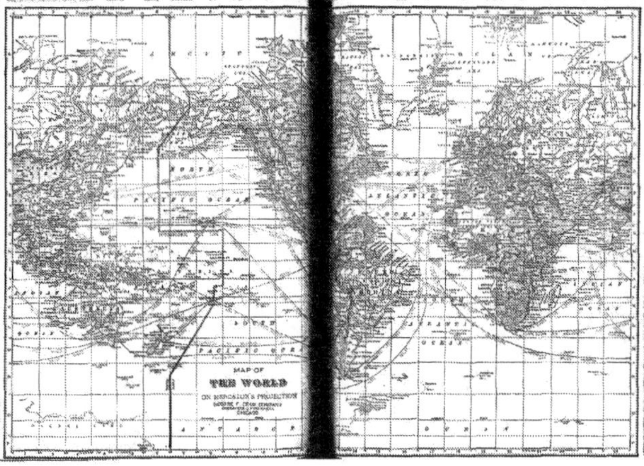
MAP OF
THE WORLD
ON MERCATOR'S PROJECTION
CHICAGO

PATRONS' REFERENCE DIRECTORY

OF

Calhoun County, Michigan

EXPLANATION.—The date following a name indicates the length of time the party has been a resident in the county. The abbreviations are as follows: S. for Section; T. for Township; P. O. for Post-office address. When no Section Number or Township is given, it will be understood that the party resides within the limits of the village or city named, and, in such cases, the post-office address is the same as the place of residence, unless otherwise stated.

Abbey, M. B., Farmer, S. 22, T. Pennfield, P. O. Battle Creek. Mr. Abbey was born in Calhoun County in 1866.

Abbott, Mrs. Effie O., Farming, S. 5, T. Emmet, P. O. Battle Creek, General Delivery. 1900.

Abbott, W. O., Farmer, S. 17, T. Albion, P. O. Albion. Mr. Abbott was born in 1850.

Ackett, John & Son, General Store, Eckford.

Ackley, C. E., County Secretary Calhoun County Y. M. C. A., Marshall.

Ackley, E. R., Real Estate, Battle Creek.

Adams, G. W., Farmer, S. 20, T. Pennfield, P. O. Battle Creek. Mr. Adams was born in Calhoun County in 1884.

Adams, Orwin, Farmer, S. 26, T. Battle Creek, P. O. Battle Creek. Mr. Adams was born in 1879.

Albion, City of,

Albion Garage, The, Automobiles, Bicycles and Supplies, Albion.

Albion Lumber Co., Lumber Dealers, Albion.

Albion State Bank, General Banking, Albion.

Albion Township, J. L. Barkley, Township Clerk, S. 28, T. Albion, P. O. Albion.

Aldrich, C. A., Farmer, S. 32, T. Eckford, P. O. Eckford. Mr. Aldrich was born in Calhoun County in 1877.

Allen, J. Edward, Farmer, S. 16, T. Eckford, P. O. Eckford. 1893.

Allen, Irvie L., Proprietor Maple Leaf Dairy Farm, Breeder of Holstein Cattle, S. 29, T. Sheridan, P. O. Albion. Mr. Allen was born in Michigan in 1865 and settled in Calhoun County in 1893. He is married to Clara Stoddard. Mr. Allen has served as Road Commissioner.

Allen, John R., Farmer and Stock Breeder, S. 2, T. Eckford, P. O. Marshall. 1893.

Allman, Geo., Farmer, S. 11, T. Albion, P. O. Albion. Mr. Allman was born in 1855.

Allwardt, Fred, Farmer, S. 16, T. Newton, P. O. Ceresco.

Allwardt, F. A., Vice President City Bank of Battle Creek and Secretary Battle Creek Public Schools, Battle Creek.

Amberg & Murphy, Druggists, Battle Creek.

American Motor Co., Automobiles and Garage, Battle Creek.

Andre, Frank, Farmer, S. 9, T. Eckford, P. O. Marshall. 1862.

Andrews, W. B., Town Clerk and Photographer, Homer.

Ankney, S. P., Farmer, S. 19, T. Pennfield, P. O. Battle Creek. Mr. Ankney was born in 1868.

Ansell, W. J., Farmer, S. 35, T. Lee, P. O. Marshall. Mr. Ansell was born in 1864.

Ansterburg, Wm. E., Farmer, S. 34, T. Albion, P. O. Homer. Mr. Ansterburg was born in 1856.

Arnold, Henry, Farmer, S. 31, T. Tekonsha, P. O. Tekonsha. Mr. Arnold was born in Indiana in 1889 and settled in Calhoun County in 1914.

Arthur & Beck, Attorneys, Battle Creek.

Ashdon, M. H., Farmer, S. 21, T. Le Roy, P. O. East Leroy. 1892.

Ashley, F. B., Farmer, S. 23, T. Burlington, P. O. Burlington.

Athens State Bank, General Banking, Athens.

Atkins Edward, Farmer, S. 2, T. Marengo, P. O. Marshall. Mr. Atkins was born in 1884.

Austin, A. R., Real Estate and Insurance, Albion.

Avery, C. H., Livery and Sale Stables, Battle Creek.

Avery, F. A., Farmer, S. 34, T. Marengo, P. O. Marshall. 1856.

Avery, L. L., Farmer and Stock Breeder, S. 1, T. Albion, P. O. Albion. Mr. Avery was born in 1874.

Backofen, B. A., Farmer, S. 26, T. Pennfield, P. O. Battle Creek. Mr. Backofen was born in Calhoun County in 1852.

Badger, D., Farmer, S. 26, T. Pennfield, P. O. Battle Creek. Mr. Badger was born in Calhoun County in 1860.

Badger, Mrs. E., Farming, S. 23, T. Pennfield, P. O. Pennfield. 1913.

Badger, J. H., Farmer, S. 22, T. Pennfield, P. O. Pennfield. Mr. Badger was born in Calhoun County in 1868.

Badger, W. H., Farmer, S. 8, T. Pennfield, P. O. Battle Creek. Mr. Badger was born in Calhoun County in 1866.

Baird, R. M., Farmer, S. 21, T. Lee, P. O. Marshall. 1914.

Baker, Elmer, Farmer, S. 2, T. Emmet, P. O. Battle Creek. Mr. Baker was born in Calhoun County in 1868.

Baker, L. J., Farmer, S. 32, T. Fredonia, P. O. Marshall. 1898.

Ball, James B., Grocer, Battle Creek.

Ball, La Vern, Farmer, S. 16, T. Eckford, P. O. Eckford. Mr. Ball was born in 1897.

Barker, Samuel R., Farmer, S. 32, T. Emmet, P. O. Battle Creek. 1903.

Barkley, James, Farmer, S. 6, T. Albion, P. O. Albion. Mr. Barkley was born in 1880.

Barkley, J. L., S. 28, T. Albion, P. O. Albion. Mr. Barkley has served as Township Clerk.

Barnes, Geo., Ex-County Treasurer, Marshall.

Barnes, W., Farmer, S. 17, T. Eckford, P. O. Eckford. 1906.

Barnum, E. L., Farmer, S. 36, T. Marengo, P. O. Albion. 1880.

Barry, Frank M., General Insurance, Battle Creek.

Bartholomew, Noah, Farmer, S. 21, T. Eckford, P. O. Eckford. 1861.

Bartholomew, S. C., Farmer, S. 4, T. Eckford, P. O. Marshall. Mr. S. C. Bartholomew, was born in Northampton County, Pennsylvania, April 21, 1857, and in 1876 came to Homer, Mich., where he made his home for ten years with an uncle who resided five miles southwest of Homer in Eckford Township. In 1886 he was married to Miss Alice C. Miller of Eckford Township, Calhoun County, where they resided for seven years, then moved to Burlington Township and remained for sixteen years. In Burlington Township he owned a fine farm of 44 acres which he sold and moved back to Eckford Township and bought the 80 acres on which he now lives and which is known as Pleasant View Farm.

Bartlett, E. B., Farmer, S. 9, T. Clarendon, P. O. Homer.

Bartlett, W. Henry, Farmer, S. 22, T. Clarendon, P. O. Homer. Mr. Bartlett was born in 1863.

Bascom, S. A., Dairyman and Breeder of Jersey Cattle, 220 Pearl St., Albion. 1866.

Batdorff, E. H., Real Estate, Battle Creek.

Bates, Ed E., Farmer, S. 6, T. Marengo, P. O. Marshall. 1868.

Battle Creek Gas Co., Gas, Coke and Gas Fixtures, Battle Creek.

Battle Creek Hack & Bus Co., Hack and Livery, Battle Creek.

Battle Creek Lumber Co., Lumber Dealers, Battle Creek.

Battle Creek Public Schools, Secretary Board of Education, Battle Creek.

Battle Creek Sanitarium, M. W. Wentworth, Steward, Battle Creek.

Battle Creek Sanitarium, Store Department, Battle Creek.

Battle Creek Storage & Carting Co., L. B. Alexander, Manager, Packers, Movers and Storers of Household Goods, Battle Creek.

Battle Creek Taxicab Co., Battle Creek.

Battle Creek Township, F. W. Van Valland, Clerk, Engineer Water Works, S. 13, T. Battle Creek, P. O. Battle Creek. Mr. Von Valland was born in 1872.

Baty, E., Farmer, S. 33, T. Clarence, P. O. Albion. 1865.

Bauer, P. A., General Auctioneer, Athens.

Baurs, August, Farmer, S. 35, T. Bedford, P. O. Battle Creek. 1907.

Beach, O. H., Farmer, S. 22, T. Pennfield, P. O. Battle Creek. Mr. Beach was born in 1873.

Beardsley, C. E., Farmer, S. 27, T. Pennfield, P. O. Battle Creek. Mr. Beardsley was born in Calhoun County in 1864.

Beardsley, G. R., Farmer, S. 27, T. Pennfield, P. O. Battle Creek. Mr. Beardsley was born in 1876.

Beattie, Rodger, Farmer, S. 7, T. Marengo, P. O. Marshall. 1867.

Beck, Ira A., Lawyer, Battle Creek.

Beckley, Mrs. L. A., Farming, S. 2, T. Le Roy, P. O. Battle Creek. 1867.

Beckwith, J. C., Grain Elevator, Marshall.

Belcher, C. P., Retired Farmer, Albion. Mr. Belcher was born in 1851.

Bemer, Wm., Blacksmith and Supervisor, Albion.

Bentley, B. K., Farmer, S. 29, T. Marshall, P. O. Marshall. Mr. Bentley was born in Calhoun County in 1868.

Bentley Shoe Co., Battle Creek.

Betterly, Walter, Farmer, S. 10 and 11, T. Battle Creek, P. O. Battle Creek. Mr. Betterly was born in Calhoun County in 1889.

Binder, Robt. Co., Meats, Battle Creek.

Bingham, Ralph, Farmer, S. 3, T. Clarence, P. O. Olivet. 1875.

Bird, Mattie E., Farmer, S. 21, T. Pennfield, P. O. Battle Creek. Mr. Bird was born in 1856.

Blake, C. L., Plumber, Marshall.

Blake, H. D., Machine Shop Work, S. 22, T. Marengo, P. O. Marshall. Mr. Blake was born in 1871.

Blanck, T. J. & Sons, Farmers and Stock Breeders, S. 34, T. Emmet, P. O. Ceresco.

Blowers, N. A., Farmer, S. 15, T. Athens, P. O. Athens.

Boehmer, August, Farmer and Stockraiser, S. 36, T. Lee, P. O. Marshall. Mr. Boehmer was born in 1852.

Bolster, R. J., Dry Goods, Battle Creek.

Boos, J. B., Wines and Liquors, Battle Creek.

Bosley, W. E., Shelf and Heavy Hardware, Marshall.

Boughton, C., Farmer, S. 14, T. Marengo, P. O. Marengo. 1838.

Bourreau, A. C., Printer, S. 21, T. Emmet, P. O. Battle Creek. 1896.

Bowen, L. H., Clerk, S. 10, T. Bedford, P. O. Bedford. Mr. Bowen was born in 1888.

Boyne, F. N., The Ideal Laundry, Battle Creek.

Bradley, Eugene, Farmer, S. 1, T. Eckford, P. O. Marshall. Mr. Bradley was born in 1881.

Bradley, R. A., Farmer, S. 12, T. Eckford, P. O. Albion. Mr. Bradley was born in 1884.

Bradley Brothers, Dealers in Coal and Hardware, Battle Creek.

Bradstreet, Geo., Farmer and Gardener, S. 3, T. Le Roy, P. O. Battle Creek. Mr. Bradstreet was born in 1882.

Brazie, M. L., Proprietor Palace Livery, Battle Creek.

Brewer, C. R. Lumber Co., Lumber and Building Material, Battle Creek.

Briggs, H. A., Real Estate, Battle Creek.

Briggs, M. L., Farmer and Dairyman, S. 34, T. Pennfield, P. O. Battle Creek.

Bristol, Glenn R., Farmer, S. 28, T. Eckford, P. O. Eckford. 1913.

Brockett, L. B. & Sons, Dealers in Hardware, Battle Creek.

Bromeling, G. M., Farmer, S. 9, T. Clarendon, P. O. Homer.

Brooks, J. P., Dairy Farm, S. 33, T. Burlington, P. O. Union City.

Brooks Appliance Co., Manufacturers of Surgical Appliances, Marshall.

Brown, C. W., Farmer, S. 30, T. Eckford, P. O. Eckford. 1864.

Brown, M. B., Daily Moon Newspaper, Battle Creek.

Brown, V. and R. D., Farmers, S. 25, T. Pennfield, P. O. Battle Creek.

Broxholm, Geo. C., Farmer, S. 7, T. Marengo, P. O. Marshall. 1911.

Brunner, George, Road Commissioner, S. 9, T. Bedford, P. O. Battle Creek. 1891.

Bryant, C. S., Farmer, S. 18, T. Albion, P. O. Albion. Mr. Bryant was born in 1872.

Bryant, Mrs. H. M., Farming, S. 18, T. Albion, P. O. Albion.

Buckley, J. J., Farmer and Dairyman, S. 11, T. Homer, P. O. Homer. 1863.

Bugden, James, Farmer, S. 17, T. Eckford, P. O. Eckford. 1902.

Burkhardt, Chas., Farmer, S. 14, T. Burlington, P. O. Burlington.

Burrell, E. D., Farmer, S. 5, T. Convis, P. O. Bellevue. 1863.

Burrows, Wm., Farmer, S. 12, T. Pennfield, P. O. Pennfield. Mr. Burrows was born in Calhoun County in 1847.

Burt, Wm., Farmer, S. 11, T. Convis, P. O. Bellevue. 1914.

Burton, A., Farmer, S. 4, T. Convis, P. O. Bellevue. 1870.

Bushnell, H. D., Farmer, S. 6, T. Marengo, P. O. Marshall. 1889.

Buskirk, Henry, Farmer, S. 27, T. Eckford, P. O. Eckford. 1854.

Buskirk, Wm., Farmer, S. 24, T. Eckford, P. O. Eckford. 1899.

Butler, Alfred, Farmer, S. 30, T. Marengo, P. O. Marshall. Mr. Butler was born in 1878.

Butt, James, Farmer, S. 17, T. Eckford, P. O. Eckford. 1885.

Butterfield, Wm., Farmer, S. 6, T. Clarence, P. O. Olivet. 1882.

Cable Piano Co., The, F. R. Lawrence, Manager, Pianos, Battle Creek.

Cahalan, Rev. James, Catholic Priest, Marshall.

Calhoun County Abstract Co., L. S. Page, Proprietor, Marshall.

Calhoun County Officers:—Circuit Judge, Walter H. North; Judge of Probate, Wm. H. Porter; Sheriff, E. J. Mallory; Clerk, Will A. Cady; Deputy Clerk, Agnes M. Sterling; Treasurer, William A. Lane; Register of Deeds, C. Howard Daskam; Prosecuting Attorney, Robert H. Kirchman; Assistant Prosecuting Attorney, A. F. Cooper; Court Stenographer, Roy R. Bildred; School Commissioner, Emma S. Willitts; Drain Commissioner, L. C. Williams. Court Commissioners:—A. N. Ford, Battle Creek; Chas. O. Miller, Marshall. County Road Commissioners: Frank Mabrie, Chairman, Marshall; Geo. R. Peet, Battle Creek; E. H. Puffer, Battle Creek. Board of Supervisors:—Albion Township, C. W. Kimer, Albion; Athens Township, Erwin Watson, Athens; Battle Creek Township, Clinton Rhodes, Battle Creek; Bedford Township, B. G. Morgan, Battle Creek; Burlington Township, Frank Pulliam, Burlington; Clarence Township, W. A. Kreneriek, Albion; Clarendon Township, Lewis R. Mead, Homer; Convis Township, J. R. Walkinshaw, Bellevue; Eckford Township, Lewis J. Decker, Marshall; Emmet Township, Chas. Hutchinson, Battle Creek; Fredonia Township, Fred Kotz, P. O. Marshall; Homer Township, Wm. T. Hamilton, Homer; Lee Township, George Rundle, Olivet; Le Roy Township, B. D. Bushnell, East Leroy; Marengo Township, Frank E. Smith, Marshall; Marshall Township, John Lee, Marshall; Newton Township, Ira Hagleshaw, Ceresco; Pennfield Township, Wm. S. Fruin, P. O. Battle Creek; Sheridan Township, J. E. O'Hara, Albion; Tekonsha Township, Bert Shedd, Tekonsha.

Calhoun State Bank, General Banking, Homer.

Callahan, J. H., Clifton and Bismark Hotels, Battle Creek.

Callahan, Wm. H., Farmer, S. 9, T. Pennfield, P. O. Battle Creek. Mr. Callahan was born in 1877.

Carpenter, L., Farmer, S. 24, T. Bedford, P. O. Battle Creek. 1885.

Carr, E. S., Farmer and Stock Breeder, S. 33, T. Albion, P. O. Homer. Mr. Carr was born in 1863.

Carver, Elias, Farmer, S. 5, T. Marengo, P. O. Marshall. Mr. Carver was born in 1881.

Case, C. B., Farmer, S. 27, T. Burlington, P. O. Union City.

Case, Jos., Florist, Battle Creek.

Casey, J. T., Jr., Farmer, S. 19, T. Eckford, P. O. Eckford. 1902.

Cavanagh, Howard W., Lawyer, Battle Creek.

Cenmer, Charles W., Dry Goods, Battle Creek.

Central National Bank, General Banking, Battle Creek.

Chamber of Commerce, Battle Creek.

Chapin, E. W., Farmer, S. 22, T. Emmet, P. O. Ceresco. 1880.

Chisholm, T. J., Farmer, S. 19, T. Marengo, P. O. Marshall. Mr. Chisholm was born in 1836.

Church, T. E., Livery, Marshall.

City Bank of Battle Creek, The, General Banking, Battle Creek.

City Suburban Lot Exchange, L. E. Alderdyce, Manager, Real Estate, Battle Creek.

Clapp, F. W., Lawyer, Battle Creek.

Clarence Township, Bert C. Ringler, Township Clerk, Albion.

Clark, Frank, Farmer, S. 36, T. Marengo, P. O. Marengo. Mr. Clark was born in 1868.

Clark, Fred E., Farmer, S. 12, T. Eckford, P. O. Albion. 1887.

Clark, G. R. & Son, General Blacksmithing, S. 16, T. Bedford, P. O. Bedford. G. R. Clark was born in 1860 and W. S. Clark was born in 1894.

Clark, Jacob, Farmer, S. 18, T. Eckford, P. O. Eckford. 1872.

Clark, O. S., Lawyer, Battle Creek.

Clark, Warren J., Farmer and Breeder of Jersey Cattle, S. 8, T. Fredonia, P. O. Marshall. 1883. Mr. Clark has served as Town Clerk.

Clayman, B. T., Farmer and Stock Feeder, S. 13, T. Emmet, P. O. Ceresco. 1900.
Cline, Eli, Farmer, S. 30, T. Pennfield, P. O. Battle Creek. 1851.
Clothier, Geo., Farmer, Burlington.
Clute, Geo., Farmer, S. 25, T. Convis, P. O. Marshall. Mr. Clute was born in 1874.
Clute, Homer, Farmer, S. 31, T. Lee, P. O. Marshall. Mr. Clute was born in 1872.
Cobb, N. A., Lawyer, Battle Creek.
Coca-Cola Bottling Co., Manufacturers and Bottlers of Soda and Mineral Waters, Battle Creek.
Coggan, S. W., Florist, Battle Creek.
Cole, S. B., Contractor, Battle Creek.
Coleman, Mrs. Geo., Marshall.
Collyer, Geo. E., Farmer and Stockraiser, S. 27, T. Albion, P. O. Homer. Mr. Collyer was born in 1868.
Collyer, Geo. W., Farmer, S. 20, T. Burlington, P. O. Union City.
Comfort, T. G., Farmer, S. 26, T. Le Roy, P. O. Climax. 1907.
Commercial & Savings Bank, The, General Banking, Albion.
Commercial Savings Bank, The, General Banking, Marshall.
Consolidated Ice Co., Limited, C. D. Peters, Manager, Battle Creek.
Converse, F. H., Farmer, S. 7, T. Burlington, P. O. Union City.
Convis, C. R., Farmer, S. 32, T. Pennfield, P. O. Battle Creek. Mr. Convis was born in Calhoun County in 1874.
Convis Township, J. R. Walkinshaw, Supervisor; Walter Scott, Justice; Thos. Hamilton, Clerk, Marshall.
Cook, Geo. W., Farmer, S. 16, T. Eckford, P. O. Eckford. 1874.
Cook, R. H. & Co., Stock Breeders and Fruit Growers, S. 36, T. Eckford, P. O. Eckford. 1889.
Coon, W. A., Farmer, S. 4, T. Pennfield, P. O. Battle Creek. Mr. Coon was born in 1872.
Cooper, C. D., Farmer, S. 21, T. Marengo, P. O. Marshall. 1868.
Corey, Elbert, Farmer, S. 29, T. Newton, P. O. Union City.
Cornell, E., Farmer, S. 31, T. Emmet, P. O. Battle Creek. Mr. Cornell was born in 1877.
Cornell, W. R., Business College, Battle Creek.
Coss, A. B., Farmer, S. 4, T. Pennfield, P. O. Battle Creek. Mr. Coss was born in 1868.
Cotton, P. D., Farmer, S. 18, T. Newton, P. O. Battle Creek.
Courtright, Ray, Farmer, S. 15, T. Clarence, P. O. Springport. Mr. Courtright was born in Calhoun County in 1873.
Coy, James, Farmer, S. 4 and 5, T. Battle Creek, P. O. Battle Creek. 1911.
Craig, J. P., Real Estate, S. 11, T. Clarendon, P. O. Homer. Mr. Craig was born in Pennsylvania in 1837 and settled in Calhoun County in 1906. *He is a Veteran of the Civil War, having enlisted in 1862* and was discharged in 1865. He served as Sergeant in Company G 4th Michigan Cavalry.
Crampton, O., Farmer, S. 16, T. Marengo, P. O. Marshall. 1903.
Crane, Guy E., Harness, Battle Creek.
Creps, W. B., Farmer, S. 22, T. Albion, P. O. Albion. Mr. Creps was born in Calhoun County in 1884.
Crofoot, George, Farmer, S. 6, T. Pennfield, P. O. Battle Creek. Mr. Crofoot was born in 1848.
Cronin, H. L., Grocer, Marshall.
Cronkhite, R. S., Farmer, S. 33, T. Bedford, P. O. Battle Creek. Mr. Cronkhite was born in 1885.
Crosby, J. B., Farmer, 400 Lake Ave., Battle Creek. Mr. Crosby was born in 1853.
Culver, P. W., Real Estate, Insurance and Supervisor, Albion.
Culver, R. A., Farmer, S. 33, T. Burlington, P. O. Union City.
Cummings-Allen Realty Co., Real Estate, Battle Creek.
Curtis, L. D., *Farmer and Dairyman*, S. 18, T. Marengo, P. O. Marshall. Mr. Curtis was born in 1873.
Cushman, Charles, Farmer, S. 36, T. Lee, P. O. Marshall. Mr. Cushman was born in 1851.
Custer, August, Farmer, S. 7, T. Clarence, P. O. Springport. 1907.
Cutting, A. F., Farmer, S. 28, T. Eckford, P. O. Eckford. Mr. Cutting was born in 1854.
Cutting, Cleve, Farmer, S. 26, T. Eckford, P. O. Eckford. Mr. Cutting was born in 1884.

Daniels, Jerome, Superintendent of Calhoun County Farm, S. 19, T. Marengo, P. O. Marshall. 1913.
Daskam, C. H., Register of Deeds, Marshall.
Davis, E. G., Farmer, S. 25, T. Athens, P. O. Athens.
Davis, J. Wendel, Rector Trinity Church, Marshall.
Davis, Mary E., Real Estate, Albion.
Davis-Fisher Co., The, Real Estate, Battle Creek.
Day, Joseph, Farmer, S. 15, T. Eckford, P. O. Eckford. Mr. Day was born in 1886.
Dean, H. W., Furniture, Tekonsha.
Dean, J. H., Proprietor Prospect Hill Farm, S. 25, T. Sheridan, P. O. Albion. Mr. Dean was born in Calhoun County in 1879. He is married to Bertha Ringler. Mr. Dean has served as Justice of Peace.
DeBow, C. C., Farmer, S. 8, T. Athens, P. O. Athens.
Decker, L. J., Farmer and Supervisor, S. 4, T. Eckford, P. O. Marshall. Mr. Decker was born in 1880.
Dehl, Jesse, Farmer, S. 2, T. Eckford, P. O. Marshall. Mr. Dehl was born in 1883.
Demott, Ed, Farmer, S. 8, T. Battle Creek, P. O. Battle Creek. Mr. Demott was born in Calhoun County in 1864.
Demott, Roy, Farmer, S. 8, T. Battle Creek, P. O. Battle Creek. Mr. Demott was born in Calhoun County in 1897.
DePuy, Edward, Farmer, S. 4, T. Pennfield, P. O. Battle Creek. 1882.
Dewey, John A., Farmer, S. 6, T. Clarence, P. O. Springport. 1902.
DeWitt, C. C., Wines, Liquors and Cigars, Battle Creek.
Dibble, W. J., President Commercial Savings Bank, Marshall.
Dickie, Samuel, President Albion College, Albion.
Dinger, S., Farmer, S. 20, T. Pennfield, P. O. Battle Creek. Mr. Dinger was born in 1860.
Disbro, Ora L., Farmer, S. 11, T. Burlington, P. O. Burlington.
Dobbins Hardware Co., Dealers in Hardware, Battle Creek.
Doly, Robert, Farmer, S. 30, T. Clarendon, P. O. Homer.
Donovan, R. A., Real Estate, Battle Creek.
Doobleday, Lee, Farmer, S. 33, T. Le Roy, P. O. East Leroy. Mr. Doobleday was born in 1888.
Doolittle, B. G., Cashier First State Bank, Tekonsha.
Doubleday, W., Farmer, S. 33, T. Le Roy, P. O. East Leroy. 1882.
Dowling, Ben, Farmer, S. 33, T. Eckford, P. O. Eckford. 1866.
Dowding, Geo., Farmer, S. 28, T. Eckford, P. O. Eckford. Mr. Dowding was born in 1860.
Dowding, Henry, Farmer, S. 31, T. Lee, P. O. Marshall. 1857.
Dowding, Mary, Farming, S. 30, T. Lee, P. O. Marshall. Born in 1880.
Doyle, J. E., Farmer, S. 11, T. Tekonsha, P. O. Tekonsha. Mr. Doyle was born in Rochester, N. Y., in 1858 and settled in Calhoun County in 1877. He is married to Emily Thunder.
Dryer, James, Drain Dredging Contractor, S. 29, T. Lee, P. O. Marshall. 1893.
Dunn, H. T., Farmer, S. 14, T. Eckford, P. O. Eckford. 1874.
Dykeman, A. A., Mason, S. 23, T. Bedford, P. O. Battle Creek. Mr. Dykeman was born in 1849.

Eastman, O. V., Livery, Albion.
Eaves, E., Insurance, Battle Creek.
Eckford Township, C. E. Miller, Township Clerk; L. J. Decker, Supervisor; F. L. Sanders, Justice of Peace, S. 30, T. Eckford, P. O. Eckford.
Eddy, Frank, Farmer, S. 1, T. Lee, P. O. Springport. Mr. Eddy was born in 1884.
Eells, C. F., Farmer and Gardening, S. 3, T. Battle Creek, P. O. Battle Creek. Mr. Eells was born in 1875.
Eitniear, G. A., Farmer, S. 17, T. Burlington, P. O. Burlington.
Eitniear, R., Farmer and Road Commissioner, S. 23, T. Athens, P. O. Athens.
Ellis, B., Farmer and Breeder of Thoroughbred Durham Cattle, S. 6, T. Tekonsha, P. O. Burlington. 1857.
Emmet Township, Wm. H. Pierce, Township Clerk; Charles Hutchinson, Supervisor, Ceresco.
Emmerson Truck & Storage Co., Movers, Packers and Shippers of Household Goods and Storage, Battle Creek.
Enos, Z. H., Farmer, S. 19, T. Eckford, P. O. Eckford. Mr. Enos was born in 1862.
Enquirer, The, Newspaper, Battle Creek.
Ettson, C. H., Farmer, S. 4, T. Pennfield, P. O. Battle Creek. Mr. Ettson was born in 1835.
Evans, Mrs. E., Farming, S. 20, T. Pennfield, P. O. Battle Creek. Mrs. Evans was born in 1866.
Evening Chronicle, The, Newspaper, Marshall.
Evening Statesman, The, Newspaper, Marshall.

Fanning, C. W., Farmer, S. 13, T. Newton, P. O. Ceresco.
Farley, W. D., Furniture and Undertaking, Battle Creek.
Farman, J. L., Farmer, S. 6, T. Athens, P. O. Athens.
Farr, H., Farmer, S. 31, T. Fredonia, P. O. Burlington. 1910.
Fenton, A., Farmer and Breeder, S. 21, T. Eckford, P. O. Eckford. 1861.
Fenton, Ed M., Farmer, S. 15, T. Emmet, P. O. Battle Creek. 1901.
Ferguson, Mrs. Marion, Farming, Marshall.
Findley, Chas. C., Farmer, S. 1, T. Albion, P. O. Albion. 1910.
Findley, H. L., Farmer and Stockraiser, S. 30, T. Homer, P. O. Homer. Mr. Findley was born in 1879.
Finley, Clelbur A., Farmer and Stockraiser, S. 3, T. Homer, P. O. Homer. 1877.
Fisher, Geo. B., Farmer, S. 29, T. Burlington, P. O. Union City.
First National Bank, General Banking, Marshall.
First State Bank, General Banking, Tekonsha.
Fisher, E. C., Books and Stationery, Battle Creek.
Fisher, J. W., Farmer, S. 29, T. Lee, P. O. Marshall. 1900.
FitzJohn, D. C., Farmer, S. 12, T. Emmet, P. O. Ceresco. 1863.
Flynn, J. J., Farmer and Stock Breeder, S. 5, T. Marengo, P. O. Marshall. 1168.
Ford, D. D., Real Estate, Battle Creek.
Forman, Wm. G., Farmer, S. 9, T. Marengo, P. O. Marshall. Mr. Forman was born in 1882.
Foss, Clarence, Farmer and Stock Feeder, S. 32, T. Emmet, P. O. Battle Creek. Mr. Foss was born in 1888.
Foss, J. W., Farmer and Stock Feeder, S. 32, T. Emmet, P. O. Battle Creek.
Foster, Ed, Farmer, S. 11, T. Bedford, P. O. Battle Creek. 1862.
Fox, John H., Farmer, S. 5, T. Newton, P. O. Burlington.
Fox, Dr. P. S., Physician, Athens.
Fox, M. C., Farmer, S. 35, T. Emmet, P. O. Battle Creek. 1900.
Fox, Samuel, Farmer, S. 22, T. Fredonia, P. O. Marshall. 1849.
Fox, W. A., Farmer, S. 27, T. Pennfield, P. O. Battle Creek. Mr. Fox was born in 1888.
Frasier, F., Farmer, S. 13, T. Pennfield, P. O. Pennfield. Mr. Frasier was born in Calhoun County in 1847.
Freer, L. H., Farmer and Breeder of Thoroughbred Durham Cattle, S. 17, T. Fredonia, P. O. Marshall. Mr. Freer was born in Michigan in 1886 and settled in Calhoun County in 1907.
French, Tom, Farmer, S. 10, T. Burlington, P. O. Burlington.
French, W. S., Photographer, Battle Creek.
Frost, F. V., Farmer, S. 17, T. Eckford, P. O. Eckford. 1881.
Frost, W. S., Farmer, S. 30, T. Eckford, P. O. Eckford. Mr. Frost was born in 1882.
Frain, Wm S., Supervisor and Farmer, S. 29, T. Pennfield, P. O. Battle Creek. Mr. Frain was born in 1876.
Fuller, A. M., Farmer, S. 22, T. Athens, P. O. Athens.
Fuller, Mrs. M. M., Farming, S. 2, T. Athens, P. O. Athens.

Galloup, J. O., Iron Pipe, Fittings and Valves, Steam Fitters, Tools and Mill Supplies, Battle Creek.
Garland, W. L., Contractor and Builder, S. 20, T. Albion, P. O. Homer. Mr. Garland was born in 1857.
Garratt, P. B., Farmer, S. 20, T. Pennfield, P. O. Battle Creek. Mr. Garratt was born in 1856.
Gartner Baking Co., Wholesale Bakers, Battle Creek.
Gauss, C. E., Gauss' Combined Treatments for Catarrh, Marshall.
Gifford, John, Farmer, S. 20, T. Clarence, P. O. Olivet. Mr. Gifford was born in 1873.
Gildart, Wm. B., Editor Albion Leader and Dealer in Real Estate, Albion.
Good, Alva, Farmer and Breeder of Thoroughbred Holstein Cattle, S. 27, T. Fredonia, P. O. Marshall. Mr. Good was born in Michigan in 1877.
Goodrich, John C., Farming and Dealer in General Merchandise, S. 29, T. Fredonia, Ellis, P. O. Marshall. 1895.
Gorham, C. E., President First National Bank, Marshall.
Gould, O. H., Farmer, S. 4, T. Le Roy, P. O. Climax. 1878.
Granger, C. B., Livery, Albion.
Grant, W., Photographer, Albion. 1910.
Green, B. K., Farmer, S. 2, T. Tekonsha, P. O. Tekonsha. Mr. Green was born in Calhoun County in 1859. He is married to Sabina Bretton.
Greenfield, L. V., Farmer and Stockraiser, S. 4, T. Lee, P. O. Olivet. 1903.
Greenfield Real Estate Co., Real Estate, Marshall. 1890.
Greenman, D. R., Farmer, S. 9, T. Marshall, P. O. Ceresco. Mr. Greenman was born in Calhoun County in 1860.
Grill, Wm. L., Garage, Athens.
Groesbeck, E., Farmer, S. 31, T. Emmet, P. O. Battle Creek. Mr. Groesbeck was born in 1863.
Grundemann, Emil, Farmer, S. 1, T. Eckford, P. O. Marshall. Mr. Grundemann was born in 1887.
Guile, Stephen, Farmer, S. 17, T. Marengo, P. O. Marshall. Mr. Guile was born in 1869.
Gurnfo, F., Livery, Battle Creek.

Haas, John, Farmer, S. 3, T. Eckford, P. O. Marshall. 1885.
Hackett, Willard, Farmer, S. 14, T. Pennfield, P. O. Pennfield. Mr. Hackett was born in 1835.
Hadwin, H. W., Farmer, S. 36, T. Newton, P. O. Union City.
Hagelshaw, Ira, Supervisor and Farmer, S. 22, T. Newton, P. O. Ceresco. Mr. Hagelshaw is one of the representative farmers of Newton Township. He was born Nov. 25, 1875, on the old homestead where he now resides. He received a limited education in the district school of Newton and later attended High School at Battle Creek. He worked by the month on a farm for about eight years and at the age of 21 he took up the carpenter's trade which he followed for thirteen years with success. Mr. Hagelshaw, as the saying goes, is a "Jack at all Trades," as he says, and has gained a great many friends throughout the county. In 1910 he moved to the home farm with his parents. Mr. Hagelshaw was married to Miss Bessie Mallow of Athens Township, to this union have been born four children. His father, aged 82 years, is the oldest resident of Newton Township. He has resided on the old farm 47 years. Mr. Hagelshaw has been chosen by the people of his township to fill several offices and served them as Township Treasurer for the years 1910 and 1911 and as Supervisor for 1913 and until the present time. In politics he is a Republican.
Haight, R. L., Farmer, S. 12, T. Eckford, P. O. Albion. 1905.
Halbert, J. G., Farmer, S. 16, T. Bedford, P. O. Battle Creek. Mr. Halbert was born in 1856.
Hale, W. F., Farmer, S. 14, T. Clarence, P. O. Springport. 1874.
Hall, E. H., Real Estate, Battle Creek.
Hall, Frank, Farmer, S. 36, T. Lee, P. O. Marshall. Mr. Hall was born in 1879.
Hall, G. H., Farmer, S. 15, T. Emmett, P. O. Battle Creek. Mr. Hall was born in 1851.
Hall, Homer, Farmer, S. 11, T. Le Roy, P. O. Battle Creek. 1854.
Halladay, J. F. & Son, Wholesale Grocers, Battle Creek.
Halladay & Wilcox, Real Estate, Battle Creek.
Halsey, H., Breeder of Jersey Cattle, S. 30, T. Homer, P. O. Homer, 1913.
Hamilton, Barritt, Lawyer, Battle Creek.
Hamons, H. J., Farmer, S. 22, T. Burlington, P. O. Union City.
Hammond, J., Farmer and Stockman, S. 16, T. Sheridan, P. O. Albion. Mr. Hammond was born in Pennsylvania in 1859 and came to Calhoun County in 1864. He is married to Miss Rose Keck. Mr. Hammond has served as Highway Commissioner and School Director.
Hanchett, H. G., Farmer, S. 15, T. Eckford, P. O. Marshall. Mr. Hanchett was born in 1883.
Hardt, Chas. and Frank, Farmers, S. 1, T. Homer, P. O. Homer. 1884.
Harmon, Joe W., Market Gardener, S. 26, T. Bedford, P. O. Battle Creek. Mr. Harmon was born in 1879.
Harris Brothers, Manufacturers of and Dealers in Harness and Horse Furnishings, Battle Creek.
Hartman, Mrs. S. B., Fruit Grower, Athens.
Hatton, James, Farmer, S. 10, T. Albion, P. O. Albion. 1885.
Hattrantt, Peter, Farmer, S. 34, T. Emmet, P. O. Ceresco. 1890.
Hartson, Edward, Farmer, S. 27, T. Lee, P. O. Marshall. Mr. Hartson was born in 1862.
Harvey, Charles, Livery, Athens.
Haskins, R., Farmer, S. 17, T. Pennfield, P. O. Battle Creek. Mr. Haskins was born in 1844.
Hatch, J. M. & Sons, Lawyers, Marshall.
Hebble, A. C., Funeral Director, Battle Creek.
Henry, Charles J., Standard Bred Poultry, S. 23, T. Burlington, P. O. Burlington.
Henry, Karl, Farmer, S. 5, T. Marengo, P. O. Marshall. 1887.
Hermon, Reni, Farmer, S. 17, T. Marengo, P. O. Marshall. 1898.
Herron, Mrs. Etta C., Farming, S. 4, T. Tekonsha, P. O. Tekonsha, 1883. Married to Pete E. Herron.
Hess, Charles H., Farmer and Stockraiser, S. 28, T. Marengo, P. O. Marshall. Mr. Hess was born in 1873.
Hess, Edward A., Farmer, S. 28, T. Marengo, P. O. Marshall. Mr. Hess was born in 1889.
Hess, Mrs. J. J., Farming, S. 28, T. Marengo, P. O. Marshall.
Hess, John P., Farmer, Breeder of Shorthorn Cattle and Shipper of Stock, S. 5, T. Fredonia, P. O. Marshall. 1874.
Hess, L. D., Farmer, Breeder of Thoroughbred Poland China Hogs and Barred Plymouth Rock Chickens, S. 6, T. Fredonia, P. O. Ceresco. 1877.
Hess, Philip, Farmer and Stock Breeder, S. 25, T. Emmet, P. O. Ceresco. Mr. Hess was born in 1879.
Hicks, Richard, Farmer, S. 8, T. Lee, P. O. Olivet. 1860.
Hicks, T. V., Farmer, S. 16, T. Pennfield, P. O. Battle Creek.
Hill, Addison, Truck Farmer, S. 28, T. Emmet, P. O. Ceresco. 1903.
Hillard, G. E., Farmer, S. 8, T. Lee, P. O. Olivet. 1897.
Hiscock, R. U., Farmer, S. 4, T. Le Roy, P. O. Battle Creek. Mr. Hiscock was born in 1869.
Hiscock, Fred C., Farmer, S. 9, T. Le Roy, P. O. Climax. Mr. Hiscock was born in 1871.
Hisler, Wm., Farmer and Stockraiser, S. 22, T. Homer, P. O. Homer.
Hobart, R. N., Farmer, S. 28, T. Albion, P. O. Homer. 1905.
Hobbs, L. D., Grocer, Battle Creek.
Hodwin, H. W., Farmer, S. 36, T. Newton, P. O. Union City.
Hoffman, Christopher, Breeder, S. 26, T. Bedford, P. O. Battle Creek. 1915.
Hoffman, W. H., Farmer, S. 1, T. Marengo, P. O. Marshall. Mr. Hoffman was born in 1880.
Holmes, S. W., Farmer, S. 26, T. Athens, P. O. Athens.
Holmes, T. F., Farmer, S. 12, T. Emmet, P. O. Ceresco. Mr. Holmes was born in 1865.
Hooper, J. L., Lawyer, Battle Creek.
Hoover, R. T., Farmer, S. 30, T. Emmet, P. O. Battle Creek. 1915.
Houghton, R. G., Merchant, East Leroy.
Hovey, E. T., Shoe Salesman, S. 21, T. Emmet; P. O. Battle Creek. 1906.
Howell, A. E., Veterinary, S. 31, T. Albion, P. O. Homer. Mr. Howell was born in 1858.
Howes, Saml. A., Real Estate, Battle Creek.
Hoyt, L., Farmer, Breeder of Percheron and Norman Horses, S. 33, T. Fredonia, P. O. Tekonsha. Mr. Hoyt was born in 1841.
Hubbard, O. L., Farmer, Marshall.
Huff, Geo. S., Real Estate, Battle Creek.
Huggett, Fred L., Farmer, S. 34, T. Pennfield, P. O. Battle Creek. Mr. Huggett was born in 1868.
Hughes, Ed, Farmer, S. 16, T. Pennfield, P. O. Battle Creek. Mr. Hughes was born in Calhoun County in 1861.
Hughes, James M., Retired Farmer, Marshall.
Humphrey, J. C., Farmer, S. 35, T. Eckford, P. O. Eckford. Mr. Humphrey was born in 1853.
Hutchinson, Charles, Supervisor and Farmer, S. 34, T. Emmet, P. O. Ceresco. Mr. Hutchinson was born in 1856.
Hyney & Young, Real Estate, Albion.

Imus, Frank, Farmer, S. 17, T. Battle Creek, P. O. Battle Creek. 1885.

Jackson, John, Grain, Seeds and Wool Dealer, Homer. 1865.
Jackson, John J., Farmer, S. 9, T. Athens, P. O. Athens.
Johns, H. W., Dyeing and Cleaning, Battle Creek.
Johnson, A. G., Farmer, S. 2, T. Le Roy, P. O. Battle Creek. Mr. Johnson was born in 1854.
Johnson, A. Morgan, Farmer, S. 11, T. Le Roy, P. O. Battle Creek. Mr. Johnson was born in 1887 and Mrs. Johnson was born in 1886.
Johnson, Edwin, Farmer, S. 28, T. Emmet, P. O. Ceresco. 1905.
Jones, C. A., Farmer, S. 7, T. Newton, P. O. Battle Creek.
Jones, C. A., Farmer and Dairyman, S. 3, T. Emmet, P. O. Battle Creek. 1896.
Jones, Walter, Farmer, S. 8, T. Pennfield, P. O. Battle Creek. Mr. Jones was born in 1876.
Jones, William, Farmer, S. 32, T. Marengo, P. O. Marshall. 1875.
Joslyn, V. H., Farmer, S. 32, T. Battle Creek, P. O. Battle Creek. 1874.
Jourdan, J. W., Farmer, S. 22 and 27, T. Battle Creek, P. O. Battle Creek, 1876.
Joy, Phillip B., Superintendent Electric and Water Department, Marshall.
Judd & Simons, Livery, Battle Creek.

Kahler, Henry, Farmer, S 29, T. Athens, P. O Athens.

Kapp Clothing Co., Clothiers, Hatters and Furnishers, Battle Creek.

Kaiz, Frank O., Farmer and Carpenter, S. 10, T. Fredonia, P. O. Marshall. 1875.

Katz, Joseph, Farmer, S. 15, T. Burlington, P. O. Burlington.

Keating, Scott, Farmer, S. 12, T. Lee, P. O. Springport. 1884.

Keck, James L., Farmer and Stockman, S. 4, T. Sheridan, P. O. Albion. Mr. Keck was born in Calhoun County in 1880. He is married to Miss Hattie Litka. Mr. Keck has served as School Director.

Keet-Davis Co., Undertakers, Battle Creek.

Kelleher, T. J. Co., E. P. Harris, Manager, Dry Goods, Battle Creek.

Kellogg, H., Farmer, S. 8, T. Marengo, P. O. Marshall. Mr. Kellogg was born in 1863.

Kellogg Toasted Corn Flake Co., Breakfast Foods, Battle Creek.

Kelly, Dennis, Manufacturer of Thermostats, Marshall.

Kenyon, W. J., Farmer, S. 28, T. Fredonia, P. O. Tekonsha. 1894.

Keys, A., Farmer and Stockraiser, S. 21, T. Homer, P. O. Homer. 1913.

Kidney, Wm., Farmer and Breeder of Thoroughbred Durham Cattle, S. 22, T. Fredonia, P. O. Marshall. Mr. Kidney was born in London, Canada, in 1846 and came to Calhoun County in 1847.

Killis, John, Farmer, S. 5, T. Pennfield, P. O. Battle Creek. Mr. Killis was born in 1859.

Kilmer, C. W., Farmer and Supervisor, S. 21, T. Albion, P. O. Albion.

Kimball, Otis, Farmer, S. 19, T. Newton, P. O. Battle Creek. Mr. Kimball is a veteran of the Civil War. He was a member of Company A First Michigan Sharp Shooters and served nearly three years. He lost his right arm at Spottsylvania Court House. He is married to Miss Florence Stolt. They have two children, Courtland A. and Leocia S. The latter graduated from the public schools and later from Northwestern University. Mr. Kimball has a splendid home, the interior of the house being finished in Cherry and Sycamore. His library contains about two thousand volumes. Mr. Kimball is a man of character and culture, esteemed by his neighbors for qualities of mind and heart.

Kimmel, M. L., Ditch Contractor and Merchant, S. 1, T. Marengo, P. O. Marshall. Mr. Kimmel was born in 1881.

Kimmer, Chas. P., Farmer and Stockman, S. 5, T. Sheridan, P. O. Albion. Mr. Kimmer was born in Ohio in 1863 and came to Calhoun County in 1867. He is married to Miss Retta Kimball. Mr. Kimmer has served as Highway Commissioner, School Director and Moderator.

King, Geo. R., Farmer, S. 10, T. Clarendon, P. O. Homer.

King, R. C., Farm Seeds, Battle Creek.

King, L. J., Farmer, S. 29, T. Albion, P. O. Homer.

Kingman, A. C., Lawyer, Battle Creek.

Kirkpatrick, W. J., Dealer in Coal, Wood and Coke, Battle Creek.

Kirschman, Robt. H., Lawyer, Battle Creek.

Kisinger, R., Farmer, S. 21, T. Le Roy, P. O. East Leroy. Mr. Kisinger was born in Calhoun County in 1870.

Kistler, L. R., Bendle Lake Resort and General Store, S. 20, T. Emmet, P. O. Battle Creek. Mr. Kistler was born in 1863.

Kistler, J. H., Farmer and Blacksmith, S. 29, T. Emmet, P. O. Battle Creek. 1860.

Klackner's Music House, Pianos, etc., Battle Creek.

Kline, Geo. W., Farmer and Stockraiser, S. 32, T. Homer, P. O. Homer. 1870.

Kline, Walter D., Lawyer, Battle Creek.

Knack, C. J., Farmer, S. 19, T. Albion, P. O. Albion. 1888.

Knapp, B. A., General Insurance, Battle Creek.

Knapp, T. C., Farmer, S. 34, T. Burlington, P. O. Union City.

Knight, W. A., and O. S. Clark, Lawyers, Battle Creek.

Knuth, Wm., Farmer, S. 21, T. Albion, P. O. Albion. 1905.

Koch, L. B., Farmer, S. 10, T. Clarendon, P. O. Homer.

Kooms, H. F., Farmer, S. 36, T. Homer, P. O. Homer. 1881.

Kopp, Fred, Farmer, S. 23, T. Clarence, P. O. Springport. 1882.

Kreserick, W. A., Supervisor and Farmer, S. 33, T. Clarence, P. O. Albion. Mr. Kreserick was born in Calhoun County in 1877.

Kyes, A. J. & Co., Groceries, Battle Creek.

Lake, Guy, Farmer, S. 10, T. Clarendon, P. O. Homer.

Lamanaco, Sam, General Store, S. 31, T. Clarence, P. O. Albion.

Lambert Machine Co., A. F. Grohens, General Manager, Designers and Manufacturers of Coffee Roasting Machinery, Peanut Butter Plants, etc., Marshall.

Larkin, W. L., Wholesale and Retail Beer, Battle Creek.

Laupp, F., Farmer, S. 35, T. Lee, P. O. Marshall. Mr. Laupp was born in 1863.

Lawrence, C. E., Livery, Feed and Sale Stable, Tekonsha. 1901.

Lawley, Thomas, Farmer, S. 7, T. Tekonsha, P. O. Burlington. 1870.

Lawton, S. W., Farmer, S. 33, T. Pennfield, P. O. Battle Creek. Mr. Lawton was born in 1867.

Layher, C. F., Farmer, S. 29, T. Marengo, P. O. Marshall. 1883.

Legge, F. H., Farmer, S. 29, T. Battle Creek, P. O. Battle Creek. Mr. Legge was born in 1861.

Leggett, H. A., Farmer, S. 17, T. Marengo, P. O. Marshall. 1864.

Leonard, Charles J., Farmer, S. 28 and 29, T. Burlington, P. O. Union City.

Leonard, F. A., Real Estate, Battle Creek.

Le Roy Township, E. B. Bushnell, Supervisor; P. M. Voyce, Clerk; C. S. Andrews, Justice of Peace, S. 21, T. Le Roy, P. O. East Leroy.

Leterme Bros., Farmers, S. 9, T. Sheridan, P. O. Albion.

Leterme, Arthur, Farmer and Stockman, S. 9, T. Sheridan, P. O. Albion. Leterme was born in Belgium in 1877 and settled in Calhoun County in 1909.

Leterme, Edmund, Farmer and Stockman, S. 9, T. Sheridan, P. O. Albion. Mr. Leterme was born in Belgium in 1881 and settled in Calhoun County in 1909.

Lewis & Prescott, Lawyers, Battle Creek.

Lincoln, H., Farmer, S. 31, T. Clarence, P. O. Albion. 1863.

Lininger, Geo., Farmer, S. 23, T. Clarence, P. O. Springport. 1847.

Linton, Ed, Farmer, Homer. 1873.

Lockhart, Tuttle & Maurer, Real Estate Dealers, Battle Creek.

Long, J. P., Farmer, S. 32, T. Lee, P. O. Marshall. Mr. Long was born in 1847.

Long, Wm. F., Farmer, S. 32, T. Marengo, P. O. Marshall. Mr. Long was born in 1868.

Lord, W. W., Farmer, S. 21, T. Marengo, P. O. Marshall. 1891.

Lowell, E. L., Farmer, S. 31, T. Newton, P. O. Union City.

Ludlum, R. M., Lawyer, Battle Creek.

Lutz, Jacob, Farmer, S. 35, T. Emmet, P. O. Ceresco. 1873.

Lybolt, C. W., Farmer, S. 4, T. Marengo, P. O. Marshall. 1902.

Lyman, C. R. Co., Insurance, Real Estate and Loans, Battle Creek.

McAllister, John, Farmer, S. 36, T. Eckford, P. O. Eckford. Mr. McAllister was born in 1871.

McAuliffe, D. W., Farm Implements, Albion.

McCaffrey, Austin, Farmer, S. 15, T. Lee, P. O. Marshall. Mr. McCaffrey was born in Calhoun County in 1896.

McClintic, B. L., Farmer and Stockraiser, S. 18, T. Homer, P. O. Homer. 1877.

McClo, Mrs. Francis, Farming, S. 36, T. Lee, P. O. Marshall. Mrs. McClo was born in 1830.

McClure, John H., Farmer, S. 36, T. Marengo, P. O. Marshall. 1910.

McCormick, H. N., Farmer, S. 23, T. Marengo, P. O. Marshall. Mr. McCormick was born in 1877.

McCutcheon, A. L., Justice of the Peace, Real Estate and Insurance, Albion.

McDonald, Geo. C., Farmer, S. 1, T. Clarence, P. O. Springport. 1913.

McGee, Guy, Farmer, S. 1, T. Albion, P. O. Albion. Mr. McGee was born in 1880.

McGee, S. A., Real Estate, Loans and Insurance, Battle Creek.

McKay, Alex A., Civil Engineer, Battle Creek.

McKee, J. R., Monument Works, Battle Creek.

McKenzie, Chas. F., Lawyer, Battle Creek.

McKenzie, Mrs. Mary L., Farming, S. 18, T. Pennfield, P. O. Battle Creek. Mrs. McKenzie was born in 1833.

McKinney, D. H., Farmer, S. 6, T. Albion, P. O. Albion. Mr. McKinney was born in 1864.

McMillin, Geo. H., Publisher, Athens.

McMurtrie, Frank, Farmer, S. 18, T. Marengo, P. O. Marshall. Mr. McMurtrie was born in 1883.

McNaughton, A. J., Monuments, Battle Creek.

Machin, R., Farmer, S. 17, T. Pennfield, P. O. Battle Creek. Mr. Machin was born in 1832.

Mack, A. F., Farmer, S. 17, T. Burlington, P. O. Union City.

Mains, A. J., Farmer, S. 34 and 35, T. Lee, P. O. Marshall. Mr. Mains was born in 1892.

Mains, Fred, Farmer, S. 6, T. Lee, P. O. Olivet. Mr. Mains was born in 1873.

Mains, Harvy, Farmer, S. 8, T. Lee, P. O. Olivet. Mr. Mains was born in 1866.

Mains, John, Farmer, S. 3, T. Marengo, P. O. Marshall. Mr. Mains was born in 1863.

Mandoka, Sam, Farmer, S. 20, T. Athens, P. O. Athens.

Mannings, M. A., Farmer, S. 1, T. Pennfield, P. O. Bellevue. Mr. Mannings was born in 1860.

Mapes, A. H., Farmer, S. 21, T. Battle Creek, P. O. Battle Creek. Mr. Mapes was born in 1868.

Maple City Dairy Co., D. S. Birdsall, Owner, Creamery, Albion.

Marengo Township, Burt Oxby, Township Clerk, F. E. Smith, Supervisor, I. W. Van Sickle, Justice of Peace, S. 20, T. Marengo, P. O. Marshall.

Markham, Roy, Insurance, Battle Creek.

Markle, Colonel W. O., Real Estate and Auctioneer, Albion.

Marks, H. F., Farmer and Township Treasurer, S. 33, T. Clarence, P. O. Albion. Mr. Marks was born in Calhoun County in 1873.

Marsh, Wayne D., Wall Paper, Paints, Oils, Glass and Window Shades, Battle Creek.

Marshall, J. L., Real Estate, Battle Creek.

Marshall, City of,

Marshall News, The, D. W. Knickerbocker, Editor, Marshall.

Marshall Furnace Co., Manufacturers of Furnaces, Marshall.

Marshall Marble and Granite Works, Monuments and Markers, Marshall.

Marshall Plumbing and Heating Co., C. L. Blake and H. L. Bailey, Marshall.

Martin, Wm., Real Estate, Marshall.

Maurer, Frank J., Farmer, S. 18, T. Homer, P. O. Homer. 1914.

Mechem, Geo. W., Lawyer, Battle Creek.

Meek, F. L., Farmer, S. 3, T. Pennfield, P. O. Battle Creek. Mr. Meek was born in 1867.

Mendoka, Sam, Farmer, S. 20, T. Athens, P. O. Athens.

Merchants Savings Bank, General Banking, Battle Creek.

Merrill, D. L., Real Estate, Battle Creek.

Metzger, Harry, Farmer, S. 13, T. Emmet, P. O. Battle Creek. 1912.

Michigan Business and Normal College, Battle Creek.

Michigan United Traction Co., Battle Creek.

Milburn, E., Farmer, S. 12, T. Lee, P. O. Olivet. 1889.

Milk Producers Co., F. W. Sullivan, Milk, Cream, Ice Cream, etc., Battle Creek.

Miller, C. E., Township Clerk, S. 20, T. Eckford, P. O. Eckford.

Miller, Chas. J., Farmer, S. 8, T. Burlington, P. O. Union City.

Miller, C. D., Attorney, Marshall.

Miller, F. D., School Commissioner, Marshall.

Miller, Floyd, Farmer, S. 5, T. Eckford, P. O. Marshall. Mr. Miller was born in 1883.

Miller, Geo. L., Farmer, S. 6, T. Clarence, P. O. Springport. 1875.

Miller, H. W., Farmer, S. 5, T. Newton, P. O. Battle Creek.

Miller, Marion, Farmer, S. 22, T. Albion, P. O. Albion. 1878.

Miller, M. H., Farmer, S. 5, T. Clarence, P. O. Springport. 1853.

Miller, N. B., Farmer and Postmaster, Athens.

Mills, Elliott, Farmer, S. 8, T. Athens, P. O. Athens.

Mitchell, A., Farmer and Fruit Grower, S. 9, T. Tekonsha, P. O. Tekonsha. Mr. Mitchell was born in Calhoun County in 1883. He is married to Elsa Smith.

Mitchell, Robt., County Road Commissioner, Battle Creek.

Mix, C. C., Veterinary Surgeon, Battle Creek.

Mohrhardt, Frank, Farmer, S. 25, T. Newton, P. O. Burlington.

Moon, H. L., Farmer, S. 33, T. Bedford, P. O. Battle Creek. Mr. Moon was born in 1872.

Moore, C. W., Farmer, S. 18, T. Battle Creek, P. O. Battle Creek. 1905.

Moore, Jacob, Farmer, S. 2, T. Pennfield, P. O. Battle Creek. Mr. Moore was born in 1849.

Moore, Whitehill, Farmer, S. 28, T. Emmet, P. O. Ceresco. Mr. Moore was born in 1853.

Morehouse, R. M., Mail Carrier, S. 13, T. Pennfield, P. O. Pennfield. 1890.

Morgan, B. G., Supervisor, S. 23, T. Bedford, P. O. Battle Creek. 1872.

Morgan, R., Farmer, S. 32, T. Emmet, P. O. Battle Creek. Mr. Morgan was born in 1867.

Morgan, E. M., Farmer, S. 18, T. Emmet, P. O. Battle Creek. 1868.

Morley Bros., Farmers, S. 20, T. Tekonsha, P. O. Burlington.

Morley, Earl, Farmer, S. 20, T. Tekonsha, P. O. Burlington. Mr. Morley was born in Michigan in 1874 and came to Calhoun County in 1876.

Morley, R. J., Retail Druggist, Marshall. 1914.

Munger, N. C., Dairyman, S. 31, T. Emmet, P. O. Battle Creek. 1863.

Musser, B. F., Farmer, S. 20, T. Eckford, P. O. Eckford. 1909.

Mustard, James H., Lawyer, Battle Creek.

Newton, W., Farmer, S. 15, T. Marengo, P. O. Marshall. Mr. Newton was born in 1845.

Nichols, J. E., Real Estate, Battle Creek.

Nichols, Lloyd, Farmer, S. 20, T. Clarence, P. O. Albion. 1886.

Noneman, R. C., Farmer, S. 23, T. Marengo, P. O. Marshall. 1888.

North & Strong, Lumber, Sash, Doors, Shingles, etc., Battle Creek.

Norton, Fay, Farmer, Breeder of Thoroughbred Holstein Cattle and Poland China Hogs, S. 36, T. Tekonsha, P. O. Tekonsha. Mr. Norton was born in Calhoun County in 1882.

Nowlin, Frank E. Co., Limited, Wholesale and Retail Farm Produce, Albion.

Oberhauser, John M., Farmer and Justice of Peace, S. 18, T. Newton, P. O. Battle Creek.

Old National Bank of Battle Creek, The, General Banking, Battle Creek.

Olney, Wm., Farmer, S. 16, T. Marengo, P. O. Marshall. 1914.

Onen, Bernard J., Attorney, Battle Creek.

Osman, V. S., Farmer, S. 25, T. Marengo, P. O. Albion. 1908.

Ostrom, William, Farmer, S. 25, T. Albion, P. O. Albion. Mr. Ostrom was born in 1865.

Ott, Emil, Farmer, S. 2, T. Eckford, P. O. Marshall. Mr. Ott was born in 1888.

Ott, Thos. L., Farmer and Dairyman, S. 23, T. Marengo, P. O. Albion. Mr. Ott was born in 1866.

Overholt, F. J., Dentist, Athens.

Overley, P. E., Farmer, S. 12, T. Lee, P. O. Olivet. 1915.

Owen, A. L., Farmer, S. 15, T. Newton, P. O. Ceresco.

Owen, Vern., Farmer and Township Road Commissioner, S. 8, T. Le Roy, P. O. Climax. 1864.

Owens, Carry, Farmer, S. 35, T. Eckford, P. O. Eckford. Mr. Owens was born in 1891.

Oxby, Burt, Township Clerk and Farmer, S. 30, T. Marengo, P. O. Marshall. 1892.

Packard, Bert, Farmer, S. 15, T. Emmet, P. O. Battle Creek. 1893.

Page, H. R., Real Estate, Marshall.

Page, Geo. W., Farmer, S. 27, T. Burlington, P. O. Union City.

Page, H. J., Farmer, S. 21, T. Lee, P. O. Marshall. Mr. Page was born in 1880.

Page, J. C., Farmer and Highway Commissioner, S. 28, T. Marengo, P. O. Marshall. Mr. Page was born in 1884.

Page, L. A., Farmer and Stock Buyer, S. 33, T. Lee, P. O. Marshall. 1870.

Palmer, Frank, Automobiles, Motorcycles and Bicycles, Battle Creek.

Palmer, L. H., Farmer, S. 17, T. Marengo, P. O. Marshall. Mr. Palmer was born in 1890.

Palmer, Peter, Farmer, S. 21, T. Eckford, P. O. Eckford. Mr. Palmer was born in 1881.

Palmiter, Clarence, Farmer and Stockraiser, S. 1, T. Emmet, P. O. Battle Creek. Mr. Palmiter was born in 1887.

Palmiter, N. R., Farmer, S. 1, T. Emmet, P. O. Battle Creek. Mr. Palmiter was born in 1860.

Palmiter, W. H., Farmer, S. 34, T. Pennfield, P. O. Battle Creek. Mr. Palmiter was born in 1858.

Pamptopee, Steve, Farmer, S. 23, T. Athens, P. O. Athens.

Parker, H., Farmer, S. 8, T. Lee, P. O. Olivet. Mr. Parker was born in 1868.

Parrott, S. M., Farmer, S. 17, T. Pennfield, P. O. Battle Creek. 1891.

Parsons, Mrs. Henry, Farming, S. 33, T. Burlington, P. O. Union City.

Patterson, D. J., Farmer, S. 16, T. Eckford, P. O. Marshall. Mr. Patterson was born in 1893.

Payette, A. G., Miller, S. 10, T. Bedford, P. O. Bedford. Mr. Payette was born in 1859.

Peck, Lewis, Farmer, S. 7, T. Battle Creek, P. O. Battle Creek. 1889.

Peck, J. C., Farmer, S. 1, T. Clarence, P. O. Springport. 1866.

Peerless Fixtures Company, Store Fixtures, Marshall.

Peterson, C. A., Hardware and Plumbing, Battle Creek.

Phelps, W. C., Grocer, Battle Creek.

Phillips, B. W., Farmer, S. 21, T. Newton, P. O. Ceresco.

Phillips, Henry L., Garage, Battle Creek.

Phillips, James, Farmer, Burlington.

Philo, John H., Farmer, S. 31, T. Eckford, P. O. Eckford. 1894.

Philo, Wm. H., Farmer and Stockraiser, S. 17, T. Tekonsha, P. O. Tekonsha. 1903.

Piepkow, Gust, Farmer, S. 24, T. Clarence, P. O. Springport. 1902.

Pike, J. W., Jeweler, Athens.

Pinnow, Harry, Farmer, S. 25, T. Pennfield, P. O. Battle Creek. Mr. Pinnow was born in 1893.

Pinnow, John, Farmer, S. 25, T. Pennfield, P. O. Battle Creek. Mr. Pinnow was born in 1893.

Pitt, W. D., Farmer, S. 22, T. Pennfield, P. O. Battle Creek. Mr. Pitt was born in Calhoun County in 1866.

Ponto, Frank, Farmer, S. 11, T. Clarence, P. O. Springport. Mr. Ponto was born in Calhoun County in 1894.

Ponto, John, Farmer, S. 13, T. Clarence, P. O. Springport. Mr. Ponto was born in Calhoun County in 1884.

Ponto, Wm., Farmer, S. 14, T. Clarence, P. O. Springport. 1872.

Porter, W. H., Judge of Probate, Marshall.

Post, C. W., Postum Cereal Co., Battle Creek.

Potter, H. J., Farmer, S. 16, T. Marengo, P. O. Marshall. Mr. Potter was born in 1886.

Powers, J. M., Lawyer, Battle Creek.

Powers & Co., Flour, Feed and Seeds, Battle Creek.

Powers, Preston, Farmer, S. 26, T. Clarendon, P. O. Homer. Mr. Powers was born in 1878.

Powers, W. S., Lawyer, Battle Creek.

Prine, D. B., Farmer, S. 36, T. Pennfield, P. O. Battle Creek. Mr. Prine was born in 1862.

Pyramid Drug Co., Marshall.

Radband, C., Farmer, S. 31, T. Le Roy, P. O. Climax. 1858.

Radford, R. J., Farmer, S. 25, T. Athens, P. O. Athens.

Rendall, A. H. Mill Co., Milling, Tekonsha.

Ranger, L. J., Farmer, S. 8, T. Eckford, P. O. Eckford. Mr. Ranger was born in 1875.

Rapp, R. W., Farmer, S. 18, T. Marengo, P. O. Marshall. Mr. Rapp was born in 1880.

Rarick, Alvin A., Farmer, S. 28, T. Homer, P. O. Homer. Mr. Rarick was born in 1880.

Rarick, Geo. Wash., Farmer, S. 4, T. Homer, P. O. Homer. 1885.

Rathbun & Kraft Lumber and Coal Co., Dealers in Lumber, Coal, etc., Battle Creek.

Raushenberger, Wm., Superintendent Paint Department and Farmer, S. 19, T. Homer, P. O. Homer. 1912.

Raymond & Rice, Milk Dealers, Battle Creek.

Reade, J. L., Real Estate, Battle Creek.

Recorder Press Co., The, W. S. Kennedy, Editor, Albion.

Reed, Floyd, Farmer, S. 5, T. Battle Creek, P. O. Battle Creek. 1889.

Reed, Milton, Farmer, Gardener and Gravel Pit, Albion. Mr. Reed has served as Supervisor.

Reese, Fred, Farmer, S. 6, T. Le Roy, P. O. Climax. 1887.

Reese, James, Farmer, S. 9, T. Eckford, P. O. Eckford. 1875.

Reese, John, Farmer, S. 6, T. Le Roy, P. O. Climax. 1887.

Reichow, Charles, Farmer, S. 34, T. Albion, P. O. Homer. Mr. Reichow was born in 1899.

Reid, M. J., Farmer, S. 11, T. Convis, P. O. Bellevue. 1869.

Rendall, James, Retired, S. 32, T. Marengo, P. O. Marshall. 1866.

Reniger, O. J., General Contractor and Builder, Marshall.

Retallick, N. B., Real Estate and Insurance, Battle Creek. Newton B. Retallick was born at Climax, Kalamazoo County, Michigan on June 3rd 1857 at the farm home of his parents, John T and Hilinda Retallick, where lived until 22 years of age. On October 17th 1878 he was united in marriage with Eunice A. Eldred, daughter of John Alonzo and Polly J. Eldred and Sunday, October 17th 1915, they celebrated the 37th anniversary of their wedding. Mr. Retallick taught District School in Climax and Le Roy Townships during the winters of 1876-77 and 1880-81 inclusive, was Township Superintendent of Schools of Climax Township during the last year this law was in force and met with the other Township Superintendents in Kalamazoo, Michigan, where they elected the first County Superintendent. In the summer of 1881 he entered the service of the Chicago and Grand Trunk Railway Company in the extra gang on track work and in September of the same year was employed as freight brakeman, in which capacity he served for 18 months when he was promoted to Conductor, which position he held for a total period of about 14 years in freight and passenger service. He was in the retail grocery business for over three years and in the spring of 1902 he started in the Insurance business for the Continental Casualty Company and New York Life and his business has gradually developed into a General Insurance and Real Estate & Loan business, in

which he is still engaged at Suite 705 Post Block, Battle Creek, Michigan. He, with his wife, has been a resident of the City of Battle Creek since September 1881, during which period he served the Fifth Ward as Alderman for two years. This matrimonial union has been blessed by the arrival of a daughter and son, both of whom are married and are raising children of their own. The son, Eldred A. is associated with his father in business.
Rial, B. A., Farmer, Breeder of Holstein and Jersey Cattle, S. 29, T. Fredonia, P. O. Tekonsha. 1871.
Richardson, F. W., Farmer, S. 4, T. Athens, P. O. Athens.
Rickonite, C. A., General Secretary, Y. M. C. A., Battle Creek.
Ringler, Bert C., Township Clerk and Farmer, S. 27, T. Clarence, P. O. Albion. 1876.
Ripley, Mrs. D., Farming, S. 9, T. Lee, P. O. Olivet. 1901.
Rivers & Petrie, Independent Garage, Battle Creek.
Root, Chas. R. Music Co., Music Publishers, Pianos, Victrolas, Sheet Music, etc., Battle Creek.
Roatch, H. F., Ditch Contractor, S. 27, T. Newton, P. O. Ceresco.
Roberts, John J., Music House, Pianos, Organs and Music Merchandise, Battle Creek.
Robinson, A. J., Auctioneer, Marshall.
Robinson, D. A., Farmer, S. 9, T. Pennfield, P. O. Battle Creek. Mr. Robinson was born in Calhoun County in 1857.
Robinson, Geo., Farmer, S. 27, T. Athens, P. O. Athens.
Robinson, Tom F., Editor The Register-Weekly, Union City.
Rocco, Ed J., Farmer, S. 8, T. Tekonsha, P. O. Tekonsha. 1877.
Roche, John, Farmer, S. 9, T. Newton, P. O. Battle Creek.
Rogers, Herbert R., Farmer and Breeder of Jersey Cattle, S. 14, T. Clarendon, P. O. Homer. Mr. Rogers was born in Michigan in 1880. He is married to Jennie McKinzie.
Rook, Harry, Farmer, Breeder of Registered Hampshire Sheep and Poland China Hogs, S. 14, T. Marshall, P. O. Marshall. 1878.
Root, S. B., Farmer, S. 3, T. Homer, P. O. Homer. 1905.
Ruddock, F. E., Farmer, S. 36, T. Convis, P. O. Marshall. Mr. Ruddock was born in Calhoun County in 1858.
Rundle, Geo., Supervisor and Farmer, S. 7, T. Lee, P. O. Olivet. Mr. Rundle was born in 1878.
Russell, A. E., Farmer, S. 16, T. Battle Creek, P. O. Battle Creek. 1900. His father, A. J. Russell, came to Calhoun County in 1906.
Russell, A. G., Farmer, S. 17, T. Battle Creek, P. O. Battle Creek. Mr. Russell was born in Calhoun County in 1888.
Russell, A. W., Farmer, S. 17, T. Battle Creek, P. O. Battle Creek. Mr. Russell was born in 1879.
Russell, F. S., Farmer, S. 24, T. Lee, P. O. Marshall. 1914.
Ryan, Wm. J., Real Estate and Insurance, Battle Creek.

Sabin & Bourne, Real Estate, Battle Creek.
Salisbury, W. H., Farmer and Dairyman, S. 35, T. Emmet, P. O. Ceresco. 1900.
Sampson, Edd L., Farmer and Fruit Grower, S. 2, T. Emmet, P. O. P. O. Battle Creek. Mr. Sampson was born in 1868.
Samson, Chas. G., Farmer, S. 36, T. Lee, P. O. Marshall. Mr. Samson was born in 1861.
Samson, S. H., Farmer, S. 21, T. Marengo, P. O. Marshall. Mr. Samson was born in 1857.
Sanders, K. W., Farmer, S. 2, T. Burlington, P. O. Burlington.
Sandford Bros., Farmers and Dairymen, S. 21, T. Emmet, P. O. Ceresco.
Sandford, H. H., Farmer and Dairyman, S. 21, T. Emmet, P. O. Ceresco. Mr. Sandford was born in 1861.
Saunders, LaVerne, Farmer, S. 15, T. Clarendon, P. O. Homer. Mr. Saunders was born in Calhoun County in 1893.
Saxton, E. L., Dealer in Bicycles, Battle Creek.
Sayer, E., Farmer, S. 19, T. Marengo, P. O. Marshall. Mr. Sayer was born in 1852.
Schmidt, Emil, Farmer, S. 35, T. Clarence, P. O. Springport. 1881.
Schmidt, Geo. P., Farmer and Dairyman, S. 35, T. Emmet, P. O. Ceresco. Mr. Schmidt was born in 1865.
Schmidt, John, Farmer, S. 22, T. Clarence, P. O. Albion. 1889.
Schmidt, Wm. F., Farmer, S. 29, T. Clarence, P. O. Albion. Mr. Schmidt was born in Calhoun County in 1877.
School District No. 1, L. Ott, Director; C. P. Way, Treasurer, S. 9, T. Convis, P. O. Bellevue.
School District No. 1, Fractional District, Lee and Convis Townships, Chas. Gernes, Director; Wm. King, Treasurer; J. B. White, Moderator; Bellevue.
School District No. 1, Chas. W. Bird, Treasurer, S. 16, Frank Lonspky, S. 4, Peter Scholz, Moderator, S. 8, T. Newton, P. O. Battle Creek.
School District No. 2, Fractional, Geo. R. Romans, Moderator; D. H. McKinney, Director, T. Eckford, P. O. Albion.
School District No. 3, C. Dowding, Moderator; Jos. Ruddock, Director; Geo. C. Clute, Treasurer; S. 36, T. Convis, P. O. Marshall.
School District No. 4, Mrs. Ray Brant, Treasurer; Vern Wagner, Moderator; S. 22, T. Convis, P. O. Pennfield.
School District No. 5, E. H. Hubbart, Director; C. H. Folsom, Moderator; R. Scholz, Treasurer; T. Albion, P. O. Albion.
School District No. 5, I. H. Cleveland, Director; G. R. Everest, Moderator, S. 27, T. Battle Creek, P. O. Battle Creek.
School District No. 5, Fractional Convis and Marshall, R. Walkinshaw, Moderator, Geo. Ranger, Director, Ceresco.
School District No. 5, Fractional, Homer and Pulaski Townships, Geo. F. Weiss, Treasurer; Chas. J. Holmes, Moderator; Geo. Feighner, Director, S. 12, T. Homer, P. O. Homer.
School District No. 9, Wm. J. Manby, Moderator; A. H. Mapes, Treasurer; S. 21, T. Battle Creek, P. O. Battle Creek.
School District No. 11, J. F. Smith, Frank W. Carpenter, T. Bedford, P. O. Battle Creek.
School District No. 12, A. J. Schrag, Director, Battle Creek; Henry Randt, Moderator, S. 20, Ceresco, B. W. Phillips, Treasurer, S. 21, Ceresco, S. 20, T. Newton, P. O. Battle Creek.
Schrom, I. W., Real Estate, Battle Creek.
Schrimshaw, True, Farmer, S. 10, T. Battle Creek, P. O. Battle Creek. 1914.
Schroder Bros. Co., Department Store, Battle Creek.
Schultz, C. M., Farmer, S. 18, T. Fredonia, P. O. Marshall.
Schumacher, Herman A., Lake View Farm, S. 20, T. Sheridan, P. O. Albion. Mr. Schumacher was born in Germany in 1860 and came to Calhoun County in 1879. He is married to Miss Augusta Frederick.
Schwark, H. J., Farmer, S. 34, T. Newton, P. O. Burlington.
Scott, Adam F., Farmer, S. 3, T. Marshall, P. O. Marshall. Mr. Scott was born in Eaton County, Michigan, in 1852, and in 1853, with parents, came to Calhoun County and settled where he at present lives. His father, Archibald Scott, was born in Scotland and came to America when a young man and stopped in Canada, but in 1836 came to Michigan where he followed his profession of blacksmith. Mr. Scott has always been a farmer and successful, and has often held office of Highway Commissioner.
Scott, Walter, Farmer, S. 23, T. Convis, P. O. Marshall. 1855.
Sears, D. K., Farmer, S. 25, T. Lee, P. O. Albion. Mr. Sears was born in 1874.
Seholt, Marion, Farmer, S. 7, T. Clarence, P. O. Olivet. Born in Calhoun County in 1865.
Seedorf, J. B., Farmer, S. 4, T. Athens, P. O. Athens.
Seaton, I. M., Farmer, S. 19, T. Eckford, P. O. Eckford. 1885.
Shafer, J. K., Farmer and Stock Feeder, S. 14, T. Homer, P. O. Homer. 1910.
Sharpsteen, M. C., Farmer, S. 27, T. Pennfield, P. O. Pennfield. Mr. Sharpsteen was born in 1862.

Shaw & McLinden, Undertakers, Battle Creek.
Shebel, F. R., Farmer, S. 23, T. Marengo, P. O. Marengo. Mr. Shebel was born in 1857.
Shedd, Clyde M., Farmer, Ice Dealer and Breeder of Thoroughbred Holstein Cattle, S. 33, T. Tekonsha, P. O. Tekonsha. Mr. Shedd was born in Calhoun County in 1882.
Shedd, J. Earle, Farmer, S. 25, T. Tekonsha, P. O. Tekonsha. Mr. Shedd was born in Calhoun County in 1880. He has served as School Director.
Shelton, J. F., Farmer, S. 1, T. Pennfield, P. O. Bellevue. Mr. Shelton was born in Calhoun County in 1857.
Shepard, Mrs. W., Farming, S. 9, T. Clarendon, P. O. Homer.
Sherwin, Frank G., Dealer in Groceries, Battle Creek.
Shilling, P. B., Farmer, S. 27, T. Clarendon, P. O. Homer. 1882.
Shipp, T. J., Farmer, S. 20, T. Eckford, P. O. Eckford. Mr. Shipp was born in 1845.
Short, C. H., Farmer, S. 1, T. Lee, P. O. Olivet. Mr. Short was born in 1859.
Shoeldice Bros., Metal Work, Battle Creek.
Shoup, J. M., Farmer, S. 15, T. Pennfield, P. O. Pennfield. Mr. Shoup was born in 1857.
Shreve, F. E., Farmer, S. 5, T. Pennfield, P. O. Battle Creek. Mr. Shreve was born in 1859.
Shultz, J. A., Farmer, S. 1, T. Emmet, P. O. Ceresco. 1896.
Simon, Frank J., Attorney, Albion.
Simons, C. L., Insurance, Battle Creek.
Simons-Leedle Furnace Co., Manufacturers of Furnaces, Marshall.
Simonton, P. B., Farmer, S. 26, T. Pennfield, P. O. Battle Creek.
Sine, Arthur, Farmer and Highway Commissioner, S. 28, T. Clarence, P. O. Albion. Mr. Sine was born in Calhoun County in 1873.
Sine, H. W., Farmer and Breeder, S. 24, T. Lee, P. O. Olivet. Mr. Sine was born in 1877.
Slower, W. B., Supervisor, Albion.
Smith, Albert, Farmer and Road Commissioner, S. 31, T. Newton, P. O. Union City.
Smith, C. J., Farmer, S. 31, T. Homer, P. O. Homer. Mr. Smith was born in 1877.
Smith, Earl, Farmer, S. 32, T. Convis, P. O. Ceresco. Mr. Smith was born in Calhoun County in 1886.
Smith, Frank B., Farmer and Supervisor, S. 16, T. Marengo, P. O. Marshall. 1880.
Smith, F. P., Insurance Agent, S. 19, T. Marengo, P. O. Marshall. 1911.
Smith, G. W., Farmer, S. 25, T. Marengo, P. O. Albion. Mr. Smith was born in 1861.
Smith, H. E., and J. L. Smith, Farmers, S. 5, T. Pennfield, P. O. Battle Creek.
Smith, Huber, Farmer, S. 1, T. Pennfield, P. O. Bellevue. 1885.
Smith, James T., Carpenter, S. 23, T. Bedford, P. O. Battle Creek. 1907.
Smith, T. J., Farmer, S. 35, T. Eckford, P. O. Eckford. 1883.
Smith, V. S., Farmer, S. 30, T. Pennfield, P. O. Battle Creek. Mr. Smith was born in Calhoun County in 1884.
Smith, W. L., Farmer, S. 9, T. Battle Creek, P. O. Battle Creek. Mr. Smith was born in 1871.
Snell, James, Farmer, S. 4, T. Eckford, P. O. Marshall. 1883.
Snell, R. E., Farmer, S. 26, T. Marengo, P. O. Marshall. Mr. Snell was born in 1889.
Snell, W. B., Real Estate, Battle Creek.
Snow, A. F., Farmer, S. 16, T. Battle Creek, P. O. Battle Creek. 1877.
Snyder Abstract Co., The, A. V. Watson, Proprietor, Marshall.
Snyder, H. Harrison, Fruit Grower, S. 18, T. Bedford, P. O. Battle Creek. Mr. Snyder was born in Calhoun County in 1890.
Snyder, Carl, Farmer, S. 14, T. Eckford, P. O. Eckford. 1908.
Snyder, C. M., Farmer, S. 2, T. Pennfield, P. O. Battle Creek. 1845.
Snyder, H. V. & Son, General Contractors, Battle Creek.
Snyder, Dr. P. M., Physician, Athens.
Snyder, R. W., Manufacturer of Extracts, Battle Creek.
Snyder, Wesley, Farmer, S. 26, T. Albion, P. O. Homer. 1846.
Spaulding, Frank C., Undertaker, Battle Creek.
Spaulding, R. J., Real Estate, Battle Creek.
Spier, Roy H., Real Estate, Battle Creek.
Sperry, J. B., Real Estate, Battle Creek.
Spooner, Henry, Farmer, S. 35, T. Emmet, P. O. Ceresco. Mr. Spooner was born in 1869.
Springport State Savings Bank, General Banking, Springport.
Standford, Chas., Postmaster, Athens.
Starks, Cottrell, Farmer, S. 8, T. Clarence, P. O. Springport. Mr. Starks was born in Calhoun County in 1881.
Steel, Chas., Farmer, S. 1, T. Marshall, P. O. Marshall. 1909.
Stephens, C. M., Real Estate, Battle Creek.
Stephens, J. H., County Agent, Battle Creek.
Sterling Bros. Co., Cash Department Store, Battle Creek.
Sterling, F. G., Farmer, S. 2, T. Le Roy, P. O. Battle Creek. Mr. Sterling was born in 1857.
Steward & Sabin, Lawyers, Battle Creek.
Stewart, Eugene, Laundry, Battle Creek.
Stewart & Jacobs, Lawyers, Battle Creek.
Stiles & Bowman, Livery, Battle Creek.
Stone, H. J., Farmer and Stock Breeder, S. 34, T. Emmet, P. O. Ceresco. 1909.
Strain, B. D., Wholesale Baker, Battle Creek.
Stratton, E. H., French Dry Cleaning Works, Battle Creek.
Stratton, W. F., Farmer, S. 36, T. Homer, P. O. Homer. 1910.
Strickland, Guy E., Stock Breeder and Fruit Grower, S. 16, T. Albion, P. O. Albion. Mr. Strickland was born in 1877.
Strong, Chas. S., City Treasurer, Battle Creek.
Strong-Barker Hardware Co., Dealers in Hardware, Stoves and Implements, Battle Creek.
Stuart, F. A. Co., Dyspepsia Tablets, Marshall.
Sturgis, Joseph, Farmer, S. 27, T. Lee, P. O. Marshall. 1876.
Sweet, Charlie V., Farmer and Stock Feeder, S. 7, T. Marengo, P. O. Marshall. Mr. Sweet was born in 1882.
Sweet, F. H., Farmer, S. 27, T. Fredonia, P. O. Marshall. Mr. Sweet was born in 1844 and settled in Calhoun County in 1865.
Sweet, Jesse R., Farmer, S. 16, T. Marengo, P. O. Marshall. Mr. Sweet was born in 1885.

Taft, H. W., Real Estate, Battle Creek.
Tawner, T. R., Farmer and Stockraiser, S. 17, T. Marengo, P. O. Marshall. 1890.
Tate, Wm. E., Farmer, S. 21, T. Athens, P. O. Athens.
Tekonsha News, The, Ben. F. McMillen, Manager, Commercial and Job Printing, Tekonsha.
Thomas, S. J., Farmer, S. 3, T. Convis, P. O. Bellevue. Mr. Thomas was born in Calhoun County in 1865.
Thomas, Theo. A., Farmer, S. 35, T. Eckford, P. O. Homer. Mr. Thomas was born in 1877.
Thompson, Edgar L., Livery, Albion.
Thomson, R. R., Local Manager Commonwealth Power Co., Battle Creek.
Thunder, W. S., Farmer, S. 26, T. Emmet, P. O. Battle Creek. Mr. Thunder was born in 1884.
Tillotson, F. S., Farmer, S. 28, T. Albion, P. O. Homer.
Tobey, A. J., Proprietor Long Lake Farm, Breeder of Thoroughbred O. I. C. Hogs and Shorthorn Durham Cattle, S. 28, T. Fredonia, P. O. Marshall. Mr. Tobey was born in Michigan in 1878 and settled in Calhoun County in 1894.
Tobey, Fred, Real Estate, Battle Creek.
Tobias, J. R., Real Estate, Urbandale, P. O. Battle Creek.
Tomlinson, Ira F., Farmer, S. 25, T. Burlington, P. O. Burlington.

Torey, Charles, Farmer and Stockraiser, S. 33, T. Homer, P. O. Homer. 1906.
Townsend, O. S., Farmer, S. 19, T. Marengo, P. O. Marshall. Mr. Townsend was born in 1859.
Tuchtenhagen, Frank, Farmer, S. 7, T. Albion, P. O. Albion. Mr. Tuchtenhagen was born in 1866.
Tuchtenhagen, J. F., Farmer, S. 15, T. Eckford, P. O. Albion. Mr. Tuchtenhagen was born in 1864.
Tucker, Frank, Farmer, S. 5, T. Eckford, P. O. Marshall. Mr. Tucker was born in 1871.
Tucker, H. C., Farmer and Stockraiser, S. 29, T. Marengo, P. O. Marshall. Mr. Tucker was born in 1864.
Tuller, Geo. M., Farmer, S. 4, T. Marshall, P. O. Ceresco. 1883.

Van Aken, H. C., Attorney, Battle Creek.
Van Arman, Adam, Farmer, S. 27, T. Lee, P. O. Marshall. Born in 1865.
Van Arman, Fred B., Farmer, S. 6, T. Marengo, P. O. Marshall. Mr. Van Arman was born in 1871.
Vandegrif, H. L., Van Hurst Fruit and Poultry Farm, T. Emmet, P. O. Battle Creek.
Vandenheede, J., Farmer, S. 8, T. Marengo, P. O. Marshall. 1892.
Vannocker, Frank, Farmer, S. 18, T. Pennfield, P. O. Battle Creek. Mr. Vannocker was born in Calhoun County in 1857.
Van Schoick, D. H., Farmer, S. 34, T. Burlington, P. O. Union City.
Van Schoick, Odie, Farmer, S. 35, T. Burlington, P. O. Union City.
Van Sickle, I. W., Farmer and Justice of the Peace, S. 3, T. Marengo, P. O. Marshall. 1888.
Van Vleet, Wm., Farmer, S. 8, T. Battle Creek, P. O. Battle Creek. 1906.
Van Voorhees, Frank, Farmer, S. 31, T. Eckford, P. O. Eckford. Mr. Van Voorhees was born in 1883.
Van Wagner, W. A., Farmer, S. 17, T. Battle Creek, P. O. Battle Creek. 1892.
Veplanck, R. C., Farmer, S. 6, T. Marengo, P. O. Marshall. Mr. Veplanck was born in 1861.

Waffle, W. B., Proprietor Fairview Percheron Stock Farm, S. 25, T. Burlington, P. O. Burlington.
Wagner, F. E., Sporting Goods, Motorcycles, Bicycles and Victrolas, Battle Creek.
Wagner, James, Farmer, S. 27, T. Lee, P. O. Marshall. Mr. Wagner was born in 1855.
Wagner, John A., Lawyer, Battle Creek.
Wagner, Wm. N., Farmer, S. 19, T. Burlington, P. O. Athens.
Wagoner, John, Farmer, Stockraiser and Breeder of Shropshire Sheep, S. 13, T. Homer, P. O. Homer. 1894.
Wakley, Wm. F., Monument Works, Marshall.
Wakefield, G. W., Farmer and Road Contractor, Augusta.
Wales, Frank R., Farmer, S. 4, T. Marengo, P. O. Marshall. Mr. Wales was born in 1885.
Walker, Horace J., Farmer, S. 3, T. Clarence, P. O. Olivet. 1908.
Walker Hose Clamp Co., The, Machine Shop and Garage, Battle Creek.
Walkinshaw, C. C., Farmer, S. 13, T. Pennfield, P. O. Pennfield. Mr. Walkinshaw was born in 1854.
Walkinshaw, J. E., Farmer and Supervisor, S. 22, T. Convis, P. O. Bellevue. Mr. Walkinson was born in Calhoun County in 1866.
Ware, William E., Lawyer, Battle Creek.
Warren, Levi S., Attorney and Conveyancer, Albion.
Warsop, B. A., Farmer, S. 12, T. Athens, P. O. Athens.
Waterman, B. O., Farmer, S. 7, T. Le Roy, P. O. Climax. 1901.
Wattles Hardware Co., Dealers in Hardware and Implements, Battle Creek.
Weaver, W. H., Farmer, S. 24, T. Marengo, P. O. Albion. Mr. Weaver was born in 1854.
Webb, Mrs. Sarah E., Farming, S. 5, T. Pennfield, P. O. Battle Creek. 1844.
Weeks, E. B., Farmer, S. 21, T. Athens, P. O. Athens.
Weeks & Cooper, Attorneys, Albion.
Weickgenant, Jacob, Dry Goods, etc., Battle Creek.
Weigand, Chas., Farmer, S. 24, T. Pennfield, P. O. Pennfield. Mr. Weigand was born in 1870.
Weiss, George F., Farmer and Stock Feeder, S. 2, T. Homer, P. O. Homer. Mr. Weiss was born in 1862.
Wellington, Perl, Farmer, S. 18, T. Athens, P. O. Athens.
Wells, Frank, Farmer, S. 29, T. Eckford, P. O. Eckford. Mr. Wells was born in 1877.
Wells, Geo., Farmer, S. 1, T. Le Roy, P. O. Battle Creek. Mr. Wells was born in Calhoun County in 1879.
Wetzel, Frank, Landscape Gardener and Nurseryman, S. 4, T. Battle Creek, P. O. Battle Creek. 1909.
Wheeler, O. K., Farmer, S. 28, T. Emmet, P. Ceresco. 1914.
Wheelock, Charles H., Real Estate and Roofing Contractor, Battle Creek.
White, C. A., Farmer, S. 21, T. Burlington, P. O. Burlington.
White, J. E., Publisher, Marshall.
Whitelam, R. H., Farmer, S. 10, T. Fredonia, P. O. Marshall. 1880.
Whitford & Ashby, Real Estate, Battle Creek.
Whitmore, S. O., Farmer, Breeder and Shipper of Pure White Leghorn Chickens, S. 27, T. Pennfield, P. O. Battle Creek. Mr. Whitmore was born in 1872.
Whitney, Harlan F., Civil Engineer, Battle Creek.
Wilber, Silas W., Farmer, S. 16, T. Battle Creek, P. O. Battle Creek. 1878.
Wildey, C. E., Farmer, S. 3, T. Burlington, P. O. Burlington. Mr. Wildey has served as Chairman Board of Supervisors.
Willett, W. C., Blacksmith, Marshall.
Williams, E. S., Farmer, S. 15, T. Marengo, P. O. Marshall. Mr. Williams was born in 1888.
Williams, L. C., Drain Commissioner, Marshall.
Williams, R. C., Farmer, S. 34, T. Lee, P. O. Olivet. 1857.
Willison, J. M., Farmer, S. 29, T. Pennfield, P. O. Battle Creek. Mr. Willison was born in Calhoun County in 1849.
Winegar, H., Farmer, S. 25, T. Lee, P. O. Marshall. Mr. Winegar was born in 1878.
Witt, G. P., Farmer and Township Treasurer, S. 11, T. Battle Creek, P. O. Battle Creek. 1900.
Wolverine Auto-Cycle Co., Motorcycles, Bicycles and Sundries, Battle Creek.
Wolverine Stock Farm, W. W. Sprague, Secretary, Farmers and Breeders of Holstein Cattle, S. 33, T. Emmet, P. O. Ceresco. Mr. Sprague was born in 1873.
Wood, Bert, Farmer, S. 23, T. Convis, P. O. Marshall. 1910.
Wood, M. T., Farmer, S. 21, T. Battle Creek, P. O. Battle Creek. Mr. Wood was born in 1870.
Wood, W. D., Farmer, S. 26, T. Burlington, P. O. Burlington.
Wood & Woodruff, Dealers in Lumber, Coal, etc., Athens.
Woodruff, F. G., Dealer in Lumber and Coal, President Athens State Bank, Athens.
Woodworth, C. M., Farmer, S. 20, T. Pennfield, P. O. Battle Creek. Mr. Woodworth was born in Calhoun County in 1866.
Wright & Shepard, Real Estate and Insurance, Albion.

Yost, H. L., Farmer, S. 34, T. Albion, P. O. Homer. Mr. Yost was born in 1885.
Young, Victor, Farmer, S. 12, T. Eckford, P. O. Marshall. Mr. Young was born in 1882.

Zeigler, H. M., Pianos, Battle Creek.
Zinn, A. K., Grain and Milling, Battle Creek.
Zull, A., Farmer, S. 12, T. Emmet, P. O. Ceresco. 1908.

ADVERTISING SECTION

The Snyder Abstract Co
A. V. WATSON, Proprietor
Offices Up Stairs in Post Office Block
Corner State and Jefferson Sts.
MARSHALL, - MICH.

Walter D. Kline
Attorney and Counselor at Law
305 Post Block
Phone, Bell 499-J
BATTLE CREEK, - MICH.

Howard W. Cavanagh
Lawyer
302-315 Ward Building
BATTLE CREEK, - MICH.

S. A. McGee
Real Estate, Rentals, Loans, Insurance
Suite No. 3 Marjorie Block
Bell Phone 1311
BATTLE CREEK, - MICH.

The Marshall Daily and Weekly News
D. W. KNICKERBOCKER, Editor and Proprietor
MARSHALL, - MICH.

P. A. LEONARD
Real Estate
Office 305 Post Building
Bell Phones: Office, 2264-J Residence, 518-K
BATTLE CREEK, - MICH.

Stewart & Jacobs
Attorneys at Law
Kingman Building
Bell Phone 290-J Citizens Phone 1216
BATTLE CREEK, - MICH.

The Morning ....Enquirer
—
The Evening News
BATTLE CREEK, - MICH.

Chas. M. Stephens
Real Estate, Loan Agent and Renter
Notary Public
Bell Phone 1003-J
24 Main Street East
BATTLE CREEK, - MICH.

W. C. Phelps
Grocer
PHONES
Bell 502 Citizens 1678
16 Jefferson Avenue S.
BATTLE CREEK, - MICH.

I. W. Schram
Real Estate, Insurance, Notary Public
267 West Main Street
Bell Phone 771 Residence 1494-W
BATTLE CREEK, - MICH.

H. M. Ziegler
KIMBALL PIANOS AND PLAYER PIANOS
115 West Main Street
Bell Phone 1010-R
BATTLE CREEK, - MICH.

P. D. Wright & M. O. Shepard
Real Estate and Insurance
ALBION, - MICH.

Mrs. R. M. ..Morehouse
DEALER IN
General Merchandise
PENFIELD, - MICH.

Calhoun County Abstract Co.
MARSHALL, - MICH.

Henry L. Phillips
Jackson Automobile Garage
Bell Phone 419- R
22-24-26 E. Jackson St.
BATTLE CREEK, - MICH.

Wayne D. Marsh
Wall Paper, Paints, Oils, Glass and Window Shades
13 Jefferson Avenue North
BATTLE CREEK, - MICH.

A. K. ZINN & CO.
DEALERS IN
Grain, Hay, Flour and Mill Feeds
36 Liberty Street
Elevator: 134 South Jefferson Ave.
Phones: Bell, 1854-R; Citizens, 1050
BATTLE CREEK, - MICH.

F. E. Shaw. F. R. McLinden.
SHAW & McLINDEN
Funeral Directors
55 South Avenue
BATTLE CREEK, - MICH.

Frank G. Sherwin
The Red Headed Grocer
58 Main Street East
BATTLE CREEK, - MICH.

Commonwealth Power Company
R. R. THOMSON, Local Manager
BATTLE CREEK, - MICH.

Milk Producers Co.
Ice Cream and Ices
Both Phones
47 Kalamazoo Street
BATTLE CREEK, - MICH.

Maple City Dairy Co.
D. S. BIRDSALL, Prop.
Cash for Cream
Cans Furnished for 30 Days Trial
ALBION, - MICH.

B. A. KNAPP
General Insurance Agency
30 Main St., West
Bell Phone 347 Citizens Phone 1300
BATTLE CREEK, - MICH.

W. B. Snell
REAL ESTATE
Investments, Loans and Insurance
7 Main Street West
BATTLE CREEK, - MICH.

Stewart Laundry
EUGENE STEWART, Prop.
—
57-59 Main Street East
BATTLE CREEK, - MICH.

THE Wolverine Temperature Regulator Company
DENNIS KELLY, Proprietor
Manufacturers of Thermostats
MARSHALL, - MICH.

A. J. McNAUGHTON
Monuments
Citizens' Phone 1565
107 South Avenue
BATTLE CREEK, - MICH.

C. L. Blake. H. L. Bailey.
Marshall Plumbing and Heating Co.
209 West State Street
Bell Phone 382 Citizens Phone 13
MARSHALL, - MICH.

H. C. King Seed Co.
Growers and Distributers of Newly Propagated Farm SEEDS
55 No. Wabash Avenue
Bell Phone 475-J
BATTLE CREEK, - MICH.

R. W. SNYDER
MANUFACTURER OF
Flavoring Extracts
66 and 68 E. Jackson St.
BATTLE CREEK, - MICH.

Frank C. Spaulding
Funeral Director
Free Ambulance Service
Both Phones
Bell 324 Auto 1417
24 Marshall Street
BATTLE CREEK, - MICH.

E. L. SAXTON
DEALER IN
Bicycles and Bicycle Sundries
143 West Main Street
BATTLE CREEK, - MICH.

ALEX. A. McKAY
CIVIL ENGINEER
Plats Surveys
528 Post Building
Phone 547-W
BATTLE CREEK, - MICH.

E. R. PAGE
Real Estate Broker
Money to Loan on Real Estate
Some of the Best Farms in Calhoun County for Sale at Reasonable Prices
MARSHALL, - MICH.

L. B. Brockett & Sons
Dealers in
HARDWARE
59-61 W. Main Street
BATTLE CREEK, - MICH.

Strong-Barker Hardware Co.
Hardware, Stoves and Implements
25-27 South Jefferson Avenue
BATTLE CREEK, - MICH.

E. L. Thompson
Livery, Feed and Sales Stables
Telephone 81
Corner Superior and Ash Streets
ALBION, - MICH.

L. C. Rivers. H. E. Petrie.
Rivers & Petrie
Independent Garage
Used Cars For Sale at All Times
Bell Phone 934-J
99-101 West Main Street
BATTLE CREEK, - MICH.

Royal Livery Barn
Bus and Baggage Line
THOS. E. CHURCH, Prop.
South Eagle St. Both Phones
MARSHALL, - MICH.

P. A. Mittauer. A. A. Monroe.
Marshall Marble and Granite Works
Monuments and Markers
Bell Phone 83
MARSHALL, - MICH.

The Battle Creek Sanitarium
—
ESTABLISHED 1866
—
BATTLE CREEK, - MICH.

ADVERTISING SECTION

ADVERTISING SECTION

MERCHANTS SAVINGS BANK

Battle Creek, Michigan.

Capital, $125,000.00

Surplus, $40,000.00

OFFICERS

A. M. Minty, - President.
R. F. Hoffmaster, Vice President.
A. O. Jones, - Vice President.
H. A. Rowles, - - Cashier.

DIRECTORS

R. F. Hoffmaster, A. M. Minty.
P. H. Rose, A. O. Jones.
M. Lafever, H. A. Rowles.
L. M. Turner.

OFFICERS

Edward C. Hinman, - President.
Frank Wolf, - Vice President.
Carroll L. Post, - Vice President.
Howard B. Sherman, Vice President.
Frank G. Evans, - Cashier.
Wm. W. Smith, - Ass't Cashier.
S. D. Albertson, - Ass't Cashier.
David Miller, - - Auditor.

Safety Deposit Boxes for Rent

Form the habit of doing your banking at the

Central National Bank

BATTLE CREEK, MICH.

OFFICERS

Chas. C. Green, - President.
E. R. Morton, Vice Pres. and Cashier.
F. A. Allwardt, 2nd Vice President.
N. E. Hubbard, 3rd Vice President.
N. E. Green, - Ass't Cashier.

THE CITY BANK

of Battle Creek, Michigan

Incorporated 1871

Capital and Surplus, $200,000.00

E. P. Keep, - - President.
R. B. Waldo, - Vice President.
B. G. Doolittle, - - Cashier.
F. D. Rice, - - Ass't Cashier.

First State Bank

of Tekonsha, Michigan

Established 1877.

Incorporated 1902.

C. E. Gorham, - President.
F. A. Stuart, - Vice President.
C. H. Billings, - - Cashier.
G. R. Grant, - Ass't Cashier.

FIRST NATIONAL BANK

Marshall, Michigan

CAPITAL AND SURPLUS, $175,000.00

H. T. Halliday, - Bell Phone 1476-J
C. S. Wilcox, - Bell Phone 562-K

Halliday & Wilcox

Real Estate, Loans and Insurance

Largest Listing in the City

16 East Main Street

Bell 2100 Citizens 1275

Battle Creek, - Mich.

CUMMINGS-ALLEN REALTY CO.

Real Estate, Loans, Insurance, Home Builders, Contractors

Suite No. 3, Marjorie Block

Office, Bell Phone 1313

Residence, Bell Phone 2157-J

BATTLE CREEK, - MICH.

W. H. Bradley. F. J. Bradley.

Bradley Brothers

DEALERS IN

Fuel, Hardware, Lowe Bros. Paints

Ward Building, 43 Jefferson Ave., No.

Telephones

Battle Creek, - Mich.

THE

Evening Statesman

Oldest Newspaper in Calhoun County, Established 1859

Marshall's Daily Newspaper

Reaches more homes in and around Marshall, the county seat of a prosperous agricultural county of 75,000 people, than any other newspaper published.

Marshall, - Mich.

H. W. TAFT REAL ESTATE INSURANCE

709 POST BLDG. BATTLE CREEK, MICH.

We have a large list of city property and investments. Also make a specialty of farms. If you have a farm for sale we would like to list it.

Bell Phone 347 Citizens Phone 1300

30 Main St., West, Battle, Creek, Mich.

W. S. Keet, T. H. Davis.
W. M. Davis.

Keet-Davis Co., Inc.

Funeral Directors and Embalmers

80 East Main Street

Office Phones:

Bell 1248-J Citizens 1039

Battle Creek, - Mich.

D. M. Dobbins, S. P. Dobbins.
D. R. Petrie.

Dobbins Hardware Co.

Wolverine Furnaces, Peninsular Stoves, Builders' Hardware

Yale Art Hardware, Yale Chain Hoists, Factory Supplies

36 East Main

Battle Creek, - Mich.

City-Suburban Lot Exchange

L. I. ALDERDYCE, Mgr.

Real Estate, Fire Insurance and Loans

Suite 603 Post Building

Bell Phone 463-W

Battle Creek, - Mich.

Chas. A. Peterson

Plumbing, Hardware

Steam and Hot Water Heating

Fireproof Safes and Vault Doors a Specialty

37 Washington Ave. N.

Bell Phone 772

Residence Phone 1225-R

Battle Creek, - Mich.

FAVORITE

Black Percheron Stallion No. 79701

OWNED BY

C. A. JONES

R. F. D. No. 2

Battle Creek, - Mich.

JOHN C. GOODRICH

DRY GOODS, GROCERIES

Boots and Shoes, Hardware, Wall Paper and Gents' Furnishings

Carriages, Harness, Farm Implements and Field Fence

Shipping Point—Ceresco.

P.O. Address—Marshall, R.F.D. No. 2

Ellis, - - Mich.

S. C. Fisher, - - President.
T. P. Davis, - Sec'y and Treas.

THE

Davis-Fisher Co., Inc.

Real Estate and Fire Insurance

We Buy, Sell, Rent or Exchange City and Farm Property

30½ N. Jefferson Ave., Op. Ward Blk.

Phones: Bell, 1913; Citizens, 1471.

Battle Creek, - Mich.

COCA-COLA Bottling Co.

Manufacturers and Bottlers of

Soda and Mineral Waters

Bar Supplies and Glass Ware

55-57 Monroe Street

Bell Phone 171. Citizens Phone 1739.

Battle Creek, - Mich.

Nashville Book Co.

(Incorporated)

Southern Office, Nashville, Tenn.

Northern Distributing House, MARSHALL, MICH.

J. E. WHITE, Proprietor

Marshall, - Mich.

J. M. Moses, - - Editor.
F. H. Moses, - Business Manager.

MARSHALL EXPOUNDER, Established 1836

The Evening Chronicle

Established 1879

J. M. MOSES & SON, Publishers

Chronicle Building, 225 W. State St.

Marshall, - Mich.

L. H. Schroder, - President.
Sherman Schroder, - Secretary.

Schroder Bros. Co.

INCORPORATED

Dry Goods, Women's Garments, Millinery, Draperies

Mail Orders Solicited

33-35-37 Main Street, West

Battle Creek, - Mich.

W. J. KIRKPATRICK

Wholesale and Retail Dealer in

Coal, Wood, Coke

Cement, Lime, Brick, Plaster, White Sand, Marble Grit, Baled Hay, Straw, Feed

Office and Yards: 128-130 Jefferson Ave., S.

Bell Phone 60 Citizens Phone 1073

Battle Creek, - Mich.

The Cable Piano Co.

Factories, Chicago & St. Charles, Ill.

State Office, Detroit, Mich.

The World's Greatest Manufacturers of Pianos and Inner Player Pianos

Branch Store, 100 W. Main St.

Bell Phone 2353

F. R. LAWRENCE, Mgr.

Battle Creek, - Mich.

Wm. F. Waidely Monument Works

Manufacturer of all Grades & Styles of

Marble and Granite Monuments and Markers

All Work Neatly Done With Pneumatic Tools

Cor. Exchange and Green Sts.

Marshall, - Mich.

THE WALKER HOSE CLAMP CO.

Expert Automobile Repairing, Overhauling and Rebuilding

Sheet Metal Specialties, Fine Die Designing and Building, Machine Work to Order

53 River Street

Telephones: Bell, 1768; Auto, 1194

Battle Creek, - Mich.

Donald I. Sterling, - President.
Geo. R. Sterling, - Vice President.
Fred S. Sterling, - Sec'y and Treas.

Sterling Bros. Co.

Cash Department Store

Sterlings Sell it for Less

Battle Creek, - Mich.

Geo. W. Leedle, - President.
L. E. Brooke, - Vice President.
W. R. Simons, - Sec'y and Mgr.

Simons-Leedle Furnace Co.

MANUFACTURERS OF

The Dobbins Tubular Warm-Air Furnaces

Mantles, Grates, Tiling and Fire Place Goods

Marshall, - Mich.

E. C. Fisher & Co.

Wholesale and Retail

Books, News, Stationery, Athletic Goods and Office Supplies

Typewriters Bought, Sold and Rented

12-14 Main Street, West

BATTLE CREEK, - MICH.

F. A. Stuart, - - President.
J. C. Stuart, - Vice President.
A. B. Osborne, - Sec'y and Treas.

F. A. STUART CO.

INCORPORATED

Stuart's Dyspepsia Tablets, Calcium Wafer Compound, Charcoal Lozenges

Marshall, - Mich.

McBeth Livery and Boarding Stable

STILES & BOWMAN, Props.

Calls Answered Promptly, Special Attention Given to Boarders

52 S. McCamly St.

Bell Phone 78. Citizens Phone 1070.

Battle Creek, - Mich.

Harris Brothers

Manufacturers of and Dealers in

Harness, Horse Furnishings, Robes, Whips, Brushes, Trunks and Bags

23 Jefferson Ave., South

Bell Phone 623

Battle Creek, - Mich.

ADVERTISING SECTION

ADVERTISING SECTION

Springport State Savings Bank
GENERAL BANKING
SPRINGPORT, - MICH.

JOHN A. WAGNER
Lawyer
214 Ward Building
Bell Phone 32
BATTLE CREEK, - MICH.

William E. Ware
Lawyer
309 Post Buiding
BATTLE CREEK, - MICH.

Weeks & Cooper
LAWYERS
ALBION, - MICH.

Walter S. Powers
ATTORNEY
BATTLE CREEK, - MICH.

Chas. F. McKenzie
LAWYER
Suite 306 Post Building
BATTLE CREEK, - MICH.

Jesse Arthur, Ira A. Beck, R. G. Leitch.
ARTHUR & BECK
Counselors at Law
207-8 Ward Bldg.
BATTLE CREEK, - MICH.

CASE THE FLORIST
Ward Building
41 Jefferson Ave., N.
Bell 790 Citizens 1212
BATTLE CREEK, - MICH

ROY MARKHAM
Insurance
No. 15 West Main St.
BATTLE CREEK, - MICH.

SEE BRIGGS FOR
Real Estate and Rentals
H. A. Briggs
214 Ward Building
Bell Phone 32
BATTLE CREEK, - MICH.

DR. P. M. SNYDER
Athens, - Michigan

J. W. PIKE
Jeweler
ATHENS, - MICH.

DONOVAN'S
Real Estate, Insurance and Loans
21 West Main St. Bell Phone 376-r
BATTLE CREEK, - MICH.

The Frank M. Barry
General Insurance Agency
Fire, Life, Accident, Liability, Plate Glass
Room 405 Post Building
Bell Phone 499-J
BATTLE CREEK, - MICH.

Amberg & Murphy Drug Co., Ltd.
Prescription Druggists
BATTLE CREEK, - MICH.

Bernard J. Onen
Attorney AND Counselor
BATTLE CREEK, - MICH.

James M. Powers
ATTORNEY
Suite 2, Kingman Block
BATTLE CREEK, - MICH.

O. J. RENIGER
Gen'l Contractor and Builder
MARSHALL, - MICH.

FARLEY
UNDERTAKING
Reliable Furniture and Rugs
87 East Main Street
Bell Phone 99 Citizens Phone 1199
BATTLE CREEK, - MICH.

J. O. GALLOUP
Iron Pipe, Fittings and Valves
Steam Fitters' Tools and Mill Supplies
43, 45 E. State St.
BATTLE CREEK, - MICH.

American Motor Co.
Experts and Garage in Connection
99-101 Main St. W.
Bell Phone 141
BATTLE CREEK, - MICH.

Athens Garage
And Machine Shop
WM. I. GRILL, Prop.
Automobile Accessories, Vulcanizing, General Machine Work
ATHENS, - MICH.

Edward D. Strain
Wholesale BAKER
71-73 S. Monroe Street
BATTLE CREEK, - MICH.

CHARLES O. MILLER
Attorney at Law
MARSHALL, - MICH.

GUY E. CRANE
Horse Tailor
15 Jackson St., W.
Bell Phone 45-J
BATTLE CREEK, - MICH.

C. R. Brewer Lumber Co.
Wholesale and Retail
LUMBER
And Building Material
111 Marshall Street
BATTLE CREEK, - MICH.

P. A. BAUER
General Auctioneer
15 Years Successful Experience
Farm Property a Specialty
Satisfaction Guaranteed
Bell Phone 25
ATHENS, - MICH.

George W. Mechem
Attorney
BATTLE CREEK, - MICH.

J. R. McKEE
Monument Works
South and Virginia Avenues
BATTLE CREEK, - MICH.

Battle Creek Hack and Bus Co.
Old Reliable Hack Line
79 S. Division
Citizens Phone 1115 Bell Phone 115
BATTLE CREEK, - MICH.

Chas. W. Centner
The Style Shop
Wearing Apparel and Furnishings for Women
Bell Phone 159-J Auto. Phone 1159
BATTLE CREEK, - MICH.

C. B. GRANGER
Albion House Barn
Taxicab Service, Carriage and Auto Livery
Phone 79
ALBION, - MICH.

I. L. ALLEN
Dairyman and Breeder of Graded Holstein Cattle
ALBION, - MICH.

W. C. WILLETT
BLACKSMITH
MARSHALL, - MICH.

James H. Mustard
Lawyer
604 Post Bldg
BATTLE CREEK, - MICH.

The Ideal American Laundry
38 East Main St. Both Phones
BATTLE CREEK, - MICH.

F. GURNFLO
Livery and Boarding Stable
36-38-40 Water Street
Old Phone 1047-J Citizens' Phone 1430
BATTLE CREEK, - MICH.

C. C. DeWitt
Wines, Liquors and Cigars
BATTLE CREEK, - MICH.

Battle Creek Taxicab Co.
Micheal Dempsey, Mgr.
CARRIAGE RATES
Day and Night Service
67 East Jackson St.
Phones: Citizens 1672; Bell 71
BATTLE CREEK, - MICH.

O. V. Eastman & Son
Livery, Sale and Exchange
Michigan Ave. Telephone 24
ALBION, - MICH.

Wm. Martin
REAL ESTATE
MARSHALL, - MICH.

C. E. AVERY
Livery and Sale Stables
Good Rigs at Right Prices
24 W. Jackson Street
Bell Phone 266-R
BATTLE CREEK, - MICH.

Missing page

Missing page

ILLUSTRATIONS

SAMUEL DICKIE,
ALBION, MICH.

L. C. WILLIAMS,
MARSHALL, MICH.

CHARLES HUTCHINSON,
R. F. D. No. 3,
CERESCO, MICH.

C. G. HILLER,
MARSHALL, MICH.

ARZA L. McCUTCHEON,
Justice of the Peace,
ALBION, MICH.

PIERCE B. MITCHELL, DECEASED.
Mr. Mitchell was a veteran of the Civil War, and was a farmer for many years, then engaged in the real estate business. Mr. Mitchell was a remarkable man, having been totally blind for many years and was one of the oldest and best known citizens of Calhoun County.

VIEW OF MAIN BUILDING, BATTLE CREEK SANITARIUM,
BATTLE CREEK, MICH.

J. E. TOBIAS,
Justice of the Peace, Notary Public,
Real Estate and Insurance,
URBANDALE, BATTLE CREEK, MICH.

GUY E. STRICKLAND,
Proprietor of Indian Spring Stock Farm, R. F. D. No. 1,
ALBION, MICH.

IRA HAGELSHAW,
R. F. D. No. 2,
CERESCO, MICH.

H. C. TUCKER,
R. F. D. No. 7,
MARSHALL, MICH.

JOSEPH STURGIS,
MARSHALL, MICH.

GEORGE RUNDLE,
R. F. D. No. 1,
OLIVET, MICH.

MR. ALEX McKENZIE, DECEASED AND
MRS. MARY L. McKENZIE,
R. F. D. No. 3,
BATTLE CREEK, MICH.

MR. AND MRS. EDWARD Z. BROWN,
R. F. D. No. 5,
BATTLE CREEK, MICH.

MR. AND MRS. WM. KIDNEY,
R. F. D. No. 5,
MARSHALL, MICH.

MR. AND MRS. JOHN ROCHO,
BATTLE CREEK, MICH.

ILLUSTRATIONS

THEODORE P. DAVIS,
BATTLE CREEK, MICH.

JAMES C. PAGE,
R. F. D. No. 8,
MARSHALL, MICH.

MR. AND MRS. C. H. ETSON,
R. F. D. No. 1,
BATTLE CREEK, MICH.

L. J. KING,
Justice of the Peace, Albion Township, R. F. D. No. 3,
HOMER, MICH.

P. A. BAUER,
ATHENS, MICH.

CITY HALL, BATTLE CREEK, MICH.

GEORGE H. McMILLEN,
ATHENS, MICH.

WILLARD LIBRARY, BATTLE CREEK, MICH.

HOSON G. BECKLEY AND
LOURSA A. BECKLEY,
R. F. D. No. 10,
BATTLE CREEK, MICH.

MR. AND MRS. GEO. W. KLINE,
HOMER, MICH.

MR. AND MRS. LEWIS L. AVERY,
ALBION, MICH.

MR. AND MRS. GEO. LININGER, JR.,
SPRINGPORT, MICH.

MR. AND MRS. F. E. RUDDOCK,
R. F. D. No. 4,
MARSHALL, MICH.

MR. AND MRS. BERT C. RINGLER,
R. F. D. No. 2,
ALBION, MICH.

MR. AND MRS. ED. WHITELAM
R. F. D. No. 2,
MARSHALL, MICH.

MR. AND MRS. R. EVANS,
R. F. D. No. 1,
BATTLE CREEK, MICH.

MR. AND MRS. H. D. BUSHNELL,
R. F. D. No. 6,
MARSHALL, MICH.

ILLUSTRATIONS

PHOTOGRAPH FROM FRANK MOHRHARDT,
SCRLINGTON, MICH.

GRANDCHILDREN OF W. A. FOX,
R. F. D. No. 5,
BATTLE CREEK, MICH.

PHOTOGRAPH FROM LETERME BROS.,
R. F. D. No. 2,
ALBION, MICH.

MRS. CHAS. WEIGAND,
R. F. D. No. 1,
BATTLE CREEK, MICH.

CHAS. WEIGAND,
R. F. D. No. 1,
BATTLE CREEK, MICH.

GEO. CROFOOT,
R. F. D. No. 3,
BATTLE CREEK, MICH.

"THOMAS AND RING AFTER DINNER"
F. L. Huggett,
R. F. D. No. 5,
BATTLE CREEK, MICH.

MR. AND MRS. W. H. BADGER AND DAUGHTER,
R. F. D. No. 1,
BATTLE CREEK, MICH.

BATTLE CREEK HIGH SCHOOL, BATTLE CREEK, MICH.

FRONT ENTRANCE, SANITARIUM, BATTLE CREEK, MICH.

SCHOOL DISTRICT NO. 5,
Battle Creek Township, Photograph from I. N. Cleveland,
BATTLE CREEK, MICH.

RESIDENCE AND SCENE ON FARM OF S. W. LAWTON,
R. F. D. No. 1,
BATTLE CREEK, MICH.

PRESBYTERIAN CHURCH,
HOMER, MICH.

OLD HOMESTEAD ADJOINING TWIN CEDAR FARM OWNED BY FRED B. VAN ARMAN,
R. F. D. No. 6,
MARSHALL, MICH.

TWIN CEDAR FARM,
Fred B. Van Arman, Proprietor, R. F. D. No. 6,
MARSHALL, MICH.

SCENE ON FARM OF M. L. BRIGGS,
R. F. D. No. 5,
BATTLE CREEK, MICH.

ILLUSTRATIONS

IDA ANKNEY,
R. F. D. No. 3,
BATTLE CREEK, MICH.

CHILDREN OF E. W. CHAPIN,
R. F. D. No. 1,
BATTLE CREEK, MICH.

MR. AND MRS. F. A. AVERY AND DAUGHTER BERTHA,
R. F. D. No. 1,
MARSHALL, MICH.

C. A. JONES,
R. F. D. No. 2,
BATTLE CREEK, MICH.

POST TAVERN, BATTLE CREEK, MICH.

CATHOLIC CHURCH, BATTLE CREEK, MICH.

MASONIC TEMPLE, BATTLE CREEK, MICH.

POST TAVERN,
BATTLE CREEK, MICH.

CATHOLIC CHURCH,
BATTLE CREEK, MICH.

MASONIC TEMPLE,
BATTLE CREEK, MICH.

J. H. BADGER,
R. F. D. No. 1,
BATTLE CREEK, MICH.

RALPH R. YOST, SON OF H. L. YOST,
HOMER, MICH.

HIGHLY BRED HOLSTEIN CATTLE,
Owned by Alva Good, R. F. D. No. 5,
MARSHALL, MICH.

M. L. BRIGGS,
R. F. D. No. 5,
BATTLE CREEK, MICH.

FAIR OAKS FARM, GEO. W. HADDOCK AND ELMER BAKER, PROPRIETORS,
R. F. D. No. 5,
BATTLE CREEK, MICH.

SCENE ON FARM OF LEWIS L. AVERY,
ALBION, MICH.

SCENE ON FARM OF E. A. BACHOFEN,
R. F. D. No. 1,
BATTLE CREEK, MICH.

ILLUSTRATIONS

HIGH SCHOOL,
HOMER, MICH.

SCHOOL BUILDING,
Photograph from Jas. A. Ruddock,
MARSHALL, MICH.

M. E. CHURCH,
HOMER, MICH.

COMMERCIAL SAVINGS BANK,
MARSHALL, MICH.

RESIDENCE OF R. B. WEEKS,
R. F. D. No. 1,
ATHENS, MICH.

RESIDENCE OF JUDSON PEAK,
SPRINGPORT, MICH.

RESIDENCE OF MARION SEBOLT,
R. F. D. No. 2,
OLIVET, MICH.

FAIRVIEW PERCHERON STOCK FARM,
W. E. Waffle, Proprietor,
BURLINGTON, MICH.

HIGH SCHOOL, ALBION, MICH.

THE SANITARIUM ANNEX, BATTLE CREEK, MICH.

FARM BUILDINGS AND VIEW ON THE MAPLE BROOK FARM,
O. H. Beach, Proprietor, R. F. D. No. 5,
BATTLE CREEK, MICH.

NORTHERN EMMETT FRUIT FARM,
Residence and Barn of Edward L. Sampson, R. F. D. No. 5,
BATTLE CREEK, MICH.

FARM BUILDINGS AND STOCK OF WILLIS J. KENYON,
R. F. D. No. 1,
TEKONSHA, MICH.

HOME AND STOCK OF W. A. FOX,
On the River View Farm, R. F. D. No. 5,
BATTLE CREEK, MICH.

RESIDENCE AND BARNS OF W. D. PITT,
R. F. D. No. 1,
BATTLE CREEK, MICH.

ILLUSTRATIONS

RESIDENCE OF FRANK VANNOCKER,
R. F. D. No. 3,
BATTLE CREEK, MICH.

RESIDENCE OF B. G. MORGAN,
R. F. D. No. 3,
BATTLE CREEK, MICH.

HOME OF W. J. DIBBLE,
President of Commercial Savings Bank,
MARSHALL, MICH.

HOME OF MR. AND MRS. J. E. TOBIAS,
Corner Main St. and Stringham Ave., Urbandale,
BATTLE CREEK, MICH.

RESIDENCE OF F. L. HUGGETT,
R. F. D. No. 5,
BATTLE CREEK, MICH.

PLEASANT VIEW FARM,
Home of Sylvester C. Bartholomew, R. F. D. No. 8,
MARSHALL, MICH.

RESIDENCE OF ED. WHITELAM,
R. F. D. No. 2,
MARSHALL, MICH.

RESIDENCE OF A. H. RUSSELL,
R. F. D. No. 8,
BATTLE CREEK, MICH.

LOOKING SOUTH FROM KISTLER'S GROVE,
Beadle Lake, Emmett Township,

VIEW FROM PORTER TO ERIE STREET,
ALBION, MICH.

SCENE ON FARM OF WM. S. PRUIN,
R. F. D. No. 1,
BATTLE CREEK, MICH.

RESIDENCE OF JOHN C. GOODRICH,
R. F. D. No 2,
MARSHALL, MICH.

STORE OF JOHN C. GOODRICH AT ELLIS,
R. F. D. No. 2,
MARSHALL, MICH.

MAPLE REST,
Scene on Farm of R. W. Chapin, R. F. D. No. 1,
BATTLE CREEK, MICH.

INDIAN MILL STOCK FARM,
Gardner W. Smith, Proprietor,
MARENGO, MICH.

SCENE ON FARM OF ED. HUGHES,
R. F. D. No. 1,
BATTLE CREEK, MICH.

ILLUSTRATIONS

RESIDENCE OF RALPH BINGHAM,
R. F. D. No. 2,
OLIVET, MICH.

RESIDENCE OF ROBERT BINGHAM,
R. F. D. No. 2,
OLIVET, MICH.

RESIDENCE OF CURRELL STARKS,
R. F. D. No. 2,
SPRINGPORT, MICH.

RESIDENCE OF S. F. ANKNEY,
R. F. D. No. 3,
BATTLE CREEK, MICH.

METHODIST CHURCH, BATTLE CREEK, MICH.

MAIN STREET, LOOKING WEST, BATTLE CREEK, MICH.

SANITARIUM ANNEX, BATTLE CREEK, MICH.

SWIMMING POOL, SANITARIUM, BATTLE CREEK, MICH.

ST. MARY'S LAKE FARM,
Home of Mrs. Mary L. McKenzie, R. F. D. No. 3,
BATTLE CREEK, MICH.

RESIDENCE OF T. J. SMITH,
ECKFORD, MICH.

FARM BUILDINGS OF J. H. DEAN,
R. F. D. No. 3,
ALBION, MICH.

RESIDENCE OF H. E. AND J. L. SMITH,
R. F. D. No. 3,
BATTLE CREEK, MICH.

ILLUSTRATIONS

HOME OF C. B. CASE,
UNION CITY, MICH.

PINE LODGE.
The suburban residence of Charles H. Wheelock, who is also owner of "The Oaks," a fifty-four acre tract lying between Brownlee Park and Greenfield Park, one quarter of a mile east of Pine Lodge. The Grand Trunk R. R. shops are located on a portion of the 153 acres purchased from Mr. Wheelock off from the south end of his Pine Lodge Farm and the Flowing Wells, from which the water supply of the City of Battle Creek is obtained, are located on the north end of the farm, in close proximity to the Battle Creek River. The tract of land lying between the Pine Lodge residence shown in this cut and the river is platted and known as Wheelock's Pine Lodge Tract. Because of abundant supply of pure water, furnished under a pressure of from 90 to 100 pounds, for the use of Battle Creek, the available supply of electricity either for commercial or family use, a long stretch of the main line of the Grand Trunk Railway, with abundant room for side tracks, level land and close proximity to the Battle Creek River, with desirable boating and fishing privileges, the Pine Lodge Tract is a most desirable piece of property either for residence or manufacturies.

RESIDENCE AND BARNS ON EVERGREEN LAWN FARM
Henry Spooner, Proprietor, R. F. D. No. 2.
CERESCO, MICH.

FARM BUILDINGS OF H. C. TUCKER,
R. F. D. No. 7,
MARSHALL, MICH.

RESIDENCE OF D. E. PRINE,
R. F. D. No. 5,
BATTLE CREEK, MICH.

HOME OF R. KISINGER,
R. F. D. No. 1,
EAST LEROY, MICH.

SCENE ON THE GREEN VALLEY FARM,
A. W. Russell, Proprietor, R. F. D. No. 3,
BATTLE CREEK, MICH.

SCENES ON FARM OF J. L. SMITH
BATTLE CREEK, MICH.

SUNNYSIDE FARM.
Home of Frank B. Smith, R. F. D. No. 1,
MARSHALL, MICH.

RESIDENCE OF F. D. COTTON,
R. F. D. No. 2,
BATTLE CREEK, MICH.

RESIDENCE OF W. H. PALMITER,
BATTLE CREEK, MICH.

RESIDENCE OF MR. AND MRS. JOHN ROCHO,
BATTLE CREEK, MICH.

RESIDENCE OF JOHN A. WAGNER,
BATTLE CREEK, MICH.

RESIDENCE OF MR. AND MRS. E. W. PHILLIPS,
CERESCO, MICH.

RESIDENCE OF BERT RINGLER,
R. F. D. No. 2,
ALBION, MICH.

H. W. DEAN,
Furniture and Undertaking,
TEKONSHA, MICH.

SCENE ON FARM OF GEO. LININGER,
SPRINGPORT, MICH.

ILLUSTRATIONS

HISTORICAL INDIAN MILL,
On farm owned by Gardner W. Smith,
MARENGO, MICH.

HOME OF MR. AND MRS. CHAS. J. MILLER,
BURLINGTON, MICH.

THE IDEAL FARM, HOME OF SAMUEL DINGER,
R. F. D. No. 3,
BATTLE CREEK, MICH.

SCENE ON FARM OF O. S. TOWNSEND,
MARSHALL, MICH.

RESIDENCE OF MARTIN B. MILLER,
R. F. D. No. 2,
SPRINGPORT, MICH.

LAKEVIEW JERSEY HERD, RAISED BY H. HALSEY, HOMER, MICH.

RESIDENCE OF A. P. MACK,
R. F. D. No. 2,
UNION CITY, MICH.

SCENE ON FARM OF EDWARD BADGER,
R. F. D. No. 1,
BATTLE CREEK, MICH.

SCHOOL DISTRICT NO. 12, NEWTON TOWNSHIP,
Photograph from A. J. Schay, R. F. D. No. 2,
BATTLE CREEK, MICH.

MAPLE VIEW, SCENE ON FARM OF F. A. AVERY,
MARSHALL, MICH.

HOME OF HENRY ARNOLD,
R. F. D. No. 3,
TEKONSHA, MICH.

SCENE ON FARM OF C. H. ETSON,
R. F. D. No. 1,
BATTLE CREEK, MICH.

SCENE ON FARM OF PETER SCHULTZ,
BATTLE CREEK, MICH.

BARNS ON FARM OF JOSEPH STURGIS,
MARSHALL, MICH.

BURR OAK PLAINS,
Charles Hutchinson, Proprietor, R. F. D. No. 3,
CERESCO, MICH.

SCENE ON FARM OF CHAS. W. BIRD,
BATTLE CREEK, MICH.

ANALYSIS OF THE SYSTEM

OF

United States Land Surveys

METES AND BOUNDS

DIAGRAM 1.

UP to the time of the Revolutionary War, or until about the beginning of the present century, land, when parcelled out, and sold or granted, was described by "Metes and Bounds," and that system is still in existence in the following States, or in those portions of them which had been sold or granted when the present plan of surveys was adopted, viz.: New York, Pennsylvania, New Jersey, Delaware, Maryland, Virginia, North and South Carolina, Georgia, Tennessee, Kentucky, Texas, and the six New England States. To describe land by "Metes and Bounds," is to have a known land-mark for a place of beginning, and then follow a line according to the compass-needle (or magnetic bearing), or the course of a stream, or track of an ancient highway. This plan has resulted in endless confusion and litigation, as land-marks decay and change, and it is a well-known fact that the compass-needle varies and does not always point due North.

As an example of this plan of dividing lands, the following description of a farm laid out by "Metes and Bounds," is given: "Beginning at a stone on the Bank of Doe River, at a point where the highway from A. to B. crosses said river (see point marked C. on Diagram 1); thence 40° North of West 100 rods to a large stump; thence 10° North of West 90 rods; thence 15° West of North 80 rods to an oak tree (see Witness Tree on Diagram 1); thence due East 150 rods to the highway; thence following the course of the highway 50 rods due North; thence 5° North of East 90 rods; thence 45° East of South 60 rods; thence 10° North of East 200 rods to the Doe River; thence following the course of the river Southwesterly to the place of beginning." This, which is a very simple and moderate description by "Metes and Bounds," would leave the boundaries of the farm as shown in Diagram 1.

MERIDIANS AND BASE LINES

DIAGRAM 2

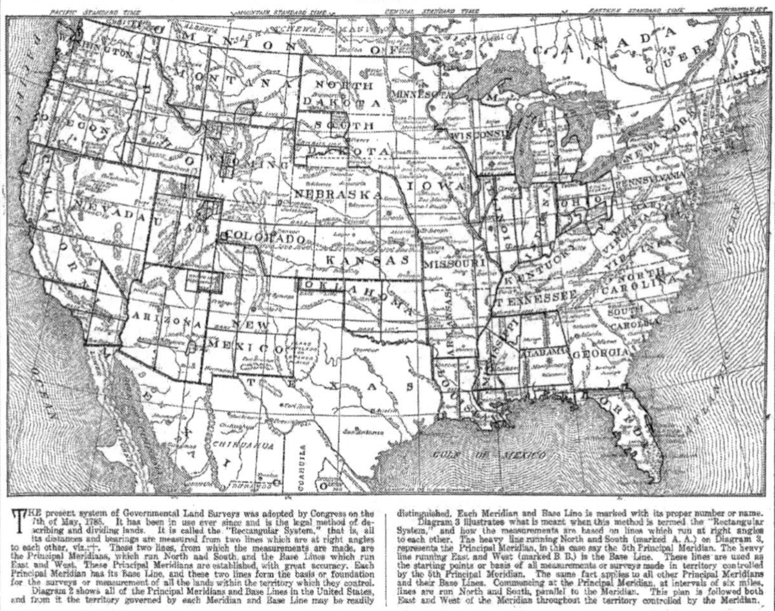

THE present system of Governmental Land Surveys was adopted by Congress on the 7th of May, 1785. It has been in use ever since and is the legal method of describing and dividing lands. It is called the "Rectangular System," that is, all its distances and bearings are measured from two lines which are at right angles to each other, viz.:┼. These two lines, from which the measurements are made, are the Principal Meridians, which run North and South, and the Base Lines which run East and West. These Principal Meridians are established, with great accuracy. Each Principal Meridian has its Base Line, and these two lines form the basis or foundation for the surveys or measurement of all the lands within the territory which they control.

Diagram 2 shows all of the Principal Meridians and Base Lines in the United States, and from it the territory governed by each Meridian and Base Line may be readily distinguished. Each Meridian and Base Line is marked with its proper number or name.

Diagram 3 illustrates what is meant when this method is termed the "Rectangular System," and how the measurements are based on lines which run at right angles to each other. The heavy line running North and South (marked A. A.) on Diagram 3, represents the Principal Meridian, in this case say the 5th Principal Meridian. The heavy line running East and West (marked B. B.) is the Base Line. These lines are used as the starting points or basis of all measurements or surveys made in territory controlled by the 5th Principal Meridian. The same fact applies to all other Principal Meridians and their Base Lines. Commencing at the Principal Meridian, at intervals of six miles, lines are run North and South, parallel to the Meridian. This plan is followed both East and West of the Meridian throughout the territory controlled by the Meridian.

UNITED STATES LAND SURVEYS

These lines are termed "Range Lines." They divide the land into strips or divisions six miles wide, extending North and South, parallel with the Meridian. Each division is called a Range. Ranges are numbered from one upward, commencing at the Meridian; and their numbers are indicated by Roman characters. For instance, the first division (or first six miles) west of the Meridian is Range I. West; the next is Range II. West; then comes Range III., IV., V., VI., VII., and so on, until the territory governed by another Principal Meridian is reached. In the same manner the Ranges East of the Meridian are numbered, the words East or West being always used to indicate the direction from the Principal Meridian. See Diagram 3.

Commencing at the Base Line, at intervals of six miles, lines are run East and West parallel with the Base Line. These are designated as Township Lines. They divide the land into strips or divisions six miles wide, extending East and West, parallel with the Base Line. This plan is followed both North and South of the Base Line until the territory governed by another Principal Meridian and Base Line is reached. These divisions or Townships are numbered from one upward, both North and South of the Base Line, and their numbers are indicated by figures. For instance: The first six mile division North of the Base Line is Township 1 North; the next is Township 2 North; then comes Township 3, 4, 5, and 6, North, and so on. The same plan is followed South of the Base Line; the Townships being designated as Township 1 South, Township 2 South, and so on. The "North" or "South" (the initials N. or S. being generally used) indicates the direction from the Base Line. See Diagram 3.

These Township and Range Lines, crossing each other, as shown in Diagram 3, form squares, which are called "Townships" or "Government Townships," which are six miles square, or as nearly that as it is possible to make them. These Townships are a very important feature in locating or describing a piece of land. The location of a Government Township, however, is very readily found when the number of the Township and Range is given, by merely counting the number indicated from the Base Line and Principal Meridian. As an example of this, Township 8 North, Range 4, West of the 6th Principal Meridian, is at once located on the square marked ★ on Diagram 3, by counting eight tiers north of the Base Line and 4 tiers west of the Meridian.

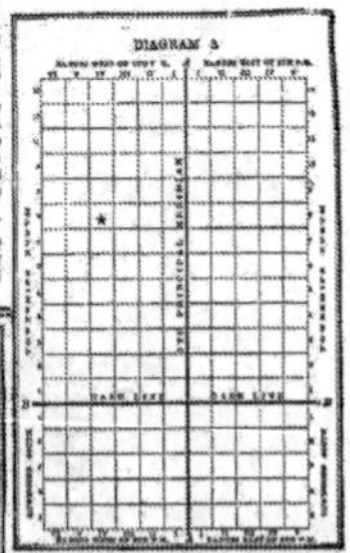

TOWNSHIPS OF LAND.

TOWNSHIPS are the largest subdivisions of land run out by the United States Surveyors. In the Governmental Surveys Township Lines are the first to be run, and a Township Corner is established every six miles and marked. This is called "Townshipping." After the Township Corners have been carefully located, the Section and Quarter Section Corners are established. Each Township is six miles square and contains 23,040 acres, or 36 square miles, as near as it is possible to make them. This, however, is frequently made impossible by: (1st) the presence of lakes and large streams; (2nd) by State boundaries not falling exactly on Township Lines; (3rd) by the convergence of Meridians or curvature of the earth's surface; and (4th) by inaccurate surveys.

Each Township, unless it is one of the exceptional cases referred to, is divided into 36 squares, which are called Sections. These Sections are intended to be one mile, or 320 rods, square and contain 640 acres of land. Sections are numbered consecutively from 1 to 36, as shown on Diagram 4. Beginning with Section 1 in the Northeast Corner, they run West to 6, then East to 12, then West to 18, and so on, back and forth, until they end with Section 36 in the Southeast Corner.

Diagram 4 shows a plat of a Township as it is divided and platted by the government surveyors. These Townships are called Government Townships or Congressional Townships, to distinguish them from Civil Townships or organized Townships, as frequently the lines of organized Townships do not conform to the Government Township lines.

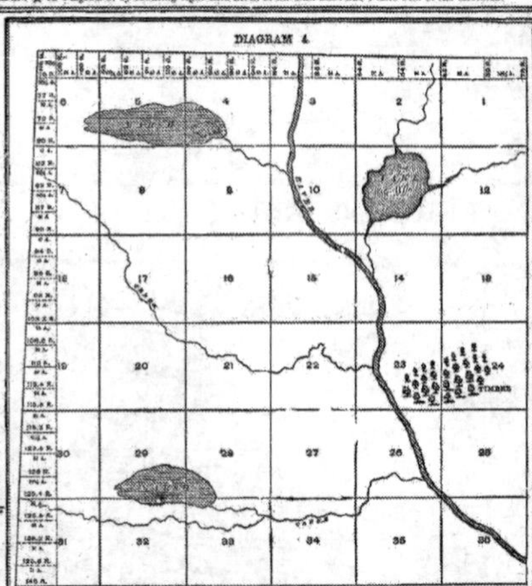

SECTIONS OF LAND.

DIAGRAM 5 illustrates how a section may be subdivided, although the Diagram only gives a few of the many subdivisions into which a section may be divided. All Sections (except fractional Sections) are supposed to be 320 rods, or one mile, square and therefore contain 640 acres—a number easily divisible. Sections are subdivided into fractional parts to suit the convenience of the owners of the land. A half-section contains 320 acres; a quarter-section contains 160 acres; half of a quarter contains 80 acres, and quarter of a quarter contains 40 acres, and so on. Each piece of land is described according to the portion of the section which it embraces—as the Northeast quarter of Section 10; or the Southeast quarter of the Southeast quarter of Section 10. Diagram 5 shows how many of these subdivisions are platted, and also shows the plan of designating and describing them by initial letters as each parcel of land on the Diagram is marked with its description.

As has already been stated, all Sections (except Fractional Sections which are explained elsewhere) are supposed to contain 640 acres, and even though mistakes have been made in surveying, as is frequently the case, making sections larger or smaller than 640 acres, the Government recognizes no variation, but sells or grants each regular section as containing 640 acres "more or less."

The Government Surveyors are not required to subdivide sections by running lines within them, but they usually establish Quarter Posts on Section Lines on each side of a section at the points marked A. B. C. and D. on Diagram 5. After establishing Township corners, Section Lines are the next to be run, and section corners are established. When these are carefully located the Quarter Posts are located at points as nearly equidistant between Section Corners as possible. These corners when established by Government Surveyors cannot be changed, even though it is conclusively shown that mistakes have been made which cause some sections or quarter sections to be either larger or smaller than others. The laws, however, of all the States provide certain rules for local surveyors to follow in dividing Sections into smaller parcels of land than has been outlined in the Governmental surveys. For instance, in dividing a quarter section into two parcels, the distance between the Government Corners is carefully measured and the new post is located at a point equidistant between them. This plan is followed in running out "eighties," "forties," "twenties," etc. In this way, if the Government division overruns or falls short, each portion gains or loses its proportion. This is not the case, however, with Fractional Sections along the North or West sides of a Township, or adjoining a lake or large stream.

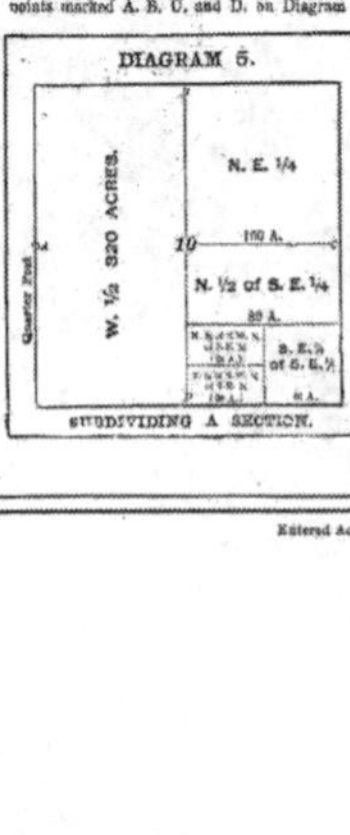

SUBDIVIDING A SECTION.

FRACTIONAL PIECES OF LAND.

CONGRESSIONAL Townships vary considerably as to size and boundaries. Mistakes made in surveying and the fact that Meridians converge as they run North cause every Township to vary more or less from the 23,040 acres which a perfect Township would contain. See Diagram 4. In arranging a Township into Sections all the surplus or deficiency of land is given to, or taken from, the North and West tiers of Sections. In other words, all Sections in the Township are made full—640 acres—except those on the North and West, which are given all the land that is left after forming the other 25 Sections.

Diagram 4 illustrates how the surplus or deficiency is distributed and the Sections it effects. It will be seen that Sections 1, 2, 3, 4, 5, 6, 7, 18, 19, 30 and 31, are the "Fractional Sections," or the Sections which are affected if the Township overruns or falls short. Inside of these Fractional Sections, all of the surplus or deficiency of land (over or under 640 acres) is carried to the "forties" or "eighties" that touch the Township Line. These pieces of land are called "Fractional Forties" or "Fractional Eighties," as the case may be. Diagrams 4 and 6 show the manner of marking the acreage and outlining the boundaries of these "Fractions."

Diagram 6 illustrates how the surplus or deficiency of land inside of these Sections is distributed and which "forties" or "eighties" it affects. From this arrangement it will be seen that in any Section that touches the North or West Township Lines, the Southeast Quarter may be full—160 acres—while another quarter of the same Section may be much larger or smaller. Frequently these fractional "forties" or "eighties" are lotted as shown in Diagram 6. They are always described as fractional tracts of land, as the "fractional S.W. ¼ of Section 6," etc. Of course those portions of these Sections which are not affected by these variations are described in the usual manner—as Southeast ¼ of Section 6. As a rule Townships are narrower at the North than at the South side. The Meridians of Longitude (which run North and South) converge as they run North and South from the Equator. They begin at the Equator with a definite width between them and gradually converge until they all meet at the poles. Now, as the Range lines are run North and South, it will at once be seen that the convergence of Meridians will cause every Congressional Township (North of the Equator) to be narrower at its North than at its South side, as stated. See Diagram 4. In addition to this fact, mistakes of measurement are constantly and almost unavoidably made in running both Township and Range lines, and if no new starting points were established the lines would become confused and unreliable, and the size and shape of Townships materially affected by the time the surveys had extended even a hundred miles from the Base Line and Principal Meridian. In order to correct the surveys and variations caused by the difference of latitude and straighten the lines, "Correction Lines" (or Guide Meridians and Standard Parallels) are established at frequent intervals, usually as follows: North of the Base Line a Correction Line is run East and West parallel with the Base Line, usually every twenty-four miles. South of the Base Line a Correction Line is usually established every thirty miles. Both East and West of the Principal Meridian "Correction Lines" are usually established every 48 miles. All Correction Lines are located by careful measurement, and the succeeding surveys are based upon them.

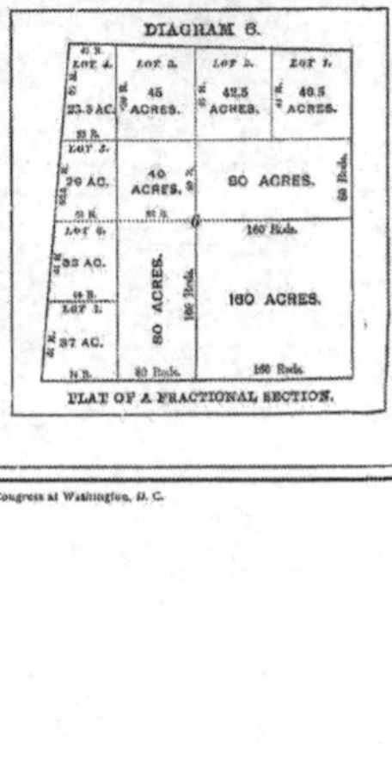

PLAT OF A FRACTIONAL SECTION.

DIGEST OF THE SYSTEM OF CIVIL GOVERNMENT

WITH A REVIEW OF THE

Duties and Powers of the Principal Officials Connected with the Various Branches of National, State, County and Township Government.

NATIONAL GOVERNMENT

THE GOVERNMENT of the United States is one of limited and specific powers, strictly outlined and defined by a written constitution. The constitution was adopted in 1787, and, with the amendments that have since been made, it forms the basis of the entire fabric of government under which we live. The constitution created three distinct branches of government, each of which is entirely separate and distinct from the others. They are the executive, legislative and judicial departments. The constitution specifically vests the executive power in the President, but all members of the cabinet are usually classed with the executive department; the legislative power is held by Congress, and the judicial authority is vested in the Supreme Court and various other courts which Congress has provided for in pursuance of the provisions of the constitution.

It has been the aim of these pages to explain each of these different branches of government, and to briefly review the duties and powers of the principal officials connected with each department.

The President and Vice-President are elected by popular vote, but the vote of each State is separate, so that a candidate may have a large majority of the aggregate popular vote of the country and yet fail to be elected. The Presidential election is held on the first Tuesday after the first Monday in November, when Presidential electors are chosen in and for the various States, each State having as many electors as it has representatives in both branches of Congress. The electors are chosen by the ballots of the people of their States, and all the electors of a State constitute an electoral college. The electors meet in each State at the capital on the first Wednesday in December following a National election and vote for President and Vice-President, certificates of which are forwarded to the President of the Senate, at Washington, who, on the second Wednesday in February opens the certificates and counts the votes in the presence of both Houses of Congress and declares the result; and the final step is the inauguration, which takes place on the 4th of March. The law provides that if neither of the candidates have a majority then the House of Representatives shall elect a President from the three candidates receiving the highest electoral vote. In elections of this kind each State is entitled to only one vote, and two-thirds of the States form a quorum.

PRESIDENT OF THE UNITED STATES.

The President is the highest executive officer of the United States. He is elected for the term of four years, and receives a salary of $75,000 per annum. He must be thirty-five years old or more, and a native-born citizen of the United States. The President is charged with a general supervision over the faithful execution of laws passed by Congress, and has supervision over all executive departments of the government. He appoints a Cabinet of nine officials who become the heads of the various departments, and these departments are intended to be managed and conducted as the President directs. The President is Commander-in-Chief of the Army and Navy. He has power to grant pardons and reprieves for all offenses against the United States, except in cases of impeachment; has power, with the advice and consent of the Senate, to make treaties. He nominates, and with the advice and consent of the Senate, appoints Ambassadors and other public Ministers and Consuls, all Judges of the United States courts, and all other executive officers of the United States, except in such cases where the appointments may be vested in the various "departments." When the Senate is not in session he can appoint, subject to its action when it reassembles. He has power, in certain extraordinary occasions, to call together both Houses of Congress, or either of them, in extra session; and is required from time to time to communicate with Congress, as to the state of the Union, and offer such suggestions or recommendations as he may deem proper. He is empowered to approve or veto all measures adopted by Congress, but it is provided that any measure may be passed over his veto by a two-thirds vote of Congress.

The President consults frequently with his Cabinet, and nearly all important official matters are discussed by that body. In case the office of President becomes vacant through the death, removal or resignation of the incumbent, the law provides that the office shall in turn be filled by the Vice-President, Secretary of State, and other Cabinet Ministers in regular order.

VICE PRESIDENT.

The Vice-President of the United States is elected for the term of four years, and receives a salary of $12,000. In case of the death, removal or resignation of the President, the Vice-President succeeds him. The chief duty of the Vice-President is to act as the presiding officer of the Senate. He has no vote in the Senate, except in case of a tie, or an equal division of the members of that body. The Vice-President administers the oath of office to the Senators.

STATE DEPARTMENT.

The head of this department is the Secretary of State, who is appointed by the President as a member of the Cabinet, and receives a salary of $8,000 per year. The law provides that in case the office of President becomes vacant, through the death, removal or resignation of both the President and Vice-President, the Secretary of State assumes the duties of the Presidency. The Secretary of State may be said to be the official Secretary of the President, and countersigns all commissions issued by the President.

The Secretary of State is the head of the Department of State and is the chief diplomatic officer of the United States. In his department and under his supervision is conducted the public business relating to foreign affairs; to correspondence, commissions or instructions to or with public Ministers from the United States; or to negotiations with Ministers from foreign States; or to memorials or other applications from foreigners, or foreign public Ministers, or citizens of this country in foreign lands, or complications arising therefrom. The Secretary of State also has charge of all other business connected with foreign affairs, extradition matters and diplomatic officers; furnishing passports to vessels going to foreign countries, etc., and has charge of the Great Seal of the United States.

Connected with the Department of State and forming a part of it in the great work of performing and caring for the duties outlined are the following bureaus:

The Diplomatic Bureau, which looks after the affairs pertaining to foreign governments.

The Consular Bureau, correspondence with consulates.

The Bureau of Indexes and Archives, the duties of which are to open the official mails, prepare an abstract of the daily correspondence and an index of it, and superintend miscellaneous work of department.

The Bureau of Accounts, in which all of the finances of the department are looked after, such as the custody and disbursement of appropriations; also indemnity trusts and bonds; also care of the building and property of the department, etc.

The Bureau of Rolls and Library, which is charged with the custody of treaties, rolls, public documents, etc.; has care of revolutionary archives, of international commissions, superintendence of library, etc.

The Bureau of Statistics, for the preparation of reports on commercial relations.

The chiefs of these bureaus receive from $2,100 per year to $2,300 per year. In addition to these there are connected with the State Department the offices of translator, at $2,100 per year; assistant secretary, $5,000; second assistant secretary, $4,500; third assistant secretary, $4,500; solicitor, $4,500; chief clerk, $3,000; clerk to Secretary of State, $2,500; passport clerk, $1,400. Besides these are the various comptrollers, auditors, clerks and assistants, which number well up into the thousands.

TREASURY DEPARTMENT.

This department was organized in 1789. The head of this department, known as the Secretary of the Treasury, is appointed by the President, is a member of the Cabinet, and receives a salary of $12,000 per annum. The Treasury Department is one of the most important branches of the national government, as it has charge of the financial affairs of the government, custody of public funds, collection of revenue and maintenance of public credit. Among the many important duties devolving upon this department are the following: It attends to the collection of all internal revenues and duties on imports, and the prevention of frauds in these departments. All claims and demands, either by the United States or against them, and all the accounts in which the United States are interested, either as debtors or creditors, must be settled and adjusted in the Treasury Department. This department also includes the Bureau of the Mint, in which the government coin and moneys are manufactured. The Treasury Department authorizes the organization of national banks and has supervision over them; has charge of the coast surveys, the lighthouses, marine hospitals, etc. It has charge of all moneys belonging to the United States; designates depositories of public moneys, keeps a complete and accurate system of accounting, showing the receipts and disbursements of the Treasury, and makes reports at stated intervals showing the condition of public finances, public expenditures and the public debt.

There are a great many important officials connected with the Treasury Department, chief among which are the following, viz.: Private secretary of the head department, at $2,500 per year; three assistant secretaries, at $5,000 each; chief clerk, $3,000; chief of appointment division, $3,000; chief of warrants division, $3,500; chief of public moneys division, $3,000; chief of customs division, $3,000; acting chief of revenue marine division, $2,500; chief of stationery division, $2,500; chief of loans and currency division, $3,000; chief of miscellaneous division, $2,500; supervising special agent, $8 per day; government actuary, $1,800; supervising architect, $4,500; steamboat inspector, $3,500; chief Bureau of Statistics, $3,000; life saving service superintendent, $4,500; assistant, $2,500; commissioner Bureau of Navigation, $3,600; superintendent United States coast and geodetic survey, $6,000; supervising surgeon-general marine hospital service, $4,000; Bureau of Engraving and Printing, director, $5,000; assistant director, $3,500; superintendent engraving division, $4,500.

The foregoing will serve to show many of the lines of work attended to in the Treasury Department, as the names of these offices explain the branch of work they are charged with attending to. There are a number of other important offices in the department that should be mentioned, among them being the following:

The Solicitor of the Treasury, or chief attorney, who receives $4,500 per year for attending to the legal matters connected with the department.

The Commissioner of Customs, who receives $4,000 per year and his deputy $2,250, has charge of all accounts of the revenue from customs and disbursements, and for the building and repairing of custom houses.

The Treasurer of the United States receives $6,000 per year, assistant treasurer $3,600, and superintendent of national banks (Red. Div.) $3,500. The Treasurer receives and keeps the government funds, either at headquarters or in the Sub-Treasuries or government depositories, paying it out upon warrants drawn in accordance with the law, and pays all interest on the national debt.

The Register of the Treasury is paid a salary of $4,000 per year and his assistant $2,500. The Register keeps the accounts of public expenditures and receipts; receives the returns and makes out the official statements of United States commerce and navigation; receives from first comptroller and Commissioner of Customs all accounts and vouchers acted on by them and files the same.

The Comptroller of the Currency receives $5,000 per year and his deputy $3,500. This bureau is charged with a general supervision of the national banks and matters connected with the issuing of paper money.

The Director of the Mint receives $4,500 per annum, and is charged with a general supervision over all the coinage of the government.

The Comptroller of the Treasury receives $5,500 per year and his assistant $4,500. This bureau has charge of the auditing system of the Treasury. With the exception of the postal revenue accounts, the comptroller prescribes the forms of keeping and rendering all public accounts.

Auditors. There are six auditors connected with the Treasury Department, each of whom receives a salary of $4,000 per year, and is allowed a deputy at a salary of $2,500 per annum. No one auditor takes rank over another. The first auditor receives and adjusts the accounts of the revenue and disbursements, appropriations and expenditures on account of the civil list and under special acts of Congress, reporting the balances to the commissioners of the customs and first comptroller respectively for their decision. The second auditor devotes most of his attention to army affairs; looks after all the accounts relating to the pay, clothing and recruiting of the army; the arsenals, armories and ordnance; all accounts relating to the Indian Department; reporting to the second comptroller. The third auditor has all accounts for subsistence of the army, military academy, military roads, fortifications, quartermaster's department, certain pensions, claims arising for military service previous to 1817; for all property lost in the military service; he reports also to the second comptroller. The fourth auditor also reports to the second comptroller, and attends to all accounts of the service connected with the navy. The fifth auditor reports to the first comptroller, and adjusts all accounts connected with the diplomatic service of the Department of State. The sixth auditor adjusts all accounts growing from the service of the Post Office Department.

WAR DEPARTMENT.

The War Department was organized in August, 1789. The head of this department is known as the Secretary of War; is appointed by the President, and receives a salary of $12,000 per annum. The War Department attends to the execution of all laws affecting the Regular Army, and carries out and performs such duties as may be provided for by law or directed by the President relative to military forces, military commissions and the warlike stores of the United States. In former years this department also had charge of Indian as well as military affairs, but this has been transferred to the Department of the Interior. The War Department is also required, among other duties, to maintain the signal service and provide for taking meteorological observations at various points on the continent, and give telegraphic notice of the approach of storms. There is also maintained a Civil Engineering Department, through the aid of which is carried out such improvements in rivers and harbors as may be authorized by Congress. The Secretary of War also has supervision over the West Point Military Academy.

The private clerk for the head of the War Department is paid $2,500 per year; assistant secretary, $5,000; chief clerk, $4,000. The most of the subordinates and assistants in the War Department, except those mentioned, are officers of the Regular Army, who are paid salaries and perquisites.

The Commanding General, next to the Secretary, looks after the arrangement of military forces, superintends the recruiting service and discipline of the army, orders courts martial, and in a general sense is charged with seeing to the enforcement of the laws and regulations of the army. The Adjutant-General keeps the rolls and the orders issued. The Quartermaster-General has charge of the barracks and the supplies, etc., that may be required for the army. The Commissary-General is the head of the Subsistence Department, and has supervision over the purchasing and issuing army rations. The Judge Advocate General is the head of the department of military justice. The Surgeon General, as the name implies, looks after the affairs of the army relating to sick, wounded, hospital, etc. The Paymaster-General is the disbursing officer for the money required by the department. There is also the Ordnance office, controlling ordnance stores, arsenals, armories, the manufacture of arms, etc. The Topographical office has charge of all plats and drawings of all surveys made for military purposes. Besides these there are the Inspector-General's Department and departments devoted to war records, publications, etc.

In this connection it may be of interest to the general reader to refer briefly to a few facts concerning the Regular Army. The United States is divided for this purpose into a number of military districts. The head of each department receives his general instructions and orders from headquarters. The term of service in the Regular Army is three years. The pay of private soldiers at the start is $15 per month and rations, and this is increased according to time of service. The pay of the officers is proportioned to their rank. The pay of officers in active service was fixed by an act of Congress May 11, 1908, as follows: lieutenant-general $11,000 per year; major-general $8,000; brigadier-general $6,000; colonels from $4,000 to $5,000; lieutenant-colonels from $3,500 to $4,500; majors from $3,000 to $4,000; captains from $2,400 to $3,360; first-lieutenants from $2,000 to $2,800; second-lieutenants from $1,700 to $2,380. In case any officer below the grade of major required to be mounted, provides himself with suitable mounts at his own expense, he receives an addition to his pay of $150 per annum if he provides one mount; and $200 per annum if he provides two mounts. The pay of retired officers was fixed as follows by the act of May 11, 1908: lieutenant-generals $8,250 per annum; major generals $6,000; brigadier-generals $4,500; colonels from $3,000 to $3,750; lieutenant-colonels from $2,625 to $3,375; majors from $2,250 to $3,000; captains from $1,800 to $2,520; first lieutenants from $1,500 to $2,100, and second-lieutenants $1,275 to $1,785.

NAVY DEPARTMENT.

The head of this department is the Secretary of the Navy, who is appointed by the President, and receives a salary of $12,000 per annum. This department is charged with the duty of attending to the construction, armament, equipment and employment of vessels of war, as well as all other matters connected with naval affairs, and appropriations made therefor by Congress. The Secretary of the Navy has direct control of the United States Naval Academy at Annapolis, Maryland; issues orders to the commanders of the various squadrons; has general authority over the Marine Corps; and has control of all the several bureaus of the Navy Department.

There are a number of bureaus organized in the Navy Department for the purpose of more thoroughly handling the work, among the most important of which may be mentioned the following: Bureau of Steam Engineering; Bureau of Medicine and Surgery; Bureau of Navigation; Bureau of Provisions and Clothing; Bureau of Yards and Docks; Bureau of Ordnance; Bureau of Equipment and Recruiting; Bureau of Construction and Repair. Attached to this department are also officials or bureaus to attend to the following matters: Marine Barracks, Washington, D. C.; Museum of Hygiene; Naval Dispensary; Board of Inspection and Survey; Navy Supplies and Accounts; Naval Observatory; Hydrographic Office; Library and War Records; Naval Intelligence; Nautical Almanac, etc.

The admiral of the navy (line) is paid $13,500 per year; the first nine rear-admirals each receive $8,000 per year and the second nine $5,500; chiefs of bureaus are paid $6,000 per year; captains $4,000; commanders $3,500; lieutenant-commanders $3,000; lieutenants $2,400; junior grade lieutenants $2,000; ensigns $1,700; chief-boatswains, gunners, carpenters, sail makers, $1,700; midshipmen at sea $1,400; midshipmen at academy $600. In the Marine Corps the major general receives $8,000 per year; colonels $4,000; lieutenant-colonels $3,500; majors, $3,000; captains (line) $2,400; captains (staff) $2,000; first lieutenants $2,000; second-lieutenants $1,700. An increase of ten per cent is allowed them when on sea duty, or on "shore duty beyond the sea." Chaplains of the rank of lieutenant-commander or higher rank receive the pay and allowance of a lieutenant-commander; those appointed prior to July 1, 1908, who have the rank of lieutenant receive $2,800; and others are paid according to their rank in the foregoing list. Naval constructors receive from $3,200 to $4,200 per year; assistant naval constructors $2,000 or the pay of rank according to the foregoing table; warrant officers $1,125 to $2,250. Petty officers and chief petty officers receive salary ranging from $33 to $77 per month. First class seamen receive $26 per month; seamen-gunners $28 per month; firemen, first class, $38; ordinary seamen $21; firemen, second-class, $33; shipwrights $27; apprentice seamen $18; coal passers $24. The term of enlistment in the United States Navy is four years.

POSTOFFICE DEPARTMENT.

This is one of the most important branches of the National Government. Its head is the Postmaster-General, who is appointed by the President, and receives a salary of $12,000 per annum. The Post Office Department has supervision over the execution of all laws passed by Congress affecting the postal service, and has general supervision over everything relating to the gathering, carrying and distribution of United States mails; superintends the distribution and disposal of all moneys belonging to or appropriated for, the department; and the instruction of and supervision over all persons in the postal service, with reference to their duties.

In providing for handling the general work of the Post Office Department it has been found necessary to create four bureaus, or offices, as they are termed, each of which is presided over by an assistant postmaster-general, who each receive $5,000 per annum; are all subject to the direction and supervision of the head of the department. A review of these various bureaus and their principal officials, with the name of the office, will show very clearly the work handled by each.

The first assistant postmaster-general is allowed a chief clerk at $2,500 per year; superintendent of salaries and allowances $4,000; superintendent of division appointments $3,000; superintendent of city free-delivery service $3,000.

The second assistant postmaster-general has charge of the following divisions, indicated by the following officials who are under his control: superintendent of railway adjustments $3,000 per year; chief of division inspection $2,000; chief of division of contracts $2,000; chief of division of mail equipment; general superintendent of railway mail service $4,000; superintendent of foreign mails $3,000.

The third assistant postmaster general controls the following divisions: superintendent of money-order division $3,500; superintendent of registry system $2,500; superintendent of division of finance $2,250; superintendent of division of stamps $2,500; also the post-card agent and the stamped-envelope agent at $2,500 each.

The fourth assistant postmaster-general controls the following divisions: Superintendent rural free delivery service $3,000; superintendent of post office supplies $2,500; superintendent of dead-letter office $2,750; topographer $2,750.

Besides the various chiefs of divisions mentioned above there are connected with the Post Office Department a law clerk, at $2,500 per year; appointment clerk, at $2,000; assistant attorney-general, $5,000; a disbursing clerk, $2,250; also the auditor of the post office department, at $4,000.

DIGEST OF THE SYSTEM OF CIVIL GOVERNMENT

DEPARTMENT OF THE INTERIOR.

The Interior Department is under the immediate control of the Secretary of the Interior. He is appointed by the President, and receives a salary of $12,000 per year. In this department, as the name implies, is conducted most of the public business relating to domestic or internal affairs, and, like most of the other executive departments, it is divided into a number of subdivisions and branches. The Secretary of the Interior is charged with a general supervision over public business connected with the following branches, viz.: 1st. The census of the United States. 2d. All matters connected with public lands. 3d. Everything relating to the Indians or Indian affairs. 4th. All matters concerning pensions or bounty lands. 5th. The issuance and filing of patents and caveats. 6th. The custody and distribution of publications. 7th. The compilation of statistics relating to educational matters in the various States. He also has oversight over several of the Government's charitable and benevolent institutions. For the purpose of handling properly the business connected with most of the subjects mentioned, there are bureaus organized for the purpose.

The salaries paid to the principal officials connected with the Interior Department are as follows: First assistant secretary of the interior, $5,000 per year; assistant secretary, $4,500; chief clerk, $3,000; assistant attorney-general (Dept. of Interior), $5,000; commissioner of the General Land Office, $5,000; commissioner of Indian affairs, $5,000; superintendent of Indian schools, $3,000; commissioner of the Pension Office, $5,000; medical referee, $3,000; commissioner of the Patent Office, $5,000; commissioner of the Education Office, $4,500; director of geological surveys, $6,000; director Reclamation Service, $7,500.

DEPARTMENT OF AGRICULTURE.

This department was formerly connected with the Interior Department, but in 1889 it was reorganized and made independent, and the Secretary of Agriculture was made a member of the Cabinet. The head of this department is appointed by the President, and receives a salary of $12,000 per annum.

The general duty and design of the Department of Agriculture is to acquire and diffuse among the people of the United States useful information on subjects connected with agriculture in the most general and comprehensive sense of that word, and to procure, propagate and distribute among the people new and valuable seeds and plants.

The following is a list of the chief officials connected with the Department of Agriculture and their salaries, and the list will also serve to indicate the various lines of work handled by and the various duties which devolve upon the department, viz.: Assistant secretary of agriculture receives $5,000 per annum; chief of Weather Bureau, $6,000; chief of Bureau of Animal Industry, $5,000; statistician, $3,500; chemist, $5,000; entomologist, $4,000; botanist, $3,240; chief of forestry division, $5,000; pomologist, $3,000; plant pathologist and physiologist, $3,500; director of the office of experiment stations, $4,000; chief of division of accounts and disbursements, $3,250; editor, $3,000; agriculturist, $3,500; director of public roads, $4,000; statistical scientist in charge of investigations of production and distribution, $3,000; chief of biological survey, $3,000; chief of bureau of soils, $3,500; chief of bureau of plant industry in charge of seed distribution, $5,000.

DEPARTMENT OF JUSTICE.

The head of the Department of Justice is the Attorney-General, who is appointed by the President, and receives a salary of $12,000 per annum. The principal assistant of the Attorney-General is the Solicitor-General, who receives $7,500 per year. There are a number of assistant attorney-generals who receive $5,000 per annum, and a special assistant attorney-general is appointed for nearly all of the various departments, including the Treasury, State, Post Office and Interior Departments. Besides these there are a number of special officials connected with the Department of Justice, such as attorney in charge of titles, $2,700; chief clerk and superintendent of buildings, $3,000; appointment clerk, $2,000; attorney in charge of pardons, $2,750; solicitor internal revenue, $4,500; superintendent of prisons and prisoners, $3,000; chief examiner, $2,750; chief of division of accounts, $2,500; disbursing clerk, $2,750; solicitor for department of commerce and labor, $5,000.

The Attorney-General is the legal adviser of the President, and it is the duty of the Department of Justice to give all opinions and render all services requiring the skill of persons learned in the law necessary to enable the President and other officers of the various Government departments to discharge their respective duties. This department is also required to prosecute or defend all suits or proceedings in which the United States is interested. The Attorney-General has general supervision over all the solicitors for the various departments; and also exercises general superintendence and direction over all United States marshals and United States district attorneys of all the districts of the United States and Territories.

DEPARTMENT OF COMMERCE AND LABOR.

The Department of Commerce and Labor was established in February, 1903. The general design of this department is to collect, assort and systematize statistical details relating to the different branches of labor and commerce in the United States. The head of this department, known as the Secretary of Commerce and Labor, is appointed by the President, is a member of the Cabinet and receives a salary of $12,000 per annum. The following are the principal officials under his control together with the salary paid: The commissioner of the bureau of manufacturers, $4,000 per year; commissioner of the bureau of corporations, $5,000; commissioner of the bureau of labor, $5,000; director of bureau of the census, $7,000; superintendent of the coast and geodetic survey, $6,000; chief of bureau of statistics, $4,000; supervising inspector-general of steamboat inspection service, $4,000; commissioner of bureau of fisheries, $6,000; commissioner of bureau of navigation, $4,000; commissioner-general of bureau of immigration and naturalization at $5,000; director of bureau of standards, $5,000.

INDEPENDENT DEPARTMENTS.

There are several independent departments, which, although none of them are as important as the foregoing, and their heads are not Cabinet members, yet they form a very necessary part and attend to very important branches of the National Government.

Government Printing Office. The head of this branch of public work is the Public Printer, who is appointed by the President, and receives a salary of $5,500 per year. His chief clerk is paid $2,400 per year, and there is a foreman of printing and a foreman of binding, each of whom receive $2,100 per annum.

Civil Service Commission. This commission consists of three commissioners, each of whom are paid $4,500 per year. The chief examiner connected with the commission is paid $3,000 per annum, and the secretary $2,500.

Interstate Commerce Commission. This commission was created for the purpose, and charged with the duty, of seeing that the laws regulating interstate commerce were faithfully executed and observed, and to prevent unjust discrimination on the part of railway corporations and common carriers. The commission consists of seven commissioners appointed from different sections of the United States, each of whom receives a salary of $10,000 per year. The secretary of the commission receives a salary of $5,000 per annum.

JUDICIARY.

The judicial powers of the United States are vested in the following named courts, viz.: The United States Supreme Court, consisting of one chief justice and eight associate justices; the United States Court of Claims, which consists of one chief justice and four judges; the United States Circuit Court of Appeals; and the United States Circuit and District Courts. All judges of United States Courts are appointed for life, or during "good behavior." The chief justice of the United States Supreme Court receives a salary of $13,000 per annum, and the associate justices $12,000 each. The circuit judges receive a salary of $7000 each per annum, district judges, $6000, and Court of Claims, judges receive $6,000, and chief justice $6,500 per year.

The jurisdiction of the United States Courts extends to all cases in law and in equity arising under the Constitution, the laws of the United States, and treaties; to all cases affecting ambassadors, other public ministers and consuls; to all cases of admiralty and maritime jurisdiction; to controversies to which the United States shall be a party; to controversies between two or more States; between a State and a citizen of another State; between citizens of different States; between citizens of the same State claiming lands under grants of different States. In all cases affecting ambassadors, other public ministers and consuls, and those in which a State is a party the Supreme Court has original jurisdiction. In the other cases the Supreme Court has appellate jurisdiction.

LEGISLATIVE DEPARTMENT.

The legislative powers of the United States are vested in a Congress, which consists of a Senate and House of Representatives, and which meets annually at Washington on the first Monday of December. The constitution gives to Congress the following general powers: To lay and collect taxes, duties, imposts and excises; pay the debts of the United States; borrow money on the credit of the United States; to regulate commerce; to establish uniform laws on naturalization and bankruptcy; to coin money and regulate the value thereof; fix the standard of weights and measures; to declare war; to raise and support armies (but it is provided that no appropriation for this purpose can be for a longer period than two years); to provide and maintain a navy; to grant letters of marque and reprisal, and make rules concerning captures on land and water; to make rules for the government and regulation of the land and naval forces; to establish postoffices and postroads; to promote the progress of science and the useful arts by securing for limited times, to authors and inventors, the exclusive right to their respective writings and discoveries; to constitute tribunals inferior to the Supreme Court; to define and punish piracies and felonies committed on the high seas and offense against the law of nations; to exercise exclusive legislation over the District of Columbia and places purchased for forts, magazines, arsenals, etc.; and further to make all laws necessary for the general welfare of the United States, and for "carrying into execution the foregoing powers, and all other powers vested by the Constitution in the Government of the United States, or in any department or officer thereof." The Constitution expressly *forbids* Congress making any law respecting the establishment of religion, or prohibiting the free exercise thereof, or abridging the freedom of speech, or of the press, or the right of the people peaceably to assemble, and to petition the Government for a redress of grievances. Congress cannot suspend the privilege of the writ of *habeas corpus* except in cases of rebellion or invasion when the public safety may require it. No bill of attainder or *ex post facto* law can be passed. No tax or duty can be laid on articles exported from any State. No preference can be given by any regulation of commerce or revenue to the ports of one State over those of another. No title of nobility can be granted. Every law passed by Congress must be submitted to the President for his approval. If he returns it with his objections, or vetoes it, the measure may be passed over his veto by a two-thirds vote of both branches of Congress.

The Senate, or the "Upper House of Congress," is composed of two Senators from each State in the Union. They are elected by the Legislatures of their respective States, for a term of six years, and receive a salary of $7,500 per annum. No person can be elected to the United States Senate who has not attained the age of thirty years, been nine years a citizen of the United States, and is when elected an inhabitant of the State from which he is chosen. The Senate has sole power to try all impeachments. Its consent and confirmation is necessary for all important officers appointed by the President. Its consent is also necessary to conclude any treaty.

The House of Representatives is the "Lower House of Congress." Each State in the Union is divided into congressional districts, of as nearly equal population as is practicable. In each district a representative is elected by the people for a term of two years, and each is paid a salary of $7,500 per year. Besides these, a delegate from each organized Territory is admitted to the House of Representatives, who is not entitled to a vote, but has the right to debate on all subjects in which the Territory which he represents has an interest. No person can be a representative who has not attained the age of twenty-five years, been for seven years a citizen of the United States, and is at the time of his election an inhabitant of the State from which he is chosen. All bills for raising revenue must originate in the House of Representatives.

STATE GOVERNMENT

THE method of State government throughout the United States follows very closely the general plan of government that prevails in national affairs. The various functions of government in State affairs are handled in departments, with a State officer at the head of each branch, and the lines are clearly drawn between the executive, legislative and judicial powers. All the States are governed under a constitution, which outlines and defines the powers which each of these departments shall exercise and possess. All of the most important State officials are elected by the people, but in many of the States the less important offices are filled by appointment of the Governor, by and with the consent of the State Senate.

GOVERNOR.

The Governor is the highest executive officer in all the States of the Union, and is elected by a direct vote of the people. The term of office varies materially in the different States, ranging from two to six years. As to the matter of salary that the Governor receives, it also differs widely throughout the different States and is subject to frequent change. At the present writing three States—New York, Pennsylvania and New Jersey pay their Governors $10,000 per year; Illinois $12,000; California $6,000; Minnesota, Indiana, Alabama, Colorado, Louisiana, Missouri, Montana, Virginia and Wisconsin all pay $5,000 per year; Kentucky $6,500; Massachusetts and Ohio $8,000; Nevada, Connecticut, Michigan, Tennessee, Texas and Washington, $4,000; Maryland and Oklahoma $4,500; Mississippi, Arkansas, Florida and South Carolina $3,500; Iowa, Georgia, Idaho, Kansas, North Carolina, North Dakota and Rhode Island $3,000; West Virginia $2,700; South Dakota, Nebraska and Wyoming $2,500; Delaware, Maine, New Hampshire and Utah $2,000; and Oregon and Vermont $1,500.

About the only statement concerning the qualifications required for this office that would be common to all the States is that he must be a citizen of the State in which he is elected. In most of the States, in addition to the salary named, the Governor is furnished with a residence, which is known as the "Executive Mansion."

The powers and duties that devolve upon the Governor are about the same in all of the States. He is charged with a general supervision over the faithful execution of the laws, and is the legal custodian of all the property of the State not specifically entrusted to other officers by law, and is authorized to take summary possession of such property. He is expected to communicate by message to each session of the State legislature such information or recommendations regarding State affairs as he may deem necessary and proper, and he is empowered to call extra sessions of that body whenever the public welfare may demand. He accounts to the same body for all moneys received and paid out, and presents estimates of amounts to be raised by taxation for various purposes. He has a negative (or veto) upon all laws passed by the Legislature, but it is provided that measures may be passed over his veto by a two-thirds vote of that body. The Governor is commander-in-chief of the State military or naval forces, and has authority to call out such forces to preserve peace and execute the laws when the local authorities are unable to accomplish this. He may require the opinion of the various State officers upon any subject relating to their respective offices, and examines and approves the bonds of State officials. In many States the Governor has power to grant reprieves and pardons, after conviction, for all offenses against the State except in cases of impeachment; but in a few of the States the pardoning power is vested in a board selected for that purpose, of which the Governor is generally ex-officio member. The Governor has the appointment of a number of State officers, and in many cases if an elective office becomes vacant he has the power to fill it by appointment; has power in many States to suspend a State officer, or even a county officer, pending a legal investigation. The Governor issues requisitions upon the executives of other States for parties charged with crime who escape to other States, and he has power to issue warrants for fleeing criminals upon requisition of other Governors.

LIEUTENANT-GOVERNOR.

The office of Lieutenant-Governor does not exist in all of the States in the Union, at least not under this name, as in a few of the States this officer is only known as the President of the State Senate. In some of the States the Lieutenant-Governor is paid a certain amount per day during sessions of the Legislature or General Assembly, and in others he is allowed a fixed salary, but it is provided that if the duties of Governor should devolve upon him, he shall during the continuance of such emergency be entitled to the emoluments thereof. The principal duty of the Lieutenant-Governor is to act as the presiding officer of the State Senate or Upper House of the State Legislature. In case a vacancy should occur in the office of Governor, the Lieutenant-Governor would act as Governor until such vacancy was filled by election; and in all cases where the Lieutenant-Governor is unable to act as presiding officer of the Senate, a President *pro tempore* is chosen by that body. The Lieutenant-Governor has no vote in the Senate except in cases of a tie or equal division of the members.

SECRETARY OF STATE.

The office of Secretary of State is one of the most important offices within the gift of the people of a State, and the office exists under this name in every State in the Union. The Secretary of State may be said to be the official secretary of the Governor, and countersigns all commissions issued by the chief executive, and he is the custodian of the Great Seal of the State. As a rule it is the duty of the Secretary of State to call the House of Representatives to order and preside until a temporary presiding officer, or Speaker, is elected. It is his duty to see that the halls are prepared for the Legislature or General Assembly; he prepares the legislative manual and causes it to be printed and distributed; secures the printing and distribution of the State laws; indexes and files executive documents; provides and distributes election blanks; has charge of all books, bills, papers, etc., of the Legislature, and is practically "keeper of all public acts, laws, records, bonds, etc." The Secretary of State is required to keep a register of all the official acts of the Governor, and affixes the Seal of the State to all official commissions, etc., keeps a record of them, and is obliged to give any person a copy of the same when demanded. In all of the States the Secretary of State is *ex officio* member of a number of the State boards, but no list of these could be given that would apply to all States, as they are different in the various States.

STATE AUDITOR.

The office of Auditor of State exists under one name or another in nearly every State in the Union. The title of this office, however, is not alike in all the States, as many of them, notably California, Connecticut, Florida, Georgia, Maryland, Nevada, New Jersey, New York, South Carolina, Tennessee, Texas, and a few others, it is known as State Comptroller. In a few of the States, including Michigan and Pennsylvania, the office is called Auditor-General, and in two of the States the public accounts are audited by a Board of Auditors. In all the States, however, the duties that devolve upon this branch of the State Government are practically the same, and a general explanation of the scope of work handled by the State Auditor in one State will apply, except as regards minor details, to all of the States. It is the duty of the State Auditor to keep the accounts of the State with any other State or Territory, and with the United States and all public officers, corporations and individuals having accounts with this State. He audits the accounts of all public officers who are to be paid out of the State Treasury, and all persons who are authorized to receive money out of the State Treasury. In fact, all claims against the State which are to be paid out of the State Treasury must be presented to the Auditor, who, after the same is adjusted, issues warrants therefor payable at the Treasury. A complete record of each warrant is kept by the Auditor, who also keeps an account with the State Treasurer, charging him with all moneys paid into the Treasury, and giving credit for all warrants paid, and the books and vouchers of the Treasury must balance therewith, as settlements are made between these two officers at stated intervals. In a number of the States the Auditor is charged with a general supervision over certain corporations, such as insurance and banking corporations and building and loan associations, and in some States is *ex officio* a member of a number of State boards. He generally has authority to make and execute satisfactions of judgments and assignments thereof in behalf of the State.

STATE TREASURER.

This is one of the most important executive offices in the gift of the people of a State. The State Treasurer handles vast sums of the people's money, and as a rule a very heavy bond, ranging from $500,000 up into the millions, is required of him; and generally the Governor is empowered to demand additional bonds if he deems the bond insufficient to fully protect the State.

The duties of the State Treasurer are implied by the title of the office, and they are very much the same throughout all of the States of the Union. The State Treasurer is custodian of all the State funds. He deposits these funds in banks, which give bonds to secure the Treasurer or State against loss, and which pay interest on daily balances. The Treasurer pays out State funds only on warrants issued or signed by the State Auditor, or other proper official, and a full record of all warrants is kept in both the auditing office and Treasurer's office. The plan by which the Treasurer receives the revenues of the State is different in different States. In some States the Auditor issues an order for him to receive the same and charges the amount against the Treasurer. In others he is charged with all moneys which he is entitled to receive, and then given credit for delinquencies. In still other States the Treasurer issues duplicate receipts for all moneys paid in, which must be countersigned by the Auditor to be valid, and one of these must be deposited with the Auditor, so he may charge the amount against the Treasurer. In this way a double system is carried on—both Auditor and Treasurer keeping a full account of all moneys received and paid out, and their books and accounts must balance, as at stated intervals the Treasurer must make settlements with the Auditor and submit books, vouchers, etc., to the Legislature. In most of the States the State Treasurer is required to publish at stated times, in the newspapers at the capital, an itemized statement of the public accounts, expenditures, funds, receipts and disbursements. He is also required to make a complete report and itemized statement to each session of the Legislature. In nearly all of the States the law is very explicit in outlining the duties of the State Treasurer, the following being very common provisions in relation to the office, viz.: That a complete record of all moneys must be kept, showing what is received or paid out of the various "funds," which "funds" must be exhibited in separate accounts. In several of the

DIGEST OF THE SYSTEM OF CIVIL GOVERNMENT

States the Governor and one or two other State officials constitute a board, which must at certain times examine and check up the accounts, books and vouchers of the State Treasurer and ascertain the amount of funds in the Treasury.

ATTORNEY-GENERAL.

The Attorney-General, as the name implies, is the general legal counsel or lawyer for the various branches of the State government. *In all of the States the powers and duties of the Attorney-General are very similar.* It is his duty to appear for the State in all actions and proceedings in the Supreme Court in which the State has an interest, to institute and prosecute in all courts all actions, either for or against a State officer, in which the State has an interest; to consult with and advise the various county or state's attorneys in matters relating to their official duties, and when public interest requires he assists them in criminal prosecutions. *It is his duty to consult with* and advise the Governor and other State officers, and give, when requested, written opinions on legal or constitutional questions relating to their official duties, and to give written opinions when requested by the Legislature or any committee thereof. It is also his duty to prepare, when necessary, drafts for contracts or other writings relating to subjects in which the State is interested. He is required to enforce the proper application of funds appropriated *to the various State institutions*, and prosecute breaches of trust in the administration of the same; and when necessary to prosecute corporations for failure or refusal to comply with the laws; to prosecute official bonds of delinquent officers or corporations in which the State has an interest. The Attorney-General is required to keep a record of all actions, complaints, opinions, etc.

STATE SUPERINTENDENT OR SUPERINTENDENT OF PUBLIC INSTRUCTION.

This is an office which exists in nearly every State in the Union. In three or four of the States the management of the educational interests of the State is vested in a State Board of Education, but in these cases the secretary of the board assumes most of the detail work that in most of the States devolve upon the State Superintendent. The full title given to this office is not the same in all of the States, but it is generally called "State Superintendent of Public Instruction or Public Schools." In Ohio, Maine and Rhode Island, and a few others, this officer is termed "Commissioner of Schools."

The duties of the State Superintendent are very much alike in all of the States, as he is charged with a general supervision over the educational interests of the State and of the public schools. In many States his authority is not limited to the public schools, and he is authorized by law to demand full reports from all colleges, academies or private schools. It is his duty to secure at regular intervals reports from all such educational institutions and file all papers, reports and documents transmitted to him by local or county school officers. He is the general adviser and assistant of the various county superintendents or school officers, to whom he must give, when requested his written opinion upon questions rising under the school law. It is also his duty to hear and determine controversies arising under the school laws coming to him by appeal from a county superintendent or school official. He prepares and distributes school registers, school blanks, etc., and is generally given the power to make such rules and regulations as are necessary to carry into efficient and uniform effect the provisions of the laws relating to schools. The State Superintendent is required to make a detailed report to each regular session of the State Legislature, showing an abstract of the common school reports; a statement of the condition of public schools and State educational institutions; the amount of money collected and expended, and all other matters relating to the schools or school funds that have been reported to him. He is forbidden from becoming interested in the sale of any school furniture, book or apparatus.

STATE LIBRARIAN.

In nearly all of the States the laws provide for a State officers under the title of "State Librarian." As a rule the office is filled by appointment of the Governor, although in a few States it is an elective office *and is filled by direct vote of the people.* The State Librarian is the custodian of all the books and property belonging to the State Library, and is required to give a bond for the proper discharge of his duties and safekeeping of the property intrusted to his care, as in many of the States the State Library is an immensely important and valuable collection. In some of the States the Supreme Court judges prescribe all library rules and regulations. In others *they have a Library Board of Trustees, which is sometimes made up* of the Governor and certain other State officials, who constitute a board of commissioners for the management of the State Library.

ADJUTANT-GENERAL.

In nearly all of the States provision is made for an Adjutant-General, who is either elected by the people or appointed by the Governor. The name of the office implies the branch of work which is handled by its incumbent. It is the duty of the Adjutant-General to issue and transmit all orders of the Commander-in-Chief with reference to the militia or military organizations of the State. He keeps a record of all military officers commissioned by the Governor, and of all general and special orders and regulations issued, and of other matters relating to the men, property, ordinance, stores, camp and garrison equipage pertaining to the State militia or military forces.

PUBLIC EXAMINER OR BANK EXAMINER.

This is a State office that is found in only about one-half of the States. In some States it is known as Bank Comptroller and in others the duties which devolve upon this officer are handled by a "department" in the State Auditor's office. The general duties and plan of conducting this work, in many respects, is very similar, but there is a great difference between the various States in the officers who attend to it. Where this made a separate State office, generally speaking, the requirements are that he must be a skilled accountant and expert bookkeeper, and cannot be an officer of any of the public institutions, nor interested in any of the financial corporations which it may be his duty to examine. He is charged with the duty of visiting and inspecting the financial accounts and standing of certain corporations and institutions organized under the State laws. In several of the States it is made his duty to visit certain county officials at stated intervals, and inspect their books and accounts, and enforce a uniform system of bookkeeping by State and county officers.

COMMISSIONER OR SUPERINTENDENT OF INSURANCE.

In all of the States of the Union the department relating to insurance has grown to be an important branch of State government. The method of controlling the insurance business differs materially in many of the States, although they are all gradually moving in the same direction, viz., creating a department or State office in which all matters relating to insurance and insurance companies are attended to. In former years, in nearly all of the States, the insurance business formed a department in the State Auditor's office, and was handled by him or his appointees. Now, however, in nearly all the Northern States and many of the Southern States, they have a separate and distinct insurance department, the head of which is either elected by the people or appointed by the Governor. The duties and powers of the insurance department of the various States are very similar. A general provision is that the head of this department must be experienced in insurance matters, and he is prohibited from holding an interest in any insurance company. The Commissioner or Superintendent of Insurance has extensive powers concerning insurance matters, and it is his duty to see that all laws respecting and regulating insurance and insurance companies are faithfully observed; he issues licenses to insurance companies, and it is his duty to revoke the license of any company not conforming to law. Reports are made to him at stated times by the various companies, and he has power to examine fully into their condition, assets, etc. He files in his office the various documents relating to insurance companies, together with their statements, etc., and at regular intervals makes full reports to the Governor or Legislature.

COMMISSIONER OF LABOR STATISTICS.

In several of the States a "Commissioner of Labor Statistics" is appointed by the Governor, who is the head of what may be termed the labor bureau. In a great majority of the States, however, this branch of work is taken care of by a board of labor commissioners, a bureau of statistics or by the State Auditor and his appointees. The general design of this bureau or commission is to collect, assort and systematize, and present in regular reports to the Legislature, statistical details relating to the different departments of labor in the State, and make such recommendations as may be deemed proper and necessary concerning the commercial, industrial, social, educational and sanitary conditions of the laboring classes.

OTHER STATE OFFICERS.

In all of the States there exist one or more other State officers *in addition to those already mentioned, which are made necessary by* local condition or local business interests. It is, therefore, unnecessary to mention any of these at length in this article. It may be stated, however, that in all of the States may be found two or more of the following State officers, and further, that each one of the following named officers is found in some State in the Union, viz.: Superintendent or commissioner of agriculture, commissioner of mines, secretary of agricultural *board, secretary of internal affairs, clerk and* reporter of the Supreme Court, commissioner of railways, commissioner of immigration, State printer, State binder, land agent or commissioner, commissioner, register or superintendent of State land office, register of lands, commissioner of schools and lands, surveyor-general, inspector-general, State oil inspector-general, State oil inspector, dairy commissioner.

STATE BOARDS.

Besides the officers and departments which have already been mentioned, there are a number of State boards or bureaus that are necessary in carrying on the complex business connected with the government of a State. The following list of such State boards and bureaus includes all that can be found in the majority of the States; some of them, however, are only found in a few of the States, because they are of a local nature and are only made necessary by the existence of certain local conditions or business interests. It will also be observed that some of the boards named cover the same line of work that has already been mentioned as belonging to some State officer. This grows from the fact that a few of the States place the management of certain lines of work in the hands of a State board, while in others, instead of having a State board they delegate the powers and duties to a single State official. All of the States, however, have a number of the State boards mentioned in this list, the names of which imply the line of work each attends to, viz.: Railroad and warehouse commissioners, board of equalization, board or commission of agriculture, university trustees, board or commissioners of public charities, canal commissioners, penitentiary commissioners, board of health, dental examiners, trustees of historical library, board of pharmacy, commission of claims, live stock commissioners, fish commissioners, inspectors of coal mines, labor commissioners, board of education, board of public works, board of pardons, assessment commissioners.

LEGISLATURE OR GENERAL ASSEMBLY.

The law-making power of every State is termed the "Legislative Department." The legislative power, according to the constitutions of the various States, is vested in a body termed the Legislature or General Assembly which consists of an Upper and Lower House, designated usually as the Senate and House of Representatives. In a few of the States the Lower House is called "The Assembly." In most of the States the Legislature meets in regular session every two years, but this is not the universal rule, as in a few of the States the law provides for annual sessions. In all of the States, however, a provision is made whereby the Governor may, on extraordinary occasions, call special session by issuing a proclamation.

The Legislative Department has the power to pass all such laws as may be necessary for the welfare of the State, and carry into effect the provisions of the constitution. The Legislature receives the reports *of the Governor, together with the reports of the various other State* officers; they provide by appropriation for the ordinary and contingent expenses of the government; at regular times provided by law they apportion the State into political districts, and make all other provisions for carrying on the State government. There is a general prohibition against the passage of any *ex post facto* law, or law impairing the obligation of contracts, or making any irrevocable grant of special privileges *or immunities.* Any measure to become a law must be passed by both branches of the Legislature, and then be presented to the Governor for his approval. If he withholds his approval (or vetoes it), the measure may be repassed by a two-thirds vote of the Legislature, when it will become a law notwithstanding the Governor's veto.

SENATE.

The Senate is the Upper House of the Legislature or General Assembly. The various States are divided into senatorial districts, in each of which a Senator is elected—the term of office varying from two to four years. Except in three or four of the States the presiding officer of the Senate is the Lieutenant-Governor, although a President *pro tem.* is usually elected, who acts as presiding officer during the absence of the Lieutenant-Governor. The presiding officer has no vote, however, in the Senate, *except when that body is equally divided.* Every Senator has one vote upon all questions, and the right to be heard in advocating or opposing the passage of any measure brought before the Legislature. In filling all of the most important State offices that are to be appointed by the Governor, the appointments must be approved or confirmed by the Senate.

HOUSE OF REPRESENTATIVES.

The Lower House of the State Legislature, in nearly if not quite all the States of the Union, is termed the House of Representatives. Like the Senators, every member of the House has the right to be heard in advocating or opposing any measure brought before the body of which he is a member. The House is given the sole power of impeachment, but all impeachments must be tried by the Senate. As a general rule, there is a provision that all bills for raising revenue must originate in the House.

JUDICIARY.

The "Judicial Department" is justly regarded as one of the most important and powerful branches of government of either the State or Nation, as it becomes the duty of this department to pass upon and interpret, and thereby either annul or give validity to all the most important measures and acts of both the legislative and executive branches of the government.

It is impossible in a general article to give a detailed review or description of the construction and make-up of the judicial departments of the various States. The courts are so differently arranged both as to their make-up and jurisdiction that it would be useless to try to give the reader a general description that would accurately cover the ground.

In all of the States, except, possibly, one or two, the highest judicial authority of the State is known as the Supreme Court, and unless questions are involved which give the United States Courts jurisdiction, it is the court of last resort. The Supreme Court is made up of a chief justice and the several associate justices or judges as may be provided for by the laws of the various States, usually from four to six. Generally these officers are elected by the people, either from the State at large or (in three of the States) *as representing certain districts,* but this is not the case always, as in several States they are chosen by the Governor or Legislature. In all of the States the Supreme Court has appellate jurisdiction both in law and in equity, and has original jurisdiction in remedial cases, *mandamus, habeas corpus* and cases relating to the revenue, but there is no trial by jury in this court.

Various other courts are provided for by the laws of the different States, such as appellate courts, *circuit or district courts, probate courts,* county courts, superior courts, municipal courts, courts of justices of the peace, etc. The jurisdiction of all these courts is, of course, inferior to that of the Supreme Court, and varies greatly in the different States. Besides these, where there are large cities, various other courts are also established to aid in caring for the enormous amount of judicial work that arises from such vast and complex business interests. The various courts are also provided with the necessary *officials for carrying on the* judicial business—such as clerks of court, court reporters, bailiffs, etc.

COUNTY GOVERNMENT

So far as the principal county offices *are concerned, the general* arrangement and method of handling the public business is very much the same in all of the States; but the offices are called by different names, and in minor details—such as transferring from one office to another certain minor lines of work—there are a number of points in which the method of county government in the various States differs. The writer has adopted the names of the principal county offices which are most *common in the* Northern States, as in the Southern and New England States there are scarcely any two States in which the names or titles of all the county offices are identical.

AUDITING OFFICE AND CLERK OF THE COUNTY BOARD.

Generally the principal auditing officer of the county is known as the "county auditor" or "county clerk." In Illinois, Kansas, Missouri, Nebraska, Oklahoma, Wisconsin and many other States the office is called "county clerk." In Indiana, Iowa, Minnesota, North Dakota, South Dakota, Ohio and others it is termed "county auditor." In a few of the States under certain conditions this office is merged with some other county office. A notable example of this is in the State of Michigan, where they have one official, under the simple title of "clerk," who looks after about all of the work which in most of the States devolves upon both the county clerk and also clerk of court. In all of the States a bond in a moderate sum is required of the county clerk or auditor, and he is paid a salary of from \$1,500 to \$3,500 per year, besides in some States being allowed certain fees, unless it is in a very large and heavily populated county, where the salary paid is of necessity much higher than this amount. No county treasurer or member of the county board is eligible to this office. In general terms it may be stated as a rule the auditor acts as the clerk or secretary of the official county board, although in a few of the States the court clerk is required to look after this matter. The clerk of the county board keeps an accurate record of the board's proceedings and carefully preserves all documents, records, books, maps and papers which may be brought before the board, or which the law provides shall be deposited in his office. In the auditing office an accurate account is kept with the county treasurer. Generally they file the duplicates of the receipts given by the county treasurer, charging him with all money paid into the treasury and giving credit for all warrants paid. The *general plan* of paying claims against a county is as follows: If the claim is one in which the *amount due* is fixed by law, or is authorized to be fixed by some other person or tribunal, the auditor issues a warrant or order which will be paid by the treasurer, the certificate upon which it is allowed being duly filed. In all other cases the claim must be allowed by the county board, and the chairman or presiding officer issues a warrant or order which is attested by the clerk. A complete record of all these county warrants or orders is kept, and the accounts of the county treasurer must balance *therewith.* The above in general terms outlines the most important branch of work which the county clerk or county auditor looks after in most of the States, but in all of the States the law requires him to look after a number of other matters, although in these there is no uniformity between the various States, and no general description of these minor or additional duties could be given that would apply to all the States.

COUNTY TREASURER.

This is an office which exists in all of the States, and it is one of the most important of the various offices necessary in carrying on the business of a county. It is an elective office in all of the States, and the term of office is usually either two or four years, but a very common provision in the various States is that after serving for one term as county treasurer a party shall be ineligible to the office until the intervention of at least one term after the expiration of the term for which he was elected. This provision, however, does not exist in all of the States, as in some of them the county treasurer is eligible for reelection for any number of terms.

The general duties of the county treasurers throughout the various States is very similar. The county treasurer is the principal custodian of the funds belonging to the county. It is his duty to receive and safely keep the revenues and other public moneys of the county, and all funds authorized to be paid to him, and disburse the same pursuant to law. He is required to keep proper books of accounts, in which he must keep a regular, just and true account of all moneys, revenues and funds received by him, stating particularly the time, when, of whom and on what fund or account each particular sum was received; and also of all moneys, revenues and funds paid out by him according to law, stating particularly the time when, to whom and on what fund payment is made from. The books of the county treasurer must always be subject to the inspection of the county board, which, at stated intervals, examines his books and makes settlements with him. In some of the States the provisions of the law relating to county treasurer are very strict; some of them provide for a county board of auditors, who *are* expected, several times a year, to examine the funds, accounts and vouchers of the treasury without previous notice to the treasurer; and in some it is provided that this board, or the county board, shall designate a bank (or banks) in which the treasurer is required to keep the county funds deposited—the banks being required to pay interest on daily or monthly balances and give bond to indemnify the county against loss. As a general rule the county treasurer is only authorized *to pay out county funds on warrants or orders* issued by the chairman of the county board and attested by the clerk, or in certain cases on warrants or orders of the county auditing office. A complete record of these warrants or orders is kept, and the treasurer's accounts must balance therewith. In most of the States the law is very explicit in directing how the books and accounts of the county treasurer shall be kept.

COUNTY RECORDER OR REGISTER OF DEEDS.

In a few of the States the office of county recorder or register of deeds is merged with some other county office, in counties where the population falls below a certain amount. A notable example of this is found in both the States of Illinois and Missouri (and there are others), where it is merged with the office of circuit clerk in many counties. *The title of the joint office is "circuit clerk and recorder,"* and the duties of both offices are looked after by one official.

The duties of the county recorder or register of deeds are very similar in the various States, although in some of the Eastern and Southern States the office is called by other names. The usual name, however, is county recorder or register of deeds. In Illinois, Indiana,

DIGEST OF THE SYSTEM OF CIVIL GOVERNMENT

Iowa, Missouri, Ohio and many other States, it is called "county recorder." In Kansas, Michigan, Minnesota, North Dakota, Wisconsin and many more it is called "register of deeds." In all of the States this office is the repository wherein are kept all records relating to deeds, mortgages, transfers and contracts affecting lands within the county. It is the duty of the recorder or register, as soon as practical after the filing of any instrument in writing in his office entitled to be recorded, to record the same at length, in the order of the time of its reception, in books provided by the county for that purpose; and it is his duty to endorse on all instruments a certificate of the time when the same was filed. All of the States have *some* of the following provisions concerning the duties of the recorder, but these provisions are not common to *all* of the States, viz.: The register or recorder is not allowed to record an instrument of any kind unless it is duly executed according to law; he is not obliged to record any instrument unless his fees are paid in advance; *as a rule*, it is unlawful for him to record any map, plat or subdivision of land situated within any incorporated city, town or village until it is approved by the proper officers of the same. In many States he is forbidden to enter a deed on the records until it has been endorsed "taxes paid" by the proper official; he is required to exhibit, free of charge, all records, and allow copies to be made; he is authorized to administer oaths and take acknowledgments.

CIRCUIT OR DISTRICT CLERK, OR CLERK OF COURT.

In nearly all of the States, each county elects a "clerk of court or courts," sometimes also known as circuit clerk or district clerk, indicating the court with which the office is connected. In some of the States, as has already been stated, the office of clerk of court is merged with some other county office. This is the case in Illinois and Missouri, where in many counties it is connected with the office of county recorder. In Michigan, one official under the name of "clerk" handles the business which usually is given to the clerk of court and county clerk or auditor. In Wisconsin, Missouri, Illinois and other States the name used is "circuit clerk;" in Kansas, Nebraska, Minnesota, North Dakota and many others the office is called "clerk of district court;" while in many of the States, including Indiana, Ohio, Iowa, South Dakota and others, it is called simply "clerk" or "clerk of the court or courts."

The chief duty of this official is to act as clerk of the district or circuit court, and sometimes other courts of inferior jurisdiction. It is the clerk's duty to keep the seals and attend the sessions of their respective courts, preserve all the files and papers thereof, make, keep and preserve complete records of all the proceedings and determinations thereof, and carry out such other duties as may be required by the rules and orders of their respective courts. They must enter of record all judgments, decrees and orders of the court as soon as possible after they are rendered; keep all indictments on file as a public record, have authority to administer oaths, take acknowledgments; take and certify depositions, and are required to exhibit all records free of charge. In nearly all the States the law defines the character of the record books which the clerk of court must keep. Although there is no settled rule in this matter, the general provisions are that he shall keep: First, a general docket or register of actions, in which is entered the title of each action in the order in which they are commenced, and a description of each paper filed in the cause and all proceedings therein; second, a plaintiff's index and defendant's index; third, a judgment book and execution docket, in which he enters the judgment in each action, time of issuing execution, satisfaction, etc., and such other books as the courts or the laws may prescribe.

SHERIFF.

In all of the States the office of sheriff is one of the most important of the county offices. The term of office varies in different States, being usually either two or four years, and in several of the States one party cannot hold the office a second term consecutively. The general provisions outlining the duties pertaining to this office are very much alike in the various States, and the following *resume* of his duties may be said to apply to all of the various States except in a few minor and unimportant details. The sheriff is charged with the duty of keeping and preserving the peace in his county; or, as has been written, "he is the conservator of peace," and it is his duty to keep the same, suppress riots, affrays, fighting, breaches of the peace and prevent crime, and may arrest offenders "on view" and cause them to be brought before the proper magistrate; and to do this, or to execute any writ, warrant, process, order or decree, he may call to his aid when necessary any person or the "power of the county." It is the duty of the sheriff to serve and execute within his county, and return, all writs, warrants, process, orders and decrees of every description that may be legally directed and delivered to him. He is a court officer, and it is his duty to attend, either in person or by deputy, all courts of record held in his county; by virtue of his office he has custody of the jail. It is his duty to pursue and apprehend felons and persons charged with crime and has custody of prisoners. He is not allowed to purchase any property exposed for sale by him as sheriff.

COUNTY SUPERINTENDENT OR COMMISSIONER OF SCHOOLS.

This is an office which exists under one name or another in nearly every State in the Union. The title of the officer in a great majority of the States is "county superintendent," but in Michigan, Missouri, Ohio, New York, and possibly one or two other States, the office is termed "school commissioner," and in several of the States the laws provide for a board of county examiners of school commissioners, who are given considerable of the work that in most of the other States is handled by the county superintendent.

The name of this office implies the duties which devolve upon it, and they are very much alike in all of the States. The incumbent of this office is charged with a general supervision over the schools of the county, and must be a fitting person as to education and moral character. As a rule it is their duty to examine and license teachers, but in a few of the States provision is made for a board of examiners. County superintendents are required to visit and inspect the schools at regular intervals, and give such advice and instruction to teachers as may be deemed necessary and proper. They are required to organize and conduct institutes for the instruction of teachers if deemed necessary, and encourage teachers' associations. They introduce to the notice of teachers and the people the best modes of instruction, the most approved plans of building and ventilating school-houses, etc., stimulate school officers to the prompt and proper discharge of their duties. They receive reports from the various school officers, and transmit an abstract of these reports to the State Superintendent, adding a report of the condition of the schools under their charge. In nearly all the States they are forbidden having any interest in the sale of any school furniture, apparatus or books used in the schools. In many States they have authority to annul a teacher's certificate for proper cause, and in general to take such steps and enforce such methods as will elevate and make more efficient the schools under their control.

COUNTY, PROSECUTING OR STATE'S ATTORNEY.

There is a great difference between the various States in the method of handling or attending to the legal business relating to county matters or growing from county affairs. In many of the States the official who attends to this line of work is known as the "county attorney," in other States he is called the State's attorney or prosecuting or district attorney. In a few of the States they divide the State into districts embracing a number of counties, and a district attorney is elected in each district, who in some cases attends to all the legal work of the various counties, and in others he assists the county attorneys in their most important duties and prosecutions. But whatever plan may be followed in the various States, and whatever title may be given to this office, the general duties of the office are very much the same throughout all of the States. It is the duty of the county attorney to commence and prosecute all actions, suits, indictments, and prosecutions, civil and criminal, in any court of record in his county in which the "people of the State or county" may be concerned; to prosecute all forfeited bonds and recognizances, and all actions for the recovery of debts, revenues, moneys, fines, etc., accruing to his county; to commence and prosecute all actions and proceedings brought by any county officer in his official capacity; to defend all actions and proceedings brought against his county, or against any county officer in his official capacity; to give legal opinions and advice to the county board or other county officers in relation to their official duties; to attend, if possible all preliminary examinations of criminals. When requested, he is required to attend sessions of the grand jury, examine witnesses in their presence, give legal advice and see that proper subpœnas and processes are issued; draw up indictments and prosecute the same. The county attorney is required, when requested by the Attorney-General, to appear for the State in cases in his county in which the State is interested. The county attorney makes an annual report to his superior State officer of all the criminal cases prosecuted by him.

PROBATE OR COUNTY JUDGE.

The method of handling probate matters is not uniform throughout the various States. In many States the higher courts are given jurisdiction over probate matters, and in others they have created districts in which are held probate courts, whose jurisdiction extends over several counties and takes in other matters besides purely probate affairs. In a majority of the States, however, particularly the Western and Northern States, they elect a county or a probate judge, who holds court and handles the probate matters which arise within his county. The jurisdiction of these county or probate courts is not always confined exclusively to probate affairs, being frequently extended to many other matters, and they generally include such matters as apprenticeship affairs, adoptions, minors, etc. In some of the States they have both a county judge and a probate judge, and in these cases the jurisdiction of the latter is confined to such matters as are in line with probate affairs. In Missouri they have a probate judge, and also a county court, composed of county judges, in whom the corporate powers of the county are vested—as the official county board. In Michigan they have a probate judge and a probate register. The probate judge is generally given original jurisdiction in all matters of probate, settlement of estates of deceased persons, appointment of guardians and conservators and settlement of their accounts. They take proof of wills, direct the administration of estates, grant and revoke letters testamentary and of administration, appoint and remove guardians, etc.

COUNTY SURVEYOR.

This is an office which is common to nearly all of the States. It is the duty of the county surveyor to execute any survey which may be ordered by any court, or upon application of any individual or corporation, and preserve a record of the surveys made by him. Nearly all of the States provide that certain records shall be kept by the county surveyor, and provide penalties for his failure to place on record the surveys made by him. While he is the official county surveyor, yet the surveys made by him are not conclusive, but may be reviewed by any competent tribunal, and the correctness thereof may be disputed.

COUNTY CORONER.

This is another county office which exists in *nearly* all of the States. In the average county there is not much work for the coroner, but in the counties in which large cities are located the office is a very important one. In general terms it may be stated that the coroner is required to hold inquests over the bodies of persons supposed to have met with violent or unnatural deaths. In most States he has power to impanel a jury to enquire into the cause of death; but in some of them this is not the case, and he is given power to act alone. He can subpœna witnesses; administer oaths; in certain cases provide for a decent burial, and can bind over to the proper court any person implicated in the killing of the deceased.

OTHER COUNTY OFFICES.

The county offices that have already been mentioned are the principal ones found in all of the States. There are, however, a few other county officials besides those mentioned which exist in many of the States, and which should be briefly mentioned in this connection. These are such offices as county physician, county assessor, county collector, county poor commissioner or superintendent of the county poor-house, master in chancery or court commissioner, county examiners, board of equalization, board of review, etc. The names of these offices imply the duties. These offices do not exist in all of the States, but in nearly every State the law provides for one or more of these county officials.

COUNTY BOARD.

The powers of every county as a body politic and corporate are vested in a county board. This official county board is generally termed the county "board of supervisors," or "board of commissioners," but there are some exceptions to this, like Missouri, where the county board is known as the "county court." There is considerable difference in the make-up of the county board in the various States. In some it is made up of one member from each township in the county. In others the counties are divided into districts, and one member of the county board is chosen from each district. No general description of this could be given that would be accurate, as some of the States follow both of these plans. For instance, in Illinois some of the counties are governed by a board of supervisors, which is made up of one member from each township, while other counties in the same State are governed by a board of county commissioners, consisting of three or more members, each representing districts into which the counties in question are divided.

The general powers of the county board throughout all of the States is about the same, except in minor details. It represents the legislative and corporate powers of the county. One of their number is always chosen as chairman or president, and acts as the presiding officer. The county board has general charge over the affairs of the county. It is their duty to provide county offices, provide desks, stationery, books, fuel, etc.; examine, investigate and adjust claims against the county, and have general care and custody of all the real and personal estate owned by the county. At regular intervals they settle with the county treasurer; examine accounts and vouchers. They locate county roads; determine the amount of county tax, and regularly publish a statement of their proceedings; make statements of receipts, expenditures, etc.; and make all contracts, and do all other acts in relation to the property and concerns of the county necessary to exercise its corporate powers that are not specifically delegated to other county officials.

TOWNSHIP GOVERNMENT

THE method of township government throughout the different States varies so much that it is impossible in this article to treat of it more than in a general way. In many of the States the townships are not organized as bodies corporate, and in other States in some counties they may have township organization, while in other counties in the same State it does not exist. In cases where there is no township organization the law provides that certain county officials shall attend to the local work, or that work which in other localities is assumed by the township officials. But even where they have township organization the plan of township government in the different States where it exists differs so widely that scarcely any two States may be said to be alike. About the only statements concerning the organized townships that could be made which would apply to all the States are the following: Every organized township in its corporate capacity has power to sue and be sued; to acquire by purchase, gift or devise, and hold property, both real and personal, for the use of its inhabitants, and again to sell and convey the same; and to make all such contracts as may be necessary in the exercise of its powers *as a township*.

In a great many of the States the township government is carried on after a plan very similar to the county and State governments, having various executive officers and a township board in which the corporate and legislative powers, of the township are vested. In other States they follow a plan which reserves to the people all corporate and legislative powers, and therefore have no need for a township board, but have various other township officers to carry out the wishes and orders of the voters. Where this plan prevails they hold what is generally termed "town meetings," at which every legal voter of the township has a voice. At these meetings reports are had from the various township officials, and the necessary measures are adopted and directions given for carrying on the township business.

Still other States combine good features from both of the plans above mentioned, and besides the other usual township officials they maintain a township board, which is given certain *restricted* powers, such as those of a review or an auditing board; but they are not vested with the complete corporate and legislative powers of the township, this being reserved in a large measure to the voters, and all questions calling for the exercise of such authority are acted upon at the town meetings. In many of the States the township board just described is made up of three or more of the other township officers, who are ex-officio members of the township board, and they meet at certain times, perform the work required of them, and report to the town meetings.

The *principal* officials in township organizations in nearly all the States are the following: "Supervisors, or trustees," "clerk," "treasurer," "assessor," "collector," "justices of the peace," "constables," "overseers, supervisors or commissioners of the highways," and "poundmasters," although as has been stated, many of the States do not have all of these officials.

SCHOOL DISTRICT GOVERNMENT

THE "common school system," or, to speak with greater accuracy, the method of governing school districts, in the various States, differs widely, yet all follow in a general way one of two separate and clearly defined methods, being amended in minor respects to meet local conditions and ideas. All of these methods have their excellent points, and yet it has been claimed by eminent educators that no one of them is free from fault and objection, nor has reached perfection. It will be the aim of this article to briefly explain the principal features of the several methods, but it is not possible to go into detail in the matter of giving the system of school government that is followed in each of the many States of the Union. The constitution and statutes of all the States agree, however, upon several points. They aim to provide for a thorough and efficient system of free schools, whereby all the children of the States may receive a thorough common school education; they provide that all lands, moneys and other property donated, granted or received for school, college, seminary or university purposes, and the proceeds thereof, shall be faithfully applied to the objects stated, with two or three exceptions they provide that no appropriation shall be made or public funds applied in aid of any church or sectarian purpose, or to support or sustain any school, academy, seminary, college or university controlled or run in the interest of any church or for a sectarian purpose; and they prohibit the various school officials from holding any interest in the sale, proceeds or profits of any book, apparatus or furniture used in the schools in which they, as officers, are interested.

In many of the States they follow what may be termed the "independent school district" method, inasmuch as each district, so far as its corporate powers are concerned, is entirely separate and independent of other districts. Where this plan is followed the boundaries of each district are clearly defined, and each district is complete within itself. They elect a full set of district officials, and exercise their corporate powers and manage their district affairs within themselves. In this plan the corporate powers of the district are usually vested in a district board, which has general charge of the interests of the district, hires teachers, and makes such contracts, and carries into effect such methods as is deemed necessary to raise the grade or aid in the efficiency of the schools. The measure of the authority given to these district boards is not the same in all the States, and in many States it is restricted, and a part of the corporate power is reserved to the people themselves, the officials being required, in all important matters, to carry out the wishes and orders of the people of the district as expressed and decided upon at the "district school meetings."

Another method which is followed in many of the States may be termed the "township system." In such States the law provides for the organization of each township for school purposes, or as one large "district," and each township, so far as its educational interests are concerned, is organized, has the necessary officials and becomes a body politic and corporate. As a general rule, where this method prevails, the townships are divided into three or more sub-districts. All of these sub-districts are a part of the whole, and the finances and general business is generally managed by a township board made up of representatives from each sub-district. This board is generally clothed with the corporate powers, hires teachers, provides fuel and supplies and makes all the contracts necessary to carry on the various schools in the township. As with independent districts, the powers of this board are not alike in all States where the township system prevails, for in some States their power is very much restricted, and is limited to certain official matters, the corporate powers and right to make important contracts being reserved to the people, who decide on these questions at what are termed the school meetings. In a few of the States where they follow the township system they have no official board. This is the case in Indiana, where they elect a township trustee, whose duty it is to look after all the educational interests of the township, subject to the approval of the people at the regular meetings. In most of the States where the township system prevails the law provides for the organization, under certain conditions, of sub-districts into independent districts, which gives them the power to elect their own officers and act independently of the other schools in the township.

In nearly all of the States one of the two general methods given above is followed, with certain changes to make the plan more efficient and satisfactory, and to better meet the desires and needs of the people of the different States. Many of the States combine good features from both these systems, as some of the States have the township system, wherein each sub-district has its own board, and so far as controlling its own affairs is concerned, is independent of all other districts. But local conditions have in many instances made special and local provisions necessary that are different in each State, and while there may be a vast difference in the methods followed, their aim is the same, and, as a whole, the various systems have accomplished the result of giving throughout the length and breadth of the Union the grandest and most efficient system of free schools that the world has ever known.

CITIES AND VILLAGES

IN all of the States the laws provide for the local government of school matters and civil authority. In school affairs provision is pendent of, the township in which they are located, both as to they may be separated from, and thus manage their affairs independently; cities and villages, so that when they attain a certain population made for handling the more complex educational interests of villages and cities—the school boards being made larger, and in many cases the scope of their authority is very much extended. In civil matters provision is made in all of the States for the organization of villages and cities as corporate bodies, separate and distinct from the townships and providing for the necessary officers to carry on the affairs of the municipality.

GENERAL INFORMATION ON Banking and Business Methods.

RELATIONS BETWEEN A BANK AND ITS CUSTOMERS.

In business life there is no more complex or important relation than that which exists between the business men generally and the banks, and it should be guarded with jealous care, so that both may retain the full confidence of the other. Business development in the United States has progressed with such gigantic strides that it has long since passed the stage where it is even possible to carry on business without the agency of banks. They are today a necessity in the transaction of business and making exchanges. It has been said, and with a great deal of truth, that in the present day the entire and sole object and result of business is the transfer of credits on the books of the banking houses; and that about the only use to which money is put is in making small change or paying balances. Business, in the most general and comprehensive sense, is almost wholly carried on by the aid of banks with checks, drafts and exchange. And it will be seen what a very important part the element of confidence plays in business life, when it is remembered that every check or draft that changes hands, implies the confidence on the part of the party receiving and accepting it, that it will be honored at the bank when presented.

OPENING AN ACCOUNT

[illegible]

DEPOSITS.

[illegible]

DISCOUNTS, LOANS, ETC.

[illegible]

COLLECTIONS.

[illegible]

STATEMENTS AND BALANCES.

[illegible]

NEGOTIABLE PAPER.

[illegible]

PROMISSORY NOTES.

[illegible]

BILLS OF EXCHANGE.

[illegible]

CHECKS.

[illegible]

DRAFTS.

[illegible]

ENDORSEMENTS.

[illegible]

GENERAL INFORMATION ON BANKING AND BUSINESS METHODS.

Another common form of limiting the endorsement is to enable the payee (when it is made payable to his order) to transfer his title in the instrument without becoming responsible for its payment, and making the party to whom it is transferred assume all responsibility concerning payment. To do this the endorser writes the words "Without Recourse" over his signature, which has the effect of relinquishing his title without making him liable to the holder in case the payer fails to take it up.

Another method of limiting the endorsement is to make it conditional, a good illustration of which is the following: "Pay to John Rine or order upon his delivering to the First National Bank a warranty deed to lot 5, block 4, etc." below which the endorser places his signature. He can also make it payable to "A. B. only," or in equivalent words, in which case "A. B." cannot endorse it over.

In fact, the endorser has the power to limit his endorsement as he sees fit, and either to lessen or increase his liability, such as either "waiving notice of demand;" making his endorsement a "general and special guaranty of payment" to all future holders, etc., but he cannot, by his endorsement, either increase or lessen the liability of any other endorser on the instrument.

An endorser, as a rule, is entitled to immediate notice in case the payer fails to pay. This is the case in nearly all of the United States as it has been a rule of the "law merchant" for many years. A few modifications, however, of the general "law merchant" have been made by statute in several of the States, relating to negotiable paper, in changing the endorser's liability by rendering his contract absolute instead of conditional, making notice unnecessary unless he suffers damage through want of it, or requiring a judgment to be first recovered before he can be held. In the absence, however, of statutory provisions of this kind, and they exist only in a few of the States, it may be said that to hold endorsers they must have prompt notice of non-payment, and it may be said to be a general rule of the "law merchant" that all parties to negotiable paper as endorsers who are entitled to notice are discharged by want of notice. The demand, notice and protest may be made according to the laws of the place where payable.

The term *Protest* is applied to the official act by an authorized person (usually a Notary Public), whereby he affirms in a formal or prescribed manner in writing that a certain bill, draft, check or other negotiable paper has been presented for acceptance or payment, as the case may be, and been refused. This, and the notice of the "Protest," which must be sent to all endorsers and parties to the paper is to notify them officially of its failure.

GUARANTY.

A "GUARANTOR" is one who is bound to another for the fulfillment of a promise, or of an engagement, made by a third party. This kind of contract is very common. According to the "statute of frauds" it must be in writing, and unless it is a sealed instrument there must be a consideration to support it. As a rule it is not negotiable, so as to be enforced by the transferee as if it had been given to him by the guarantor, but this depends upon the wording, as, if it contains all the characteristics of a note, payable to order or bearer, it will be held negotiable. A contract of guaranty is construed strictly, and if the liability of the principal be materially varied by the act of the party guaranteed, without the consent of the guarantor, the guarantor is discharged. The guarantor is also discharged if the liability or obligation is renewed, or extended by law or otherwise, unless he in writing renews the contract. In the case of a bank incorporated for twenty years, which was renewed for ten years more without change of officers, the courts held that the original sureties could not be held after the first term.

The guaranty can be enforced even though the original debt cannot, as is the case in becoming surety for the debt of a minor. A guarantor who pays the debt of the principal is entitled to demand from the creditor all the securities he holds, or of the note or bond on which declares the debt; and, in some States, the creditor cannot fall back upon the guarantor until he has collected as much as possible from these securities and exhausted legal remedies against the principal. If the debt or obligation be first incurred and completed before the guaranty is given, there must be a new consideration or the guaranty is void.

A guaranty is not binding unless the guarantor has notice of its acceptance, but the law presumes this acceptance when the offer of guaranty and acts of the party to whom it is given, such as delivery of goods or extending credit are simultaneous. But an offer to guarantee a future operation does not bind the offerer unless he has such notice of the acceptance as will afford him reasonable opportunity to make himself safe. A creditor may give his debtor some indulgence or accommodation without discharging the guarantor, unless it should have the effect of prejudicing the interests of the guarantor, in which case he would be released. Generally a guarantor may, at any time, pay a debt and so, at once, have the right to proceed against the debtor. Where there has been failure on the part of the principal and the guarantor is looked to, he must have reasonable notice—and notice is deemed reasonable if it prevents the guarantor from suffering from the delay.

It is, in many cases, difficult to say—and upon it rests the question of legal liability—whether the promise of one to pay for goods delivered to another is an original promise, as to pay for one's own goods, in which case it need not be in writing; or a promise to pay the debt of guaranty the promise of him to whom the goods are delivered, in which case it must be in writing. The question generally resolves itself into this: To whom did the seller give and was authorized to give credit? This is a question of fact and not of law. If the books of the seller show that he charged them to the party to whom he delivered them, it is almost impossible for him to hold the other party for it, but if on the other hand it is shown that he regarded the goods as being sold to the party whom it is desired to hold, but delivered them to another party and it is so shown on his books, it is not regarded as a guaranty, but an original or collateral promise, and would make the party liable. In general, a guarantor of a bill or note is not entitled to such strict and exact notice as an endorser is entitled to, but only such notice as shall save him from actual loss, as he can not make the want of notice his defense unless he can show that it was unreasonably withheld and that he suffered thereby. There is a marked difference in the effect of a guaranty of the "payment," or of the "collection" of a debt. In the first case, the creditor can look to the guarantor at any time; in the latter, the creditor must exhaust his legal remedies for collecting it.

ACCOMMODATION OF PAPER.

AN accommodation bill or note is one for which the acceptor or maker has received no consideration, but has lent his name and credit to accommodate the drawer, payee or holder. He is bound to all other parties just as completely as if there were a good consideration, for, if this was not the case, it would be of no value to the party accommodated. He is not allowed to set up want of consideration as a defense as against any holder for value. But he is not bound to the party whom he thus accommodates, no matter how the instrument may be drawn.

IDENTIFICATION.

THE mere act of identifying a party or making him known to a banker carries with it no liability on the part of the party who thus performs it, unless it can be shown there was fraud or collusion. Customers of banks are frequently asked to identify and make known to their own bankers, strangers who desire checks or drafts cashed or other accommodations. In some cases a mere introduction is all that is necessary, but only because the banker relies upon the honor and integrity of his customer, knowing that an improper person would not be introduced, for in a case of this kind the bank assumes all the risk. Generally speaking, however, it is an almost invariable rule with bankers, as it should be, to require their customer to endorse all drafts or checks which are honored for the stranger. In this case the endorser becomes personally liable to the bank if any or all of the drafts or checks prove worthless.

An endorsement which is frequently made by parties who are asked to identify others is to merely indicate that they know the party to be the payee named in the check or that the signature of the payee or party is correct. This is done by writing the words "Signature O. K." under the party's name and signing it. This has the effect of guaranteeing that the party's name is as written and that it is his proper signature. It does not guarantee that the check or draft is good or will be paid, but merely as expressed, that the signature is correct and the only liability assumed is that he will pay the amount in case the signature proves a forgery. Many banks, however, will not accept papers endorsed this way and justly so, for it throws upon them the burden of the risk.

RECEIPTS AND RELEASES.

ANY acknowledgment that a sum of money has been paid is a receipt. A receipt which reads "in full" though admitted to be strong evidence is by no means legally conclusive. If the party signing it can show an error or mistake, it will be admitted in his favor. Receipts for money will be held open to examination, and the party holding it must abide the results of such examination—the great aim of the law being to administer strict justice. A receipt may be of different degrees of explicitness, as the word "Paid" or "Received Payment" written on a bill. A "release" is simply a form of receipt, but is more binding upon the parties, inasmuch as, if properly drawn, under seal, for a consideration, it is a complete defense to any action based on the debts or claims so released. Herein, releases differ from receipts. A release is in the nature of a written contract and therefore cannot be controlled or contradicted by evidence, unless on the ground of fraud. But if its words are ambiguous, or may have either two or more meanings, evidence is receivable to determine the meaning.

INFANTS AND MINORS.

THE incapacity of a person to make a valid contract may arise from several causes, and the fact of being an infant, or minor, is one of them. The general rule of law may be stated as being that the contract of an infant or minor is not always void, but is voidable, and in many cases special exception is made, giving validity to their contracts for necessaries. By being voidable but not void in themselves, means that the infant has the right to disavow and annul the contract, either before or within a reasonable time after he reaches his majority. He may do this by word only, but a mere acknowledgment that the debt exists is not enough, and it must be substantially a new promise.

AGENCY.

THERE are a few well-settled and important rules of law governing the matter of agents and agency, which every business man should understand thoroughly. The relation of principal and agent implies that the principal acts by and through the agent. A principal is responsible for the acts of the agent only when he has actually given full authority to the agent, or when he has by his words, or his acts, or both, caused or permitted the person with whom the agent deals to believe him clothed with this authority. This is a point which is not always thoroughly understood, but it is a well-settled principle of law. There are two kinds of agents—general and special. A general agent is one authorized to represent his principal in all his business, or in all his business of a particular kind, and his power is limited by the usual scope and character of the business he is empowered to transact. If he is given out as the general agent, the principal is bound, even if the agent transcends his actual authority, but does not go beyond the natural and usual scope of the business.

On the other hand, a special agent is one authorized to do only a specific thing, or a few specified things, or a specified line of work. If the special agent exceeds his authority, it may be stated as an almost invariable rule that the principal is not bound, because the party dealing with the agent must inquire for himself and at his own peril, into the extent and limits of the authority given to the agent. Especially is this the case where the party knew that the agent had been or was engaged in attending to a particular and specified line of work connected with the business of the principal. The party, however, is not bound by any special reservations or limitations made secretly by the principal of which he had no reasonable or easy means of having notice. The authority of an agent may be given by the principal, by writing or orally, or may be implied from certain acts. Thus, if a person puts his goods into the custody of another whose business it is to sell such goods, he authorizes the whole world to believe that this person has them for sale; and any person buying them honestly, in this belief, would hold them. If one, knowing that another had acted as his agent, does not disavow the authority as soon as he conveniently can, but lies by and permits a person to go and deal with the supposed agent, or lose an opportunity of indemnifying himself, this is an adoption and confirmation of the acts of the agent.

A principal is bound by the acts of an agent even after the revocation of his agency, if such revocation has not been made public or is unknown to the party dealing with the agent. An agent can generally be held personally liable if he transcends his authority; but this is not the case if the party with whom he dealt knew that the authority was transcended.

ORIGIN AND HISTORY OF BANKING.

IN general, banks may be said to be credit institutions or dealers in credit. John Jay Knox once said that "the exchanges of the modern world are barter, effected by the indirect agency of the credit system, and banks and bankers are the machinery by which this is done." Metallic money and its representative, the circulating note, are only the small change of "Trade" employed in the settlement of balances and small purchases and payments. This fact is illustrated by the operations of the New York clearing house. The exchanges have been about 900,000 millions of dollars during the past thirty years, while the balances paid in money have only been about 38,000 millions, or about 4 per cent, of the amount of the settlements.

It has always been claimed that the business of banking originated with the Venetian money changers who displayed their wares and moneys on the streets and thus supplied those in need of change. According to the most eminent authorities the earliest banking institution in Europe was the Bank of Venice, which was founded in 1171, and was based upon a forced loan of the government. Funds deposited in it could be transferred to others on the books of the bank at the pleasure of the owner, but they could not be withdrawn. The perpetual annuities of the British debt are handled in a very similar manner at the present day. The Bank of Venice was continued until 1797. In 1401, the Bank of Barcelona was formed. At a period much earlier than this, the Jewish money-dealers had invented what was known as "foreign bills of exchange," but it is said that this bank was the first institution that made a business of negotiating and handling them. The Bank of Genoa commenced operation in 1407 and for centuries was one of the principal banks of Europe. It was the first to issue circulating notes—which were passed only by endorsement, not being payable to bearer.

The Bank of Hamburg, established in 1619, was a bank of both deposit and circulation based on the silver bars. This bank, like nearly all of that early time, had, as a principal object, the protection of the people from worn, sweated, clipped and plugged coins, or coins of certain empires that were reduced in standard value. The remedy generally adopted was to lock up the debased and depreciated coins and circulate the credit granted for them. Various other banks sprang into existence throughout Europe, many of them being powerful government agencies, and in many cases exerted a wide influence in shaping the destinies of empires.

In 1694 the Bank of England was established, and there is no banking institution in the world equal to it in the management of national finances. The Bank of France was authorized in 1800. It is not a fiscal agent of the government as is that of England. It does not collect or disburse the revenues of the exchequer, but it lends to it largely, while its credits, in the form of circulating notes and other acceptances, have borne the government safely through extraordinary needs.

It is claimed that the first organized bank in the United States had its origin in the formation of a banking company without charter June 18th, 1780, by the citizens of Philadelphia, and first action by Congress was taken June 22, of the same year, in reference to this proposed association. Two years afterward a "perpetual charter" was granted to the Bank of North America at Philadelphia. In 1784 the State of Massachusetts incorporated the Massachusetts Bank. The Bank of New York was chartered in March, 1791, although it had been doing business since 1784, under articles of association drawn by Alexander Hamilton. Most of these institutions are still running and have been converted into national banks. The Bank of the United States was organized in 1791. The most of the stock was owned by the United States Government but later the Government interest was disposed of, and in 1841 the bank failed.

State banks were organized rapidly, and private banking firms sprang into existence and the business of banking assumed immense proportions.

In 1863, the NATIONAL BANK SYSTEM was adopted and in 1864 the National Bank Bureau of the Treasury Department was organized, the chief officer of which is the comptroller of the currency. In March, 1865, an act was passed providing for a ten per cent. tax on notes of any person, or State bank issued for circulation, and making an exception of National banks. This had the effect of taxing the State bank circulation out of existence. As the National banking system has proven one of the most efficient and satisfactory methods the world has ever known, it will be of interest to review here some of its principal features. Under this act National banks may be organized by any number of persons not less than five. Not less than one-third of the capital must be invested in United States bonds, upon which circulating notes may be issued equal to 90 per cent. of the par value of the bonds. These circulating notes are receivable at par in the United States in all payments except for duties on imports, interest on the public debt and in redemption of the national currency. The National banks are required to keep a certain reserve; they are authorized to loan money at the rate of interest allowed in the various states—when no rate is fixed by the laws of the State, the banks may charge 7 per cent. Shareholders are held individually liable, equally and ratably, for all debts of the association to the extent of the amount of their stock, in addition to the amount invested therein. The banks are required, before the declaration of a dividend, to carry one-tenth part of their net profits of the preceding half year to a surplus fund until the same shall amount to 20 per cent. of the capital; and losses and bad debts must be deducted from net profits before any dividend is declared. A receiver may be appointed by the comptroller to close up under his supervision the affairs of any national bank which shall fail to keep good its lawful money reserve or which may become insolvent. While there have been national bank failures, there has never been any loss to the people whatever on the circulation. A suit may be brought for forfeiture of the charter of a bank if the directors shall knowingly violate the law; and in such cases they may be held liable in their individual capacity. There are other restrictions in the law—such as, for instance, the prohibition against loaning to any one borrower of more than ten per cent. of the capital; or the holding of any real estate except such as is required for banking purposes, or the granting of loans upon the security of the bank stock.

The national bank circulation has been gradually growing less during the past ten years, as the United States bonds available are quoted so high above par and the rate of interest so low that there is but little profit to the banks in it. All of the States have laws regulating State banks and providing certain restrictions, but as the laws of the various States are not alike it is impossible to give a general description of the matter that would apply to all the States. The laws, however, provide for and require State banks to hold a certain reserve, and at regular intervals they make full statements as to their condition and their affairs are examined into by certain State officials at frequent intervals. The laws of all the States have reached a high degree of perfection in the method of regulating and inspecting State banks, and the almost universal soundness and reliability of these institutions reflect credit upon the laws under which they exist.

CLEARING HOUSE.

THE Clearing-House is the place where the exchanges of the banks are made in all the principal cities of the world. The clearing-house system was first established in London about the beginning of the present century. It was first introduced into this country by the banks of the city of New York organizing an association, under the name of the New York Clearing-House, which commenced operations Oct. 11, 1853. At that time it consisted of fifty-two banks, but five of them were soon closed because of inability to meet its requirements. Clearing Houses have since been established in nearly all of the principal cities of the continent.

In all cities a bank receives large amounts of bills and checks on other banks, so that at the close of each day's business every bank has, in its drawers, various sums thus due it by other banks. It is, in like manner, itself the debtor of other banks, which have during the day received its bills and checks drawn upon it. Prior to the establishment of the clearing house it was necessary for each bank, every morning, to make up its account with every other bank, and to send its porter or agent to present the bills and checks so received to the debtor banks for payment. The balances were adjusted by payments in gold, which became so laborious, dangerous and complicated that the balances were settled only weekly instead of daily—a plan that resulted in great risk and evil. This was obviated by the clearing-house system, through which the settlements are so simultaneously and quickly effected that in New York the transactions in one single day have amounted to over $300,000,000, in adjusting which the exchanges were settled in the space of an hour. Besides saving a vast amount of work, bookkeeping and expense, it enabled the banks by united aid to strengthen each other in times of excitement and financial panic.

The following is the manner in which the settlements are made in about all the clearing-houses of this country: The clearing-room is provided with a continuous line of desks, one for each bank that is a member of the association, each desk bearing the name and number of the bank. Each bank is represented every morning, at the hour fixed for settlement, by two clerks, one a messenger who brings with him the checks, drafts, etc., that his bank has received during the day previous upon the other banks—called the "exchanges," and these are assorted for each bank and placed in envelopes. On the outside of each envelope is a slip on which are listed the amounts of the various items which it contains. The messengers take their places in a line outside the row of desks, each opposite the desk assigned to his bank, while at each desk is a clerk with a sheet containing the names of all the banks in the same order as the desks, with the aggregate amounts which his bank's messenger has against each bank. Just previous to the hour fixed for making the exchanges the manager takes his position and calls the house to order. At a signal the bell rings and each messenger moves forward to the desk next to his own and delivers the envelope containing the checks, etc., for the bank represented at that desk to the clerk at that desk, together with a printed list of the banks in the same order, with the amount opposite each bank. The clerk receiving it signs and returns it to the messenger, who immediately passes on to the next desk; then to the next, and so on until he has made a complete circuit and has again reached the desk of his own bank—the starting point. All the other messengers moving in the same manner, each messenger has, by this means, visited every bank and delivered to each everything his bank held for it, taking a receipt for the same; and at the same time each bank has received all the exchanges that every other bank had against it. This operation, even in the greatest clearing-houses, only consumes from ten to fifteen minutes.

This enables the banks to know at once the exact balance for or against it, as the clerks immediately enter from the slips on their own sheets the aggregate amount from each bank, and the difference between the total amount brought by them, which at once shows the balance due to or from the clearing house to each bank. This is reported to their banks, and the balance is paid to or drawn from the clearing house, thus at once settling the accounts between all the banks. The lists are "proved" carefully and certain fines are laid for all errors, tardiness, etc.

CHRONOLOGICAL ARRANGEMENT

—OF—

ANCIENT, MEDIEVAL AND MODERN HISTORY

The chief aim of this Chronological History is to give in a comprehensive and attractive form the principal events of the history of the world free from unnecessary details. For convenience this history is arranged under—I. Ancient History. II. Medieval History. III. Modern History. The latter is given—First. From the beginning of the Sixteenth Century to American Revolution. Second. From the birth of the United States to the present time by countries.

Ancient History

B. C.

[illegible]

B. C.

[illegible]

B. C.

[illegible]

B. C.

[illegible]

B. C.

[illegible]

[illegible]

A. D.

[illegible]

Medieval History

[illegible]

ANCIENT, MEDIEVAL AND MODERN HISTORY.

A. D.
1377 Richard II. King of England, June 22.
Papacy restored to Rome.
1380 Battle of the Don; Dimitri II., of Russia, defeats the Tartars.
Wycliffe's translation of the Bible published.
Thomas A. Kempis born.
Russia wars with the Tartars.
Charles VI., King of France.
1381 Wat Tyler's insurrection in London crushed.
Ghiberti, artist, born; died 1455.
1382 "Legend of Good Women," England.
1383 The Tartars burn Moscow.
1384 Death of John Wycliffe.
1386 John of Gaunt in Spain.
Battle of Sempach; defeat of the Austrians by the Swiss, and death of Duke Leopold.
1387 Genoese Empire divided.
Fra Angelico, painter, born; died 1455.
1388 Battle of Chevy Chase, or Otterburne, between Scots and English.
1389 Margaret of Norway.
1390 The Eastern Empire loses power in Asia.
Robert III. King of Scotland.
The Canterbury Tales published.
J. Van Eyck, painter, born.
1392 The Portuguese discover the Cape of Good Hope.
1395 Tamerlane, the Tartar, invades Russia.
The Wakefield and Towneley mysteries.
1396 Battle of Nicopolis; the Turks, under Bajazet I., defeat the Hungarian Christians.
1397 Persecution of the Wycliffites or Lollards.
Union of Calmar.
1399 Henry IV. crowned King of England.
[illegible]

A. D.
1595 Shakespeare's poems first issued.
1596 Conquest of Cadiz by Essex.
University of Barcelona founded.
Birth of Descartes; died 1650.
1597 Bacon's essays published.
1598 Death of Philip II., of Spain.
Philip III. King; he banishes 300,000 Moors from Spain by A. D. 1610.
The Netherlands ceded to Austria.
Edict of Nantes in favor of Protestants, by Henry IV.
Irish rebellion of O'Neil, or Tyrone; defeat of the English at Blackwater.
Henry IV. commissions De la Roche to conquer Canada, in which he fails.
The race of Rurik, who had governed Russia for 700 years, becomes extinct.
Bodleian founded.
1599 Appenzell joins the Swiss Cantons.
Birth of Vandyck, painter; died 1641.
Birth of Velasquez, painter; died 1660.

Modern History.

1600 Maurice, of Holland, invades Flanders.
The Dutch East India Company chartered with a capital of $350,000.
Chauvin's trading voyages to Tadousac, Canada.
Birth of the painter, Rembrandt; died 1669.
Birth of Claude Lorraine, painter; died 1682.
[illegible]

[illegible]